The California Gardener's
Book of Lists

The California Gardener's

BOOK OF
LISTS

❧

Catherine Yronwode
with Eileen Smith

Taylor Publishing Company
Dallas, Texas

Designed by David Timmons

Published by Taylor Publishing Company
1550 West Mockingbird Lane
Dallas, Texas 75235
www.taylorpub.com

Library of Congress Cataloging-in-Publication Data

Yronwode, Catherine, 1947–
        The California gardener's book of lists / Catherine Yronwode with Eileen Smith.
            p.   cm.
        Includes bibliographical references (p.   ) and index.
            1. Landscape plants—California. 2. Landscape gardening—California.
        I. Smith, Eileen, 1947–   . II. Title.

        635.9'09794—dc21   98–26034
                                                              CIP

Printed in the United States of America
10 9 8 7 6 5 4 3 2 1

CONTENTS

INTRODUCTION

California is not only a big state, it is a state of many climates and soils. When I was asked to prepare a list of garden plants for use by California gardeners, I was both happy and apprehensive: happy because as a California gardener myself, I know how important it is to get information tailored to our region's special needs, and apprehensive because the Golden State is big enough and diverse enough to support at least three books of lists.

Because this one book will be consulted by folks from San Diego to Del Norte counties, and from the foggy coast to the dry interior valleys—not to mention the slopes of some of the most rugged mountains in the world—you will find that some sections are for particular regions, while others can be taken as a general guide for almost anywhere in the state.

This book is intended to be a resource and workbook. Take it along with you to your local nursery and make notes on what you see there. It's not just enough to know whether a plant will grow for you—it also has to be something you like.

SOIL TYPE CAN CHANGE YOUR PLANS

The type of soil you have can make a real difference in how well certain plants will grow for you. Some want acid soil; others will tolerate alkaline. The high mineral content found in parts of the Central Valley is difficult for some varieties to handle, while others pay such conditions little mind, and in the mineral-deficient "pygmy forests" along parts of the North Coast, a few species survive and almost anything else simply gives up the ghost.

Fortunately, you do not have to become a soil scientist to have a beautiful garden. If you don't know the kind of soil you have, the easiest way to learn is to ask your gardening neighbors. Then it's up to you to adapt your plans or modify your soil. For instance, even though azaleas and rhododendrons enjoy the climate throughout California, they only do really well where the soil is on the acid side. So what do you do if your soil is alkaline? Look around your neighborhood! Chances are, if there are lots of azaleas and rhododendrons in other people's yards near you, other people have been able to modify the local soil by adding acidifying materials—and if they could do it, you can too. But if no one in your area grows azaleas or rhododendrons, you might think twice about your chances of success. The same is true of plants that like light, sandy soil. If you have heavy adobe clay, you can modify your soil by adding sand and organic matter (at least in one or two beds), or you can avoid the problem entirely by growing plants that know how to cope with clay soils.

ABOUT THE NAMES

The scientific names of plants change over time as taxonomists decide to lump species together or split them apart into new species. In fact, a botanist friend of mine once joked that the reason plant names keep changing is that "unless we botanists come up with some new lump or split every few years, we never get to fly to taxonomic conventions in Europe to discuss our theories." The standard listing of the proper names of nursery plants is a huge book called *Hortus*, a project started by Liberty Hyde Bailey many years ago and revised periodically ever since. Keeping up to date on the changes in species names is fine for taxonomists, but the truth is that nursery growers often stick with old Latin names long after they have become obsolete, simply because that's what their customers are used to. Sometimes the change is minor, as when what used to be called *Rosa wichuriana* was officially renamed *Rosa wichurana*. (Max Wichura, the botanist who first described the Memorial Rose, had no "i" in his name, and decades later, someone decided to correct the mistake.)

What I've tried to do in this book is steer a middle course, using new names when they seem to be gaining acceptance among nurseryfolks, and holding fast when it seems that you'll have a better chance of finding the plant under the older name. Just remember that when you ask for a plant and are told it does not exist, you and the nursery person may need to hit the books and come up with a common language.

VARIETIES, CULTIVARS, AND SELECTIONS

Because this is a book for the home gardener rather than the botanist, I've been a bit loose with the use of words variety, cultivar, and selection, treating them as essentially interchangeable words. As you will see when you start selecting plants at a nursery, knowing the species name will only be the beginning. Some shrubs, trees, and flowering perennials come in one form only, the "species type"—but even wild plants show a great deal of variation, and many cultivated species can be supplied in dwarf, variegated-leaf, and diversely flowered forms. It is not important to the gardener's purposes to know whether these variations are the result of cloning a selection, cross-breeding two separate lines to produce a hybrid, or line-breeding a variety to "come true from seed." What matters is that the species will grow well in your area and that you enjoy the look of the variety you select.

Some lists in this book emphasize varieties—the roses and the fruit trees, for instance—but in other lists, the species is the foundation of the choices that have been made. Once you pick a species from such a list, you will get to have the fun of walking down the nursery aisles and deciding whether to go with a double-flowered, purple-leafed, golden-margined, fragrant, weeping, or ground-creeping variety!

THERE'S ALWAYS A PLANT THAT WILL MAKE A LIAR OUT OF ME

Lois Trigg Chaplin, whose *Southern Gardener's Book of Lists* started this series, presented her readers with a quote from Glenn Morris, a landscape gardener from Greensboro, North Carolina, who said, "There's always a plant that will make a liar out of me." I think it is wise enough and true enough to be carved over the door to every gardener's toolshed, and so I pass it along. What it means is that every plant is an individual, and one might succeed while another might fail, even when planted side by side. This book is designed to help you make choices, but it is not the only or the last word. Look around you, remain open to experimentation, and remember, there's probably an exception to almost every gardening rule.

YOUR MILEAGE MAY VARY

California is a big state, and not only do its soils and climates run the gamut, but so do its gardeners. You probably won't agree with everything you read here. If you discuss these lists with local nursery people, you'll probably find that they have their own strongly held notions too. Horticulture is not an exact science, so if you have questions that are not answered here, ask around for second and third opinions. The folks with dirt under their fingernails probably know the answers.

BOOKS YOU SHOULD KNOW ABOUT

A basic library of gardening books can be one of the wisest investments you will make. If you have ever set out a plant that later died because you didn't understand its needs, you will know how valuable a garden library can be. Even if you have most of your work done by a landscaper or garden designer, it will save you money and prevent disappointment if you can read about or see pictures of the plants that are being proposed for your home.

The following books will help you in your plant selections. Your local bookstore should be able to special order them for you if they do not keep copies in stock. Good places to find regional gardening books are stores that have extensive local shelves, botanical gardens, university bookstores, or nurseries that sell books. Also ask if any pamphlets have been published by members of local garden clubs; often these humble booklets contain top-notch information on regional microclimate or soil conditions. Another source of information is your county cooperative extension service.

BASIC REFERENCE

Armitage, Alan. *Herbaceous Perennial Plants.* Athens, Ga.: Varsity Press, Inc.; Portland, Ore.: Timber Press, 1989.

Dirr, Michael. *Manual of Woody Landscape Plants.* Champaign, Ill.: Stipes Publishing Co., 1990.

Jones, Samuel R. Jr., and Leonard E. Foote. *Gardening with Native Wildflowers.* Portland, Ore.: Timber Press, 1991.

Lacy, Allen. *The Garden in Autumn.* New York: Atlantic Monthly Press, 1991. (Not entirely Californian, but very helpful.)

Mitchell, Sidney R. *Gardening in California.* Garden City, New York: Doubleday Page & Co., 1925. (Old and out of print, but it is a classic and was so popular in its time that it is not hard to find in used book stores even now.)

Mollison, Bill. *Permaculture: A Designer's Manual*. Washington, D.C.; Covelo, Calif.; Tyalgum, NSW, Australia: Island Press, Tagari Publishing, 1990.

Sunset Western Garden Book. Menlo Park, Calif.: Sunset Publishing, 1995. (Periodically revised and always in print, the best aid to understanding California's microclimates.)

Welch, William C. *Perennial Garden Color*. Dallas, Tex.: Taylor Publishing, 1989.

Others for Specific Needs

Druitt, Liz, and G. Michael Shoup. *Landscaping with Antique Roses*. Newtown, Conn.: Taunton Press, 1992.

Garden Club of America. *Plants That Merit Attention: Trees*. Portland, Ore.: Timber Press, 1984.

Phillips, Roger, and Martyn Rix. *Roses*. New York: Random House, 1988. (The largest illustrated list of roses currently in print.)

Taylor, Norman, et al. *Taylor's Pocket Guide* series. Boston: Houghton Mifflin. (These handy digest-sized photo-guides are useful if you need quick visual reference of a specific category of plant. Individual books cover topics such as evergreen shrubs, shady-area ground covers, modern roses, annuals for sunny areas, climbing vines.)

Wilder, Louise Beebe. *The Fragrant Garden*. New York: Dover Publications, 1932.

Wilson, Jim. *Landscaping with Wildflowers*. Boston: Houghton Mifflin, 1992.

THE REGIONAL CODES

This book uses its own system of codes to indicate which area of California each plant should do well in: All, SN (Sierra Nevada and Sierra Foothills), IV (Inland Valleys), HD (High Desert), LD (Low Desert), NC (North Coast), and SC (South Coast). The terms correspond to the map on page 5. No coding system for indicating growing zones is exact or flawless, not even the USDA zoning system or the Sunset codes. Zone codes provide a helpful, general guide, but cannot absolutely predict whether a particular plant will do well in your garden. Local gardeners and nurseries will be your best source of information about what plants have been successful in your area.

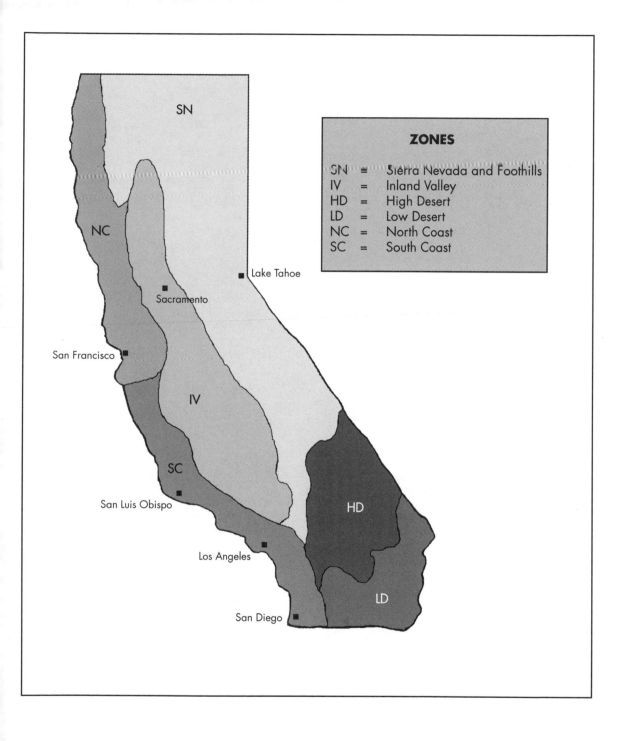

ZONES

SN = Sierra Nevada and Foothills
IV = Inland Valley
HD = High Desert
LD = Low Desert
NC = North Coast
SC = South Coast

PERENNIALS

The past few years have seen a resurgence of interest in old-fashioned perennials, inspired by romantic notions of Victorian cottage gardens and fueled by reprints of the inspirational works of the great champion of perennial borders, Gertrude Jekyll. Perhaps our busier lives have something to do with the upsurge in perennial gardening as well. Being sturdy herbaceous subjects, perennials do not need the constant fussing over and replanting that annuals do.

California is not an ideal area for many of the traditionally favored perennials that flourish in British gardens, however. Our rainless summers can put a lot of stress on plants that evolved in regions where frequent rains kept their roots from drying out. One modern solution to the problem is to install an irrigation system, using drip emitters, misters, or sprayers to supply what nature withholds. The resurgence of perennial gardening in California can be directly attributed to the increased availability of inexpensive automated irrigation systems for small gardens.

Along with the renewed interest in perennials has come a great deal of experimentation with new varieties and importations of old favorites from other regions. If any one plant epitomizes this turnabout in garden fashion to me, it is Silver King artemisia. Back in the 1960s, when I first read about its wonderfully soft gray leaves in an old British garden book, it seemed to symbolize the vanished English country gardens of the 1920s. I asked everyone about it, and only a few older gardeners even remembered its name. I believed that it was something I would never see but only dream of in nostalgic reverie. In the early 1980s Silver King artemisia showed up—much to my surprise and delight—as a very expensive subject in one-gallon pots at a specialty nursery. I spent a small fortune buying out the owner's entire stock. Shortly thereafter its charming image began to appear in California garden magazines, and the secret was out, with the result that today Silver King artemisia is so much in demand that it can frequently be found in the 4-inch perennial section at my local hardware store!

That brings me to an important point about perennials. While some species will adapt to almost any climate, others are a bit tricky. The wonderful beds of lupines one reads about in old British books did not make the same leap to renewed popularity in California that Silver King artemisia did, and for one simple reason—they require great amounts of summer water, something we tend to skimp on when we can. So before you go crazy reading books on cottage gardens of yesteryear and ordering plants from out of state just because they look great in a catalogue, ask around. Your neighbors, local nursery, garden center, botanical garden, or county agent will help you learn the limits of perennial gardening in your area.

PERENNIALS FOR POOR, SANDY SOIL

Here are some perennials that will survive and even thrive in poor, thin, sandy soil. The addition of biodegradable mulch, compost, or other organic matter will greatly improve these soils in time, but these plants will make do with what you have right now. For perennials that can endure salt spray as well as sandy soil, see the list of plants for the oceanfront on page 9.

Fleabane

Yarrow (*Achillea*)	All
Pussy toes (*Antennaria dioica*)	All
Golden marguerite (*Anthemis tinctoria*)	SN, IV, HD, NC, SC
Sea pink (*Armeria maritima*)	SN, IV, NC, SC
Columbine (*Aquilegia*)	All
Butterfly weed (*Asclepias tuberosa*)	All
Blackberry lily (*Belamcanda chinensis*)	All
Heartleaf bergenia (*Bergenia cordifolia*)	SN, IV, LD, NC, SC
Winter-blooming bergenia (*Bergenia crassifolia*)	SN, IV, LD, NC, SC
Boltonia (*Boltonia asteroides*)	All
Canna (*Canna*)	All
Lemon grass (*Cymbopogon citratus*)	NC, SC
Rosea ice plant (*Drosanthemum floribundum*)	IV, NC, SC
Pride of Madeira (*Echium fastuosum*)	IV, NC, SC
Fleabane (*Erigeron*)	All
Santa Barbara daisy (*Erigeron karvinskianus*)	IV, LD, NC, SC
Spurges (*Euphorbia*)	All
Blanket flower (*Gaillardia*)	All
Gaura (*Gaura lindheimeri*)	All
Gazania (*Gazania*)	IV, HD, LD, NC, SC
Ox-eye (*Heliopsis helianthoides, H. scabra*)	SN, IV, NC, SC
Daylily (*Hemerocallis*)	All
Red yucca (*Hesperaloe parviflora*)	HD, LD, NC, SC
Shamrock, Wood sorrel (*Oxalis*)	SN, IV, LD, NC, SC
Jerusalem sage (*Phlomis fruticosa*)	All
Plumbago (*Plumbago auriculata*)	IV, LD, NC, SC
Rudbeckia, Yellow coneflower (*Rudbeckia*)	All
Sage, Salvia (*Salvia*)	All
Purple Heart (*Setcreasea pallida* 'Purple Heart')	IV, LD, NC, SC
Goldenrod aster (*Solidaster luteus*)	SN, IV, HD, NC, SC
Goldenrod (*Solidago*)	All
Germander (*Teucrium chamaedrys*)	All
Dactil yucca (*Yucca baccata*)	All
Soapweed yucca (*Yucca glauca*)	All

Jim Balestreri of Green Point Nursery in Novato knows there is "no perfect plant," so for the beginner who wants flowering ornamentals, he suggests the "old timers" such as iris and *Dianthus barbatus,* or sweet William, which is actually a biennial. Purchase these at the blooming stage from your nursery and transplant for a natural addition to any large landscaped area in the home garden.

PERENNIALS FOR THE OCEANFRONT

Salt spray and continual wind make oceanfront gardening difficult. Beach areas where the soil is sandy can add to your problems. A windbreak will help, whether it is a wall or a few rows of trees and shrubs, so if at all possible, add one to your garden plans. Plants in this list should be suitable for North Coast and South Coast gardens.

Yarrow (*Achillea*)
Lily-of-the-Nile (*Agapanthus africanus*)
Silver King artemisia (*Artemisia albula*)
Sandhill sage (*Artemisia pycnocephala*)
Giant reed (*Arundo donax*)
Pacific coast ice plant (*Carpobrotus*)
Sea oats (*Chasmanthium latifolium*)
Chrysanthemum (*Chrysanthemum*)
Pampas grass (*Cortaderia selloana*)
Pride of Madeira (*Echium fastuosum*)
Santa Barbara daisy (*Erigeron karvinskianus*)
Sea holly (*Eryngium*)
Euryops, African daisy (*Euryops*)
Blanket flower (*Gaillardia aristata,* G. *grandiflora*)
Sunrose (*Helianthemum nummularium*)
Daylily (*Hemerocallis*)
Tropical hibiscus (*Hibiscus rosa-sinensis*)
Red-hot poker (*Kniphofia uvaria*)
Ice plant (*Lampranthus*)
Redondo creeper (*Lampranthus filicaulis*)
Sea lavender, Statice (*Limonium*)
Eulalia grass, Maiden grass (*Miscanthus*)
Switch grass (*Panicum virgatum*)
Scented geranium (*Pelargonium*)
New Zealand flax (*Phormium*)
Common reed (*Phragmites australis*)
Dusty miller (*Senecio cineraria*)
Watsonia (*Watsonia*)
Yucca (*Yucca*)

According to Sidney Hilburn, who helps caretake the Community Garden at Pt. San Pablo Yacht Harbor near Richmond, "Primroses, dusty miller, rockrose, and calendula all work beautifully in the Community Garden. They're hardy, and they love cold, damp nights. Not quite as showy, but equally sturdy, is the geranium. Just be careful to plant in well-drained soil behind a retaining wall or other structure to protect them from salt spray."

PERENNIALS FOR WET SITES

Boggy soil, stream banks, pond edges, and low areas in which water collects are ideal for growing wetland perennials. Listing all of the wet-loving plants would fill a specialty book on the subject, so what follows is only a brief list. If you are planning a wetland garden, check the other chapters in this book for trees, ferns, shrubs, and other plants that will grow in soggy soil.

Japanese sweet flag (*Acorus gramineus*)	IV, NC, SC
Showy cobra lily (*Arisaema speciosum*)	SN, IV, NC
Swamp milkweed (*Asclepias incarnata*)	All
Marsh marigold (*Caltha palustris*)	All
Camass lily (*Camassia*)	SN, IV, NC, SC
Turtlehead (*Chelone*)	SN, IV, NC
Crinum lily (*Crinum americanum*)	IV, LD, NC, SC
Umbrella plant (*Cyperus alternifolius*)	IV, LD, NC, SC
Papyrus (*Cyperus papyrus*)	NC, SC
Joe Pye weed (*Eupatorium purpureum*)	SN, IV, NC
Meadowsweet (*Filipendula*)	SN, IV, NC
Gunnera (*Gunnera*)	IV, NC, SC
Houttuynia (*Houttuynia cordata*)	SN, IV, NC, SC
Wild sunflower, Elecampana (*Inula helenium*)	SN, IV, NC, SC
Douglas iris (*Iris douglasiana*)	All
Pacific coast iris (*Iris innominata*)	All
Bog iris (*Iris laevigata*)	SN, IV, NC, SC
Yellow flag iris (*Iris pseudacorus*)	All
Blue flag iris (*Iris versicolor*)	SN, IV, NC
Fiber optics plant (*Isolepis gracilis*)	All
Rush (*Juncus*)	All
Ligularia (*Ligularia*)	SN, IV, NC, SC
Cardinal flower (*Lobelia cardinalis*)	SN, IV, LD, NC
Forget-me-not (*Myosotis semperflorens*)	All
Switch-grass (*Panicum virgatum*)	SN, IV, HD, NC, SC
Japanese coltsfoot (*Petasites japonicus*)	SN, IV, NC
Primrose (*Primula*)	SN, IV, LD, NC, SC
Rodgersia (*Rodgersia*)	SN, IV, NC
Yellow-eyed grass (*Sisyrinchium californicum*)	All
Globeflower (*Trollius*)	All
Calla lily (*Zantedeschia*)	IV, LD, NC, SC

For pond sites and boggy areas, Cindy Braley of Foothill Nursery in Shingle Springs recommends canna lilies and calla lilies. "Both bloom in late spring and early summer, and both come in lots of colors. Calla lilies prefer part shade, and they're very tall. Canna lilies are smaller, and they like full sun. Both do well in very wet places." Cindy also says that a perennial lobelia, such as *Lobelia cardinalis*, does well as a bog plant, as does Japanese iris, which will bloom in mid spring. Siberian irises, too, don't mind extra moisture. Other options for wet or boggy sites are any of the rushes, such as corkscrew, horsetail, and zebra. "Rushes reseed like mad," Cindy notes. She also recommends "Azure pickerel, which has a blue flower," as another plant for wet areas.

PERENNIALS THAT DEER DON'T USUALLY EAT

Watching deer is one of the more pleasant aspects of rural or suburban life—until they dine on your garden. Fencing to keep deer out is expensive and can be unsightly, so another way to deal with the problem is to plant perennials that deer find distasteful. A starving deer will try almost anything, but the list below contains plants that deer usually avoid.

Acanthus, Bear's breeches (*Acanthus mollis*)	All
Yarrow (*Achillea*)	All
Lily-of-the-Nile (*Agapanthus*)	SN, IV, LD, NC, SC
Agave (*Agave*)	IV, LD, NC, SC
Aloe (*Aloe*)	IV, LD, NC, SC
Belladonna lily (*Amaryllis belladonna*)	All
Columbine (*Aquilegia*)	All
Thrift, Sea pink (*Armeria*)	SN, IV, NC, SC
Artemisia, Wormwood (*Artemisia*)	All
Astilbe, False spiraea (*Astilbe*)	SN, IV, NC, SC
Bamboos (*Bambusa*)	All
Tuberous begonia (*Begonia tuberhybrida*)	IV, NC, SC
Perennial Swan River daisy (*Brachycome multifida*)	IV, NC, SC
Serbian bellflower (*Campanula poscharskyana*)	SN, IV, HD, NC, SC
Coreopsis (*Coreopsis*)	All
Crocus (*Crocus*)	All
Bleeding heart (*Dicentra*)	SN, IV, NC, SC
Foxglove (*Digitalis*)	All
Pride of Madeira (*Echium fastuosum*)	IV, NC, SC
Freesia (*Freesia*)	IV, LD, NC, SC
Blanket flower (*Gaillardia*)	All
Cranesbill (*Geranium*)	All
Hellebore (*Helleborus*)	All
Daylily (*Hemerocallis*)	All
Iris (*Iris*)	All
Red-hot poker (*Kniphofia uvaria*)	SN, IV, NC, SC
Sea lavender (*Limonium*)	SN, IV, HD, NC, SC
Lupine (*Lupinus*)	All
Daffodil, Narcissus (*Narcissus*)	All
Oriental poppy (*Papaver orientale*)	SN, IV, HD, NC
Fountain grass (*Pennisetum*)	All
Moss pink (*Phlox subulata*)	SN, IV, HD, LD, NC
New Zealand flax (*Phormium tenax*)	All
Matilija poppy (*Romneya coulteri*)	SN, IV, NC, SC
Rudbeckia, Yellow coneflower (*Rudbeckia*)	All
Santolina (*Santolina*)	All
California fuchsia (*Zauschneria, Epilobium*)	SN, IV, HD, NC, SC

PERENNIALS FOR ALKALINE SOIL

Not too many perennials tolerate alkaline soil (a pH level above 7.0), but there are some. If you live in an area with naturally alkaline soil or have been saddled with "contractor's soil" that is highly alkaline due to low organic matter plus leached lime from concrete foundations or pathways, this list should get you started. Remember, though, that adding compost or a yearly mulch of biodegradable plant matter will help bring the soil pH into a more comfortable range. Check with local nurseries for other plants that will do well under alkaline conditions.

Yarrow (*Achillea*)	All
Aloe (*Aloe*)	IV, LD, NC, SC
Columbine (*Aquilegia*)	All
Artemisia (*Artemisia*)	All
California sagebrush (*Artemisia californica*)	All
Tarragon (*Artemisia dracunculus*)	All
Aster (*Aster*)	All
Hardy begonia (*Begonia grandis*)	All
Winter-blooming bergenia (*Bergenia crassifolia*)	SN, IV, LD, NC, SC
Blue grama grass (*Bouteloua gracilis*)	All
Rattlesnake grass (*Briza media*)	All
Dusty miller (*Centaurea gymnocarpa*)	IV, HD, LD, NC, SC
Centaurea (*Centaurea montana*)	SN, IV, NC, SC
Red valerian (*Centranthus ruber*)	All
Dwarf plumbago (*Ceratostigma plumbaginoides*)	IV, NC, SC
Sea oats (*Chasmanthium latifolium*)	All
Cigar plant (*Cuphea ignea*)	NC, SC
Hair grass (*Deschampsia*)	All
Pink (*Dianthus*)	All
Gas plant (*Dictamnus albus*)	SN, IV
Purple coneflower (*Echinacea purpurea*)	All
Globe thistle (*Echinops*)	All
California poppy (*Eschscholzia californica*)	All
Blanket flower (*Gaillardia aristata, G. grandiflora*)	All
Hardy geranium (*Geranium*)	SN, IV, HD, NC, SC
Gypsophila (*Gypsophila cerastioides*)	SN, IV, NC, SC
Baby's breath (*Gypsophila paniculata*)	SN, IV, NC, SC
Ox-eye (*Heliopsis helianthoides*)	SN, IV, HD, NC, SC
Candytuft (*Iberis sempervirens*)	All
Blood grass (*Imperata cylindrica* 'Rubra')	All
African corn lily (*Ixia*)	SN, IV, LD, NC, SC
Summer snowflake (*Leucojum aestivum*)	All
Gayfeather (*Liatris*)	SN, IV, NC, SC
Sea lavender (*Limonium*)	All
Maltese cross (*Lychnis chalcedonica*)	All
Maiden grass, Eulalia grass (*Miscanthus*)	All
Jonquil (*Narcissus jonquilla*)	All
Catnip (*Nepeta cataria*)	All
Fountain grass (*Pennisetum*)	All
Moss pink (*Phlox subulata*)	All
Cape plumbago (*Plumbago ariculata*)	IV, HD, LD, NC, SC

Matilija poppy (*Romneya coulteri*)	SN, IV, HD, NC, SC
Rudbeckia, Yellow coneflower (*Rudbeckia*)	All
Bouncing Bet (*Saponaria officinalis*)	All
Harlequin flower (*Sparaxis tricolor*)	IV, LD, NC, SC
Lemon marigold (*Tagetes lemmonii*)	IV, LD, NC, SC

> If you have alkaline soil, Michael A. Parten of Orchard Nursery & Florist in Lafayette suggests Pacific Giant hybrid delphiniums, whose flower spikes reach 4 to 6 feet and may need staking. Others plants to try are African iris (also called Fortnight lily) and matilija poppies. All do well in sun; African iris can take light shade.

PERENNIALS THAT BLOOM IN WINTER

For Californians, winter is the onset of the fertile rainy season. Brown hills turn green, and many perennials that bloom in early spring in other climates burst into flower. Among the most reliable of the winter bloomers is the Crimson King iris. Neither crimson, nor large enough to merit a sovereign title, this late-19th-century hybrid is an intense royal purple with handsome white netting, a yellow beard, and narrower falls than on 20th-century hybrids. It is easily distinguished when not in bloom by a purplish tinge at the bases of its leaves and the larger than normal number of narrow leaves per fan. Crimson King propagates tremendously fast, is immune to drought, and usually begins blooming shortly after the rains begin. It can produce scattered flowers as early as late November and is almost always in full bloom by January. Plants that bloom early in winter will rebloom in late spring. This unusual iris can be found all over California in old gardens and farmsteads, but as the commercials say, it is not sold in stores. Look around your neighborhood; if you see a patch of Crimson King blooming in winter, ask your neighbor for a rhizome next July or August, and within a few years you may have enough to give starts away to all your friends.

The perennials in this list are good winter bloomers. In colder areas of California, though, blooms may be delayed until spring.

Winter-blooming bergenia (*Bergenia crassifolia*)	SN, IV, LD, NC, SC
Crocus (*Crocus*)	All
Winter cyclamen (*Cyclamen atkinsii, C. coum*)	SN, IV, NC, SC
Winter aconite (*Eranthis*)	SN, IV, NC
Crown of thorns (*Euphorbia martinii*)	All
Snowdrops (*Galanthus*)	SN, IV, NC, SC
Bearsfoot hellebore (*Helleborus foetidus*)	SN, IV, NC, SC
Lenten rose (*Helleborus orientalis*)	SN, IV, NC, SC
Chamomile sunray (*Helipterum anthemoides*)	IV, NC, SC
Reticulated iris (*Iris reticulata*)	All
Winter iris, Algerian iris (*Iris unguicularis*)	SN, IV, NC, SC
Ice plant (*Lampranthus*)	IV, NC, SC
Daffodil and narcissus, early types (*Narcissus*)	All
Japanese coltsfoot (*Petasites japonicus*)	SN, IV, NC, SC
Fairy primrose (*Primula malacoides*)	IV, LD, NC, SC
English primrose (*Primula polyantha*)	SN, IV, LD, NC, SC
Winter squill (*Scilla tubergeniana*)	SN, IV, HD, NC, SC
Aztec lily (*Sprekelia formosissima*)	IV, LD, NC, SC
Lemon marigold (*Tagetes lemmonii*)	IV, LD, NC, SC
Violet (*Viola*)	All

PERENNIALS FOR HEAVY CLAY SOIL

Adobe clay soil can be a heartbreaker; soggy in the winter and brick hard in the summer, it is not hospitable to most garden perennials. The following will tolerate clay conditions, but before you plant, modify the soil by working in sand and compost to loosen it up. You want to improve drainage and allow air in for better root growth.

Lily-of-the-Nile (*Agapanthus*)	SN, IV, LD, NC, SC
Milkweed (*Asclepias*)	All
Bergenia (*Bergenia*)	SN, IV, LD, NC, SC
Boltonia (*Boltonia asteroides*)	All
Brodiaea lily (*Brodiaea*)	SN, IV, NC, SC
Red valerian (*Centranthus ruber*)	All
Shasta daisy (*Chrysanthemum superbum*)	All
Golden star, Green and gold (*Chrysogonum virginianum*)	SN, IV, NC
Purple coneflower (*Echinacea purpurea*)	All
Mission bells (*Fritillaria biflora*)	SN, IV, NC
Perennial sunflower (*Helianthus maximilianii*)	All
Daylily (*Hemerocallis*)	All
Obedient plant (*Physostegia virginiana*)	All
Goldenrod (*Solidago*)	All
Brazilian verbena (*Verbena bonariensis*)	IV, HD, LD, NC, SC
Ironweed (*Vernonia noveboracensis*)	SN, IV, NC

PERENNIALS THAT DO WELL IN SHADE

For many urban gardeners, persistent areas of shade seem the biggest hurdle to overcome. One frequently hears discouraged folks say, "I can't grow anything in that shady spot," but in truth, the woodlands of the world are filled with wonderful perennials that are specifically adapted to live in shade. Think of the dense undergrowth found in many forests, and then think of bringing that sort of luxuriance to your shade garden.

In addition to shade-specific plants, this list includes many that are adaptable to partial sun or day-long dappled sun from the moving shadows of trees. Speaking of trees, one reason that you may be getting poor results in shady spots is that tree roots near the surface are robbing smaller plants of water and nutrients. Check the root zones of the perennials you plant under such trees and water them more frequently if necessary.

Acanthus, Bear's breeches (*Acanthus mollis*)	All
Monkshood (*Aconitum*)	SN, IV, NC, SC
Bishop's weed (*Aegopodium podagraria*)	SN, IV, NC, SC
Blue star (*Amsonia*)	All
Japanese anemone (*Anemone japonica*)	All
Wood anemone (*Anemone nemorosa*)	SN, IV, NC, SC
Columbine (*Aquilegia*)	All
Wild ginger (*Asarum caudatum*)	IV, NC, SC
Aspidistra, Cast-iron plant (*Aspidistra elatior*)	SN, IV, NC, SC
Astilbe (*Astilbe*)	SN, IV, NC, SC
Hardy begonia (*Begonia grandis*)	All

Lily-of-the-valley (*Convallaria majalis*)	SN, IV, NC, SC
Crassula (*Crassula*)	IV, LD, NC, SC
Cyclamen (*Cyclamen*)	SN, IV, NC, SC
Bleeding heart (*Dicentra*)	SN, IV, NC, SC
Indian mock strawberry (*Duchesnea indica*)	All
Trout lily (*Erythronium*)	SN, IV, NC
Sweet woodruff (*Galium odoratum*)	SN, IV, NC, SC
Gentian (*Gentiana*)	SN, IV, NC
Wood geranium (*Geranium sylvaticum*)	SN, IV, NC, SC
Hellebore (*Helleborus*)	All
Heuchera (*Heuchera micrantha*)	SN, IV, HD, NC, SC
Hosta, Plantain lily (*Hosta*)	SN, IV, LD, NC, SC
Impatiens (*Impatiens*)	All
Gladwin iris (*Iris foetidissima*)	All
English iris (*Iris latifolia*)	SN, IV, NC, SC
Leopard plant (*Ligularia tussilaginea*)	SN, IV, NC, SC
Lily turf (*Liriope*)	SN, IV, NC, SC
Perennial lobelia (*Lobelia gerardii*)	SN, IV, NC
Garden loosestrife (*Lysimachia ephemerum*)	SN, IV, NC, SC
Himalayan poppy (*Meconopsis betonicifolia*)	SN, NC
Virginia bluebells (*Mertensia virginica*)	All
Forget-me-not (*Myosotis scorpioides*)	All
Narcissus and daffodils (*Narcissus*)	All
Mondo grass (*Ophiopogon japonicus*)	SN, IV, NC, SC
Redwood sorrel (*Oxalis oregana*)	SN, IV, NC, SC
Double fernleaf peony (*Paeonia tenuifolia* 'Rubra Plena')	SN, IV, HD, NC
Jacob's ladder (*Polemonium*)	SN, IV, HD, NC
Primrose (*Primula*)	All
Rehmannia (*Rehmannia elata*)	SN, IV, LD, NC, SC
Snake plant (*Sansevieria trifasciata*)	IV, LD, SC
Saxifrage (*Saxifraga*)	SN, IV, NC, SC
Scilla, Squill (*Scilla bifolia*)	SN, IV, HD, NC, SC
Dusty miller (*Senecio vira-vira*)	All
Wake robin (*Trillium ovatum*)	SN, IV, NC
Periwinkle (*Vinca*)	All
Violets, Violas, Johnny-jump-ups, Pansies (*Viola*)	All
Calla lily (*Zantedeschia*)	IV, LD, NC, SC

Jim Mehdy of the Green Thumb Nursery in Petaluma says that their most popular perennials are the begonias and dahlias. "Begonias really need the shade," he cautions, "but dahlias prefer the sun. Both are good for summer bloom. Water both regularly." Jim notes that most begonias and dahlias are hybridized to perform well and to have good flowers.

PERENNIALS THAT DO WELL IN SUN

Sun-loving perennials can be some of the toughest plants in the garden. Even better, they tend to be bold and showy. Most are native to open areas such as meadows, and many of the best come from our sister bioregion, the Mediterranean.

Cape fuchsia

While all of the plants in this list are adapted to full sun, a couple of cautions need to be stated. These are not all going to accept the unrelenting sun and heat of the desert regions. Also, the intensity of sunlight changes as one moves south, and plants that like full sun near the Oregon border will not necessarily be able to endure the same amount of exposure down along the Mexican line. Soil condition, air moisture, and ambient temperature also affect any perennial's tolerance for sun.

Agave (*Agave*)	IV, LD, NC, SC
Golden marguerite (*Anthemis tinctoria*)	SN, IV, HD, NC, SC
Silver King artemisia (*Artemisia albula*)	All
California sagebrush (*Artemisia californica*)	All
Aster (*Aster*)	All
Baboon flower (*Babiana*)	All
Blackberry lily (*Belamcanda chinensis*)	All
Feather reed grass (*Calamagrostis acutifolia* 'Stricta')	All
Snow-in-summer (*Cerastium tomentosum*)	All
Chrysanthemum (*Chrysanthemum*)	All
Coriander, Cilantro (*Coriandrum*)	All
Fortnight lily (*Dietes, Moraea*)	IV, LD, NC, SC
Shooting star (*Dodecathion hendersonii*)	SN, IV, HD, NC, SC
Euryops, African daisy (*Euryops*)	IV, LD, NC, SC
Blue marguerite (*Felicia amelloides*)	IV, HD, LD, NC, SC
Cranesbill (*Geranium*)	All
Gladiolus (*Gladiolus*)	SN, IV, LD, NC, SC
Perennial sunflower (*Helianthus maximilianii*)	All
Curry plant (*Helichrysum italicum*)	IV, LD, NC, SC
Daylily (*Hemerocallis*)	All
Homeria (*Homeria collina*)	All
Candytuft (*Iberis sempervirens*)	All
Iris (*Iris*)	All
Blue buttons (*Knautia*)	SN, IV, NC, SC
Red-hot poker (*Kniphofia uvaria*)	SN, IV, NC, SC
Easter lily (*Lilium longiflorum*)	All
Mallow (*Malva*)	SN, IV, NC, SC
Four o'clock (*Mirabilis jalapa*)	SN, IV, LD, NC, SC
Showy catnip (*Nepeta sibirica*)	All
Switch grass (*Panicum virgatum*)	SN, IV, HD, NC, SC
Oriental poppy (*Papaver orientale*)	SN, IV, HD, NC, SC
Cape fuchsia (*Phygelius*)	SN, IV, NC, SC
Persian ranunculus (*Ranunculus asiaticus*)	All
Mexican hat (*Ratibida columnifera*)	All
Prairie coneflower (*Ratibida pinnata*)	All

Winter savory (*Satureja montana*)	SN, IV, HD, NC, SC
Scilla, Squill (*Scilla*)	All
Sedum (*Sedum*)	All
Miniature hollyhock (*Sidalcea*)	SN, IV, NC, SC
Moss campion (*Silene schafta*)	SN, IV, NC, SC
Aztec lily (*Sprekelia formosissima*)	IV, LD, NC, SC
Big betony (*Stachys macrantha*)	All
Bird of paradise (*Strelitzia*)	LD, SC
Tritonia (*Tritonia, Montbretia*)	IV, HD, LD, NC, SC
Watsonia (*Watsonia*)	SN, IV, NC, SC

Ernie G. Wasson of Berkeley Horticultural Nursery says that one of his favorite plants is the *Chondropetalum tectorum* from South Africa. "Commonly known as the Kate brush or elephant's reed, its main stems look somewhat like horsetail. This plant forms a loose mound about 4 feet tall, and when covered in mist or fog the water joins in beautiful drip formations along the stem. In the fall you'll get arching flowering stems with brown clusters at the end—perfect for dried flower arrangements. It's easy to grow in a pot or ground. Water it from fall through early spring during its maturing cycle of two years, then allow it a more natural self-feeding period. Particularly attractive in a raised clay pot, this is a striking ornamental."

DAFFODILS FOR WARM-WINTER REGIONS

Anyone who has taken the tour of Daffodil Hill in the Sierra foothills near the town of Volcano knows how inexpressibly lovely a vista of these massed flowers can be. Most people who have seen this sight cherish a fond desire to recreate it, even on a small scale. However, in the warm coastal areas and subtropical regions of California, it is difficult to grow anything that requires a period of winter chilling, and daffodils (*Narcissus*), for all their delicate grace, are naturally cold-winter plants. If you live in a warm-winter region, you need to do your homework before ordering daffodils from a catalogue, otherwise you may find that although the bulbs bloom spectacularly their first year, they may bloom a great deal less the next year, and then may disappear entirely.

This list is not foolproof for all warm-winter regions of the state, but it will get you off the treadmill of trying to grow daffodils that simply cannot survive in your area.

Avalanche
Cragford
Fortune
Ice Follies
Minnow
Paper White
Sun Disk
Trevithian
White Cheerfulness
Yellow Cheerfulness

ORCHIDS THAT CAN BE GROWN OUTDOORS

The orchids in this list from David Hannings, professor of environmental horticulture at Cal Poly in San Luis Obispo, should do well outdoors in Coastal California from San Francisco to the south. He notes, "Most gardeners in Coastal California usually have some standard-size *Cymbidiums* hanging about somewhere in the garden, but there are more interesting plants in this genus and a whole list of other orchid genera that can be grown outdoors with fairly simple care." According to Dave, newer *Cymbidium* cultivars are much improved over most of the ones commonly seen in gardens, and breeders have produced newer dwarf cultivars as well that can be grown and bloomed in 4-inch pots. Others, he says, show off pendulous spikes of flowers from hanging baskets. "Wood slat baskets work well, as do moss-lined wire baskets. Most of the pendulous types are smaller plants with smaller flowers, and some can have up to 30 flowers on a 4- or 5-inch spike. Pretty spectacular!"

Coelogyne
cristata

Among the orchids in this list, *Brassavola nodosa* stands out for its night fragrance. *Coelogyne cristata* has semipendulous spikes of flowers that look beautiful spilling out of a hanging basket. Particularly hardy and reliable are the *Dendrobium* species and hybrids. *Sobralia macrantha* and *Epidendrum ibaguense* have a bamboo-like appearance.

Orchid	Color	Bloom Season
Brassavola nodosa	White	year round
Cattleya aurantiaca	Orange	spring
Cattleya Chit Chat 'Tangerine'	Orange	spring
Cattleya skinneri	Pink	spring
Coelogyne cristata	White	winter
Dendrobium kingianum	Several	winter/spring
Dendrobium speciosum	Several	winter/spring
Disa uniflora	Red, Red-orange	winter/spring
Encyclia nemorale	Lavender	summer
Epidendrum ibaguense	Several	year round
Laelia anceps	Several	fall/winter
Laelia purpurata	Several	spring
Lycaste	Several	fall/winter
Masdevallia coccinea	Several	year round
Maxillaria tenuifolia	Red	year round
Oncidium cavendishianum	Yellow	spring
Oncidium luridum	Yellow	spring
Oncidium splendidum	Yellow	spring
Rossioglossum grande	Orange and brown	fall
Sarchochilus hartmannii	White to pink	spring
Sobralia macrantha	Pink	spring/summer
Zygopetalum	Several	winter

BULBS AND CORMS FOR WARM-WINTER REGIONS

None of these bulbs and corms needs winter chilling, which makes them ideal for gardens of the North Coast, South Coast, and Inland Valleys.

Allium (*Allium*)
Crinum amaryllis (*Amarcrinum memoria-corsii*)
Belladonna lily (*Amaryllis belladonna*)
Diodiaea lily (*Brodiaea*)
Meadow saffron (*Colchicum*)
Crinum lily (*Crinum*)
Pineapple lily, Pineapple flower (*Eucomis*)
Spanish bluebell (*Endymion hispanicus, Scilla hispanica*)
Freesia (*Freesia*)
Summer hyacinth (*Galtonia candicans*)
Habranthus amaryllis (*Habranthus*)
Blood lily (*Haemanthus katherinae*)
Amaryllis (*Hippeastrum*)
Peruvian daffodil (*Hymenocallis narcissiflora, Ismene calathina*)
African corn lily (*Ixia*)
Asian amaryllis (*Ixiolirion tataricum*)
Summer snowflake (*Leucojum aestivum*)
Grape hyacinth (*Muscari*)
Guernsey lily (*Nerine sarniensis*)
Star of Bethlehem (*Ornithogalum arabicum*)
Peruvian scilla (*Scilla peruviana*)
Harlequin flower (*Sparaxis tricolor*)
Aztec lily (*Sprekelia formosissima*)
Sternbergia (*Sternbergia lutea*)
Tiger flower (*Tigridia pavonia*)
Tritonia, Flame freesia (*Tritonia, Montbretia*)
Scarborough lily (*Vallota speciosa, Cyrtanthus*)
Zephyr lily (*Zephyranthes*)

Summer
snowflake

According to Warren Roberts of the UC Davis Arboretum, "Narcissus and daffodils are excellent for our climate. They don't need any water, yet they'll tolerate it." Warren says that, in terms of harshness, California's summer is the equivalent of winter in the eastern United States. "California is green all winter, brown all summer, in the lower elevations. Above 2,000 feet, the snow pack is 12 to 20 feet high, and the melt is stored in the soil and waterways." The harsh season begins in June, but the Davis area has abundant groundwater, he notes, "and watering plants every 2 weeks keeps things going in the hot summer." When the first rains start in October, "That's our spring. Things come into bloom."

PERENNIALS WITH VERTICAL SPIKES OF FLOWERS

For devotees of the Gertrude Jekyll school of perennial borders, the following list is indispensable. These are plants for the back row, the foundation of a good border. Most of them form tidy clumps of foliage that don't compete for visual attention with foreground plants until they shoot up their tall spikes of colorful blossoms.

Not all of these spike-flowered plants are equally suited to every border, however. Some—like foxglove—prefer shade, while others—like red-hot poker, bear's breeches, and pride of Madeira—are so large that they may crowd out more delicate subjects. If you select them wisely, though, they will reward you with some of the most dramatic displays of bloom your perennial beds can offer.

Bear's breeches (*Acanthus mollis*)	All
Canna (*Canna*)	IV, LD, NC, SC
Giant Pacific delphinium (*Delphinium elatum* 'Giant Pacific')	SN, IV, NC, SC
Gas plant, Fraxinella (*Dictamnus albus*)	SN, IV
Foxglove (*Digitalis*)	All
Pride of Madeira (*Echium fastuosum*)	IV, NC, SC
Foxtail lily, Desert candle (*Eremurus*)	SN, IV, NC
Summer hyacinth (*Galtonia candicans*)	All
Gladiolus (*Gladiolus*)	SN, IV, LD, NC, SC
Coral bells (*Heuchera micrantha, H. sanguinea*)	SN, IV, HD, NC, SC
Hyssop (*Hyssopus officinalis*)	All
Red-hot poker (*Kniphofia uvaria*)	SN, IV, NC, SC
Liatris, Gayfeather (*Liatris*)	SN, IV, NC, SC
Cardinal flower (*Lobelia cardinalis*)	SN, IV, LD, NC
Big blue lobelia (*Lobelia siphilitica*)	SN, IV, NC
Spike catmint (*Nepeta sibirica*)	All
Tuberose (*Polianthes tuberosa*)	All
Betony (*Stachys officinalis*)	All
Mullein (*Verbascum*)	SN, IV, HD, NC, SC

Ginny Hunt, of Seedhunt in Freedom, specializes in seeds that are unusual or hard to find. Among the favorites that she grows are salvias, or sages. "A new one from Mexico, *Salvia darcyi,* has beautiful big red flowers. The plant dies to the ground in winter, then comes back. *Salvia ringens,* from the Mediterranean region, has blue flowers, is cold hardy, and does well here." Both salvias bear their flowers on stalks rising about a foot and a half above the foliage. Ginny says that for success in growing plants from seed, "Buy the kinds that aren't tricky." She says that most salvias are easy to grow. "Wait till warm, and plant. Cover with soil to a depth equal to the size of the seed."

PERENNIALS FOR HOT, DRY SITES

For an area of the garden that is an especially hot, dry challenge to plants, consider the following perennials.

Yarrow (*Achillea*)	All
Aloe (*Aloe*)	IV, LD, NC, SC
Belladonna lily (*Amaryllis belladonna*)	All

Perennial anchusa (*Anchusa azurea*)	All
Pussy toes (*Antennaria dioica*)	All
Anthemis (*Anthemis*)	SN, IV, HD, NC, SC
Artemisia, Wormwood (*Artemisia*)	All
Borage (*Borago officinalis*)	All
Blue grama grass (*Bouteloua gracilis*)	SN, IV, HD, NC, SC
Red valerian (*Centranthus ruber*)	All
Golden aster (*Chrysopsis*)	All
Coreopsis (*Coreopsis*)	All
Purple coneflower (*Echinacea purpurea*)	All
Hedgehog cactus (*Echinocereus*)	All
Wild buckwheat (*Eriogonum*)	All
Crown of thorns (*Euphorbia martinii*)	All
Blanket flower (*Gaillardia*)	All
Sneezeweed (*Helenium autumnale*)	All
Hesperaloe (*Hesperaloe parviflora*)	HD, LD, SC
Hyssop (*Hyssopus officinalis*)	All
Algerian iris (*Iris unguicularis*)	SN, IV, NC, SC
Blackfoot daisy (*Melampodium leucanthum*)	SN, HD, LD
Bamboo muhly grass (*Muhlenbergia dumosa*)	IV, HD, LD, NC, SC
Deer grass (*Muhlenbergia rigens*)	All
Catnip (*Nepeta cataria*)	All
Mexican evening primrose (*Oenothera speciosa*)	All
Fountain grass (*Pennisetum setaceum*)	IV, HD, LD, NC, SC
Russian sage (*Perovskia*)	All
Matilija poppy (*Romneya coulteri*)	SN, IV, HD, NC, SC
Mexican petunia (*Ruellia brittoniana*)	IV, NC, SC
Lavender cotton (*Santolina chamaecyparissus*)	All
Rosemary santolina (*Santolina rosmarinifolia*)	All
Southwest pincushion flower (*Scabiosa columbaria*)	All
California Indian pink (*Silene californica*)	SN, IV, HD, NC, SC
Betony (*Stachys officinalis*)	All
Germander (*Teucrium chamaedrys*)	All
Cat thyme (*Teucrium marum*)	All
False lupine (*Thermopsis*)	SN, IV, NC
Thyme (*Thymus*)	All
Verbena (*Verbena*)	All

Cactus and succulents are perennials that withstand desert conditions. "Succulents have very shallow roots, and most of them have large leaves or stems that store water for times of drought," says Joe Clements, curator of the Desert Gardens at the Huntington Botanical Gardens in San Marino. "A cactus will store water in its stem. Jade plants store water in their leaves and stem. The ponytail palm, *Beaucarnea recurvata*, highly recommended as a shrub or tree for desert conditions, stores water in its base."

A FEW BULBS, CORMS, AND TUBERS OF FILOLI

The Filoli estate in Woodside is renowned for its formal gardens and spring blooms. Located about 25 miles south of San Francisco, its 654 acres experience a microclimate that is part Inland Valley and part North Coast. Lucy Tolmach, director of horticulture at Filoli, says the area has some ocean influence, and average low temperatures are 16 to 26 degrees F. The bulbs, corms, and tubers in this list from Lucy reflect only a few of the delightful plants in the 16 acres of gardens around the Georgian manor house.

"We take a historic approach at Filoli," explains Lucy, and the garden plantings tend to be those typically found surviving in old estate gardens on the Peninsula. Daffodils, or *Narcissus*, are important to the collection. "Narcissus bulbs naturalize beautifully in full sun with no summer water in our Mediterranean climate," Lucy says. "They are certainly one of the best values of all the bulbs because they keep on going year after year. Old-time tazetta types like the golden, fragrant 'Soleil d'Or' and white and orange 'Cragford' and 'Geranium' were planted in a field under olive trees at Filoli, and after many years they still bloom reliably." Lucy recommends planting daffodils near rosemary for a pleasing color combination, and planting scilla or squill nearby too. The tall lavender blooms of Spanish squill follow the yellow daffodils and cover their spent foliage.

In April come the orange, yellow, and red blooms of harlequin flower and tall white spikes of watsonia. Both plants naturalize easily at Filoli. Lucy also praises summer snowflake, which blooms through winter with the early daffodils and camellias. "It thrives with little care in our zone and naturalizes in shady places in the shrub beds and woodlands. The white flowers are like nodding white bells with little green tips to the petals." You'll find these and more in the groups of plants that follow, with their periods of peak bloom.

Narcissus, Daffodils	Bloom
Carlton	Feb.
Cragford	Jan./Feb.
Geranium	Jan./Feb.
Ice Follies	Feb.
King Alfred	Feb.
Soleil d'Or	Jan./Feb.
World's Favorite	Feb.

Tulips	
Angelique	Mar./Apr.
Kingsblood	Mar./Apr.
Maureen	Mar./Apr.
Mrs. John Scheepers	Mar./Apr.
Pink Diamond	Mar./Apr.
Renown	Mar./Apr.

Other Bulbs, Corms, Tubers	
Dahlia	summer/fall
Gladiolus	summer
Gladiolus tristis	Mar./Apr.
Harlequin flower (*Sparaxis*)	Apr.
Montbretia (*Crocosmia crocrosmiiflora*)	summer
Naked lady lily (*Amaryllis belladonna*)	summer
Spanish squill (*Endymion hispanica*)	Mar./Apr.

| Summer snowflake (*Leucojum aestivum*) | winter |
| Watsonia (*Watsonia pyramidata ardernei*) | Apr./May |

> Ginny Hunt of Seedhunt, in Freedom, recommends *Dierama*, or fairy wand, a South African corm that sends up long stems topped with "beautiful dangling bell flowers in dark purple. The plant is evergreen."

PERENNIALS THAT MAKE SHOWY GROUND COVERS

Ground covers are usually thought of as low-maintenance plants, preferably evergreen. But for a showy ground cover, you might consider these low-growing perennials. When massed together so closely that they cover the soil, they present a uniform appearance, and their bonuses of seasonal bloom or interesting foliage make them a great choice for beds near walkways, where they will be often admired. Also consider low-growing ferns (page 152), and see the chapter on ground covers (page 153).

Woolly yarrow (*Achillea tomentosa*)	All
Carpet bugle (*Ajuga reptans*)	All
Wood anemone (*Anemone nemorosa*)	SN, IV, NC, SC
Trailing aptenia (*Aptenia cordifolia*)	NC, SC
Creeping rockcress (*Arabis procurrens*)	SN, IV, NC, SC
Bergenia (*Bergenia*)	SN, IV, LD, NC, SC
Cumberland rosemary (*Conradina verticillata*)	SN, IV, NC
Delosperma, Ice plant (*Delosperma*)	All
Rose ice plant (*Drosanthemum floribundum*)	IV, NC, SC
Indian mock strawberry (*Duchesnea indica*)	All
Wild strawberry (*Fragaria chiloensis*)	All
Sweet woodruff (*Galium odoratum*)	SN, IV, NC
Spreading gardenia (*Gardenia jasminoides* 'Radicans')	IV, LD, NC, SC
Hybrid cranesbill (*Geranium cantabrigiense*)	All
Lenten rose (*Helleborus orientalis*)	SN, IV, HD, NC, SC
Hosta (*Hosta*)	All
Creeping St. Johnswort (*Hypericum calycinum*)	All
Candytuft (*Iberis sempervirens*)	All
Dead nettle (*Lamium maculatum*)	All
Creeping Jennie (*Lysimachia nummularia*)	SN, IV, NC, SC
Mazus (*Mazus reptans*, *M. japonicus*)	SN, IV, NC, SC
White cup (*Nierembergia repens*)	IV, NC, SC
Creeping phlox (*Phlox stolonifera*)	SN, IV, HD, LD, NC
Creeping buttercup (*Ranunculus repens*)	All
Blue Shade ruellia (*Ruellia* 'Blue Shade')	IV, NC, SC
Strawberry geranium (*Saxifraga stolonifera*)	SN, IV, NC, SC
Mauve Clusters scaevola (*Scaevola* 'Mauve Clusters')	IV, NC, SC
Purple Heart (*Setcreasea pallida* 'Purple Heart')	IV, LD, NC, SC
Golden fleece (*Solidago sphacelata* 'Golden Fleece')	SN, IV, NC, SC
Lamb's ears (*Stachys byzantina*)	All
Vancouveria (*Vancouveria*)	SN, IV, NC, SC
Spreading verbena (*Verbena* 'Sissinghurst')	All
Creeping speedwell (*Veronica liwanensis*)	SN, IV, NC, SC

PERENNIALS THAT BLOOM SIX WEEKS
OR LONGER

The greatest benefit in growing perennials is that they come back every year and can be relied on when you make your garden plans. Annuals, on the other hand, need to be replanted every year—but they bloom longer. The following list of perennials includes some that keep blooming for months. Many perennials will keep going as long as possible if you deadhead them (cut off the spent blooms) regularly and give them water.

Alstroemeria

Alstoemeria (*Alstroemeria*)	SN, IV, NC, SC
Peruvian lily (*Alstroemeria aurea*)	SN, IV, NC, SC
Golden marguerite (*Anthemis tinctoria*)	SN, IV, HD, NC, SC
Thrift, Sea pink (*Armeria maritima*)	SN, IV, NC, SC
Dwarf michaelmas daisy (*Aster dumosus*)	All
Purple aster (*Aster frikartii*)	All
Begonia (*Begonia*)	All
Bellflower (*Campanula*)	SN, IV, NC, SC
Cupid's dart (*Catananche caerulea*)	All
Painted daisy, Pyrethrum (*Chrysanthemum coccineum*)	All
Ox-eye daisy, Common daisy (*Chrysanthemum leucanthemum*)	All
Florists' chrysanthemum (*Chrysanthemum morifolium*)	All
Feverfew (*Chrysanthemum parthenium*)	All
Cheddar pink (*Dianthus gratianopolitanus*)	All
Purple coneflower (*Echinacea purpurea*)	All
Spreading euphorbia (*Euphorbia cyparissias*)	All
Euryops, African daisy (*Euryops pectinatus*)	IV, LD, NC, SC
Blue marguerite (*Felicia amelloides*)	IV, HD, LD, NC, SC
Gaura (*Gaura lindheimeri*)	All
Cranesbill (*Geranium*)	All
Gerbera daisy, Transvaal daisy (*Gerbera jamesonii*)	IV, LD, NC, SC
Geum (*Geum*)	All
Ox-eye (*Heliopsis helianthoides*)	SN, IV, HD, NC, SC
Daylily (*Hemerocallis*)	All
Rose mallow, Perennial hibiscus (*Hibiscus moscheutos*)	All
Japanese aster (*Kalimeris pinnatifida*)	SN, IV, NC, SC
Flax (*Linum*)	All
Woodland mallow (*Malva sylvestris*)	SN, IV, NC, SC
Bee balm (*Monarda*)	All
Sundrops, Evening primrose (*Oenothera fruticosa*)	All
Patrinia (*Patrinia scabiosifolia*)	SN, IV, NC
Rudbeckia, Yellow coneflower (*Rudbeckia*)	All
Mexican petunia (*Ruellia brittoniana*)	IV, NC, SC
Flowering sage, Salvia (*Salvia*)	All
Southwest pincushion flower (*Scabiosa columbaria*)	All
Showy sedum (*Sedum spectabile*)	All
Miniature hollyhock (*Sidalcea*)	SN, IV, NC, SC
Moss campion, Fire pink (*Silene virginica, Melandrium virginicum*)	SN, IV, NC, SC

California blue-eyed grass (*Sisyrinchium bellum*)	SN, IV, HD, NC, SC
Goldenrod (*Solidago*)	All
Goldenrod aster (*Solidaster luteus*)	SN, IV, HD, NC, SC
Lemon marigold (*Tagetes lemmonii*)	IV, LD, NC, SC
Verbena (*Verbena*)	All

If you're eager for spring color from flowering perennials, Ed Wright of Millards Florist & Nursery, Sonora, says bleeding hearts and alstroemeria are extremely popular in his area. "They will bloom in early March and continue all summer long." Ed says these plants offer years of vibrant flowers when planted in loose soil rich in organic materials, and are fertilized.

SOME ORNAMENTAL GRASSES FOR DRAMATIC ACCENTS

Some of the tallest perennials for gardens are ornamental grasses. Slender, arching stems rising 4 feet or more in height can create spectacular effects when used here and there in the landscape, or as border backdrops for colorful flowers. The sturdy giant reeds, which can reach 20 feet, are useful for a screen or windbreak. Grasses of smaller stature, such as the white-striped bulbous oat grass, can be used in a perennial border to complement other foliage textures, or use them in rock gardens or naturalized areas of the garden.

Tall Grasses

Giant reed (*Arundo donax*)	All
Alphonse Karr bamboo (*Bambusa multiplex* 'Alphonse Karr')	IV, HD, LD, NC, SC
Papyrus (*Cyperus papyrus*)	NC, SC
Eulalia grass (*Miscanthus sinensis*)	All
Maiden grass (*Miscanthus sinensis* 'Gracillimus')	All
Deer grass (*Muhlenbergia rigens*)	All
Fountain grass (*Pennisetum alopecuroides*)	All
Giant feather grass (*Stipa gigantea*)	SN, IV, NC, SC

Short Grasses

Bulbous oat grass (*Arrhenatherum elatius*)	SN, IV
Blue oat grass (*Avena sempervirens*)	All
Quaking grass (*Briza media*)	All
Job's tears (*Coix lacryma-jobi*)	IV, LD, NC, SC
Hair grass (*Deschampsia*)	All
Blood grass (*Imperata cylindrica* 'Rubra')	All
Fiber optics plant (*Isolepis gracilis*)	All
Purple moor grass (*Molinia caerulea*)	SN, IV, NC, SC
Bamboo muhly (*Muhlenbergia dumosa*)	IV, HD, LD, NC, SC
Hameln fountain grass (*Pennisetum alopecuroides* 'Hameln')	All

PERENNIALS FOR CRACKS AND CREVICES

For added interest, you can plant perennials between the stones or bricks of a path or in soil pockets between the stones in a wall. Remember that these areas will dry out rapidly without summer rain, so be prepared to lavish extra water on them. Also, because the soil in these pockets cannot be enriched by yearly applications of compost, start with a fertile mixture that has been loosened with the addition of plenty of organic matter to increase its fertility and its water-retaining capacity. The following perennials are traditional subjects for crevice gardening.

Woolly yarrow (*Achillea tomentosa*)	All
Warley Rose stonecress (*Aethionema warleyense*)	SN, IV, NC, SC
Trailing alyssum (*Alyssum wulfenianum*)	All
Mount Atlas daisy (*Anacyclus depressus*)	All
California rockcress, Rose cress (*Arabis blepharophylla*)	IV, NC
Sandwort (*Arenaria montana*)	SN, IV, NC, SC
Thrift, Sea pink (*Armeria maritima*)	SN, IV, NC, SC
Basket-of-Gold (*Aurinia saxatilis*)	All
Snow-in-summer (*Cerastium tomentosum*)	All
Purple ice plant (*Delosperma cooperi*)	All
Hardy ice plant (*Delosperma nubigenum*)	All
Cheddar pink (*Dianthus gratianopolitanus*)	All
Trailing gazania (*Gazania rigens*)	IV, HD, LD, NC, SC
Globe daisy (*Globularia cordifolia*)	SN, IV, NC, SC
Gypsophila (*Gypsophila cerastioides*)	SN, IV, NC, SC
Candytuft (*Iberis sempervirens*)	All
Lithodora (*Lithodora diffusa*)	SN, IV, NC
Mazus (*Mazus reptans*, *M. japonicus*)	SN, IV, NC, SC
Partridgeberry (*Mitchella repens*)	SN, IV
Moss pink (*Phlox subulata*)	SN, IV, HD, LD, NC
Trailing soapwort (*Saponaria ocymoides*)	SN, IV, HD, NC, SC
Goldmoss sedum (*Sedum acre*)	All
Hen and chicks (*Sempervivum tectorum*)	All
Caraway-scented thyme (*Thymus herba-barona*)	All
Creeping thyme (*Thymus praecox*)	All
Woolly thyme (*Thymus pseudolanuginosus*)	All
Peruvian verbena (*Verbena peruviana*)	IV, HD, LD, NC, SC
Sissinghurst verbena (*Verbena* 'Sissinghurst')	All
Prostrate speedwell (*Veronica repens*)	SN, IV, NC, SC
Creeping speedwell (*Veronica liwanensis*)	SN, IV, NC, SC
Sweet violet (*Viola odorata*)	All

A tough plant that does well in poor or rocky soil conditions is alyssum. This gray-leaved plant with fragrant yellow flowers reaches a height of about 8 inches and is easy to grow in full sun or light shade. It works well for edging borders, between paving stones, or in a rock garden.

CACTUS AND SUCCULENTS FOR THE GARDEN

Mostly natives of dry or desert regions, cactus and succulents store water in fleshy stems, leaves, or pads to get them through dry times. Many of these plants will do fine in gardens, rock gardens, and containers. This list comes from Wendy Proud, a grower at Monrovia Nursery in Azusa. Wendy is in charge of 100 acres and about 550 species at Monrovia, which keeps her busy, but in her spare time she pursues an interest in cactus and succulents. "This group of plants has two requirements that must be met for success," she advises. "These are plenty of bright light, and well-drained soil. A common myth about cacti and succulents is that they must have direct sun all the time and that they require very little to no water. Actually, cacti and succulents that receive regular watering and dappled or light shade from the afternoon heat are the healthiest plants." Wendy notes that the plants prefer to be watered well, then left to dry out before being watered again. "But they still require attention. They actively grow during the warmer months and take a rest during the cooler months, so the frequency of watering should be determined by the time of year."

Wendy says that wax flowers are fast-growing, vining succulents that can grow to 10 feet long. They bear fragrant red or pink clusters of perfect 5-point, star-shaped flowers. "Over time, the number of clusters will increase because the flowers appear from the sites of old flowers. Wax flower grows best in light afternoon shade with rich, well-drained soil and an even moisture during warm months. Let the plant assume a state of dormancy during winter, watering only enough to keep the plant from shrivelling. Wax flower blooms best when pot bound. It makes a great hanging basket."

The sea urchin cactus, which grows to 10 inches tall, will bloom spring to fall with long, tubular, multipetal flowers, and the golden barrel cactus, which grows 2 feet high but 4 feet wide, produces a crown of small flowers in spring. The tallest plant in this list is the pencil tree, which grows to shrub or tree size. Wendy notes that pencil tree, named for its pencil-thin branches, is appreciated for its odd branching structure. It can be grown indoors in very bright light. The branches produce a milky sap if broken or cut, so pencil tree is sometimes called milkbush.

Victoria regina agave (*Agave victoriae-reginae*)	LD, NC, SC
Medicinal aloe (*Aloe vera*)	IV, LD, NC, SC
Jade plant (*Crassula argentea*)	IV, LD, NC, SC
Sickle-leaved crassula (*Crassula falcata*)	IV, LD, NC, SC
Molded wax echeveria (*Echeveria agavoides*)	IV, LD, NC, SC
Hens and chicks (*Echeveria imbricata*)	IV, LD, NC, SC
Golden barrel cactus (*Echinocactus grusonii*)	IV, LD, NC, SC
Sea urchin cactus (*Echinopsis*)	NC, SC
Crown of thorns (*Euphorbia splendens*)	SC
Pencil tree (*Euphorbia tirucalli*)	LD, SC
Wax flower (*Hoya carnosa*)	NC, SC
Blossfeld kalanchoe (*Kalanchoe blossfeldiana*)	NC, SC
Pork and beans (*Sedum rubrotinctum*)	IV, LD, NC, SC
Siebold sedum (*Sedum sieboldii*)	All
String of beads (*Senecio rowleyanus*)	IV, LD, NC, SC

PERENNIALS WITH FRAGRANT FOLIAGE

Perennials with fragrant foliage usually release the most aroma when their leaves are brushed against or crushed. Some of the best fragrance may come from herbs.

Yarrow (*Achillea*)	All
Lemon verbena (*Aloysia triphylla, Lippia citriodora*)	IV, LD, NC, SC
Anthemis (*Anthemis*)	SN, IV, HD, NC, SC
Common wormwood (*Artemisia absinthium*)	All
Calamint (*Calamintha*)	SN, IV, NC, SC
Chamomile (*Chamaemelum nobile, Anthemis nobilis*)	All
Spreading cranesbill (*Geranium macrorrhizum*)	All
Curry plant (*Helichrysum italicum*)	IV, LD, NC, SC
Chamomile sunray (*Helipterum anthemoides*)	IV, NC, SC
Hyssop (*Hyssopus officinalis*)	All
Horehound (*Marrubium vulgare*)	All
Lemon balm (*Melissa officinalis*)	All
Mint (*Mentha*)	All
Bee balm (*Monarda*)	All
Catnip, Catmint (*Nepeta*)	All
Geranium (*Pelargonium*)	IV, LD, NC, SC
Rosemary (*Rosmarinus officinalis*)	All
Rue (*Ruta graveolens*)	All
Sage, Salvia (*Salvia*)	All
Yerba buena	SN, IV, NC, SC
(*Satureja douglasii, Micromeria chamissonis*)	
Santolina (*Santolina*)	All
Stokes' aster (*Stokesia laevis*)	All
Lemon marigold (*Tagetes lemmonii*)	IV, LD, NC, SC
Mexican tarragon (*Tagetes lucida*)	IV, LD, NC, SC
Tansy (*Tanacetum vulgare*)	All
Thyme (*Thymus*)	All

Salvia

PERENNIALS WITH FRAGRANT FLOWERS

A fragrant garden is one that gives the visitor an added level of enjoyment. On warm, humid days, when the perfume released by flowers is most intense, a walk down the garden path can be a heaven of sensual delight. For more fragrant plants, see the section on perennials with fragrant foliage, above. Also, be sure to look over the chapter on roses.

Stonecress (*Aethionema schistosum*)	SN, IV, NC, SC
Fragrant alyssum (*Alyssum montanum*)	All
Belladonna lily (*Amaryllis belladonna*)	All
Chocolate cosmos (*Cosmos atrosanguineus*)	SN, IV, NC, SC
Crinum lily (*Crinum*)	IV, LD, NC, SC
Pink (*Dianthus*)	All
Fragrant cyclamen	SN, IV, NC, SC
(*Cyclamen cilicium, C. purpurascens, C. europaeum*)	

Freesia (*Freesia*)	IV, LD, NC, SC
Summer hyacinth (*Galtonia candicans*)	All
Gladiolus (*Gladiolus*)	SN, IV, LD, NC, SC
Lemon daylily (*Hemerocallis lilioasphodelus*)	SN, IV, HD, NC, SC
Dame's rocket (*Hesperis matronalis*)	All
Fragrant hosta (*Hosta plantaginea*)	SN, IV, LD, NC, SC
Dutch hyacinth (*Hyacinthus orientalis*)	All
Spider lily (*Hymenocallis latifolia*)	IV, NC, SC
Peruvian daffodil, Ismene (*Hymenocallis narcissiflora, Ismene calathina*)	IV, NC, SC
Bearded iris (*Iris*)	All
Lavender (*Lavandula*)	All
Lily (*Lilium*)	All
Narcissus, Daffodil (*Narcissus*)	All
Lily-of-the-valley orchid (*Odontoglossum pulchellum*)	SC
Tuberose (*Polianthes tuberosa*)	SC
Moonlight primrose (*Primula alpicola*)	SN, IV, NC
Sweet violet (*Viola odorata*)	All

SOME PERENNIALS NATIVE TO CALIFORNIA

More and more people are becoming interested in devoting some space in the garden to a naturalized patch of native California plants, or using native plants here and there as accents. Native plants, the best for naturalizing, should grow well and take minimal care. Here is a short list of plants that are native to California. Use them as accent plants in the garden, or for meadow or natural effects.

Yarrow (*Achillea millefolium*)	All
Western columbine (*Aquilegia formosa*)	All
Seaside daisy (*Erigeron glaucus*)	NC, SC
Red buckwheat (*Eriogonum rubescens*)	NC, SC
California fescue (*Festuca californica*)	SN, IV, NC, SC
Coral bells (*Heuchera micrantha*)	All
Douglas iris (*Iris douglasiana*)	All
Humboldt lily (*Lilium humboldtii*)	All
Leopard lily (*Lilium pardalinum*)	All
Deer grass (*Muhlenbergia rigens*)	All
Matilija poppy (*Romneya coulteri*)	All
Blue-eyed grass (*Sisyrinchium bellum*)	All
Yellow-eyed grass (*Sisyrinchium californicum*)	All
California goldenrod (*Solidago californica*)	All
California fuchsia (*Zauschneria*)	SN, IV, LD, NC, SC

Blue-eyed
grass

PERENNIALS FOR CUTTING

If you like to have cut flowers in the house, here is a list of perennials that hold up well in arrangements.

Yarrow (*Achillea*)	All
Alstroemeria (*Alstroemeria*)	SN, IV, NC, SC
Pearly everlasting (*Anaphalis*)	SN, IV, NC
Poppy anemone (*Anemone coronaria*)	All
Golden marguerite (*Anthemis tinctoria*)	All
Butterfly weed (*Asclepias tuberosa*)	All
Aster (*Aster*)	All
Blackberry lily (*Belamcanda chinensis*)	All
Borage (*Borago officinalis*)	All
Brodiaea lily (*Brodiaea*)	SN, IV, NC, SC
Chrysanthemum (*Chrysanthemum*)	All
Purple coneflower (*Echinacea purpurea*)	All
Blanket flower (*Gaillardia*)	All
Gaura (*Gaura lindheimeri*)	All
Gerbera daisy (*Gerbera jamesonii*)	IV, LD, NC, SC
Geum (*Geum*)	All
Gladiolus (*Gladiolus*)	SN, IV, LD, NC, SC
Baby's breath (*Gypsophila paniculata*)	SN, IV, NC, SC
Dwarf sunflower (*Helianthus multiflorus*)	All
Ox-eye (*Heliopsis helianthoides, H. scabra*)	SN, IV, HD, NC, SC
Hellebore (*Helleborus*)	All
Coral bells (*Heuchera*)	SN, IV, HD, NC, SC
Iris (*Iris*)	All
Knautia, Blue buttons (*Knautia*)	SN, IV, NC, SC
Rehmannia (*Rehmannia elata*)	IV, LD, NC, SC
Rudbeckia, Yellow coneflower (*Rudbeckia*)	All
Southwest pincushion flower (*Scabiosa columbaria*)	All
Trachelium (*Trachelium caeruleum*)	IV, NC, SC
Watsonia (*Watsonia*)	IV, LD, NC, SC
Calla lily (*Zantedeschia*)	IV, LD, NC, SC

Lucy Tolmach, director of horticulture at the Filoli estate gardens in Woodside, says that they grow dahlias as a source of cut flowers for late summer and fall. "Dahlias grow beautifully in full sun in California, and although they do better with regular summer water, they will survive okay without it." Gladiolus supplies cut flowers during the transition between the late spring and summer flowers, Lucy notes. "A lovely old-fashioned species glad is *Gladiolus tristis*, which blooms in March and April with pale, creamy, fragrant flowers." But most glads bloom in late June and July, and they take full sun. "Glad thrips are a real problem in California, so we often will buy new corms. We irrigate the glads, although they are fairly drought tolerant."

PERENNIALS THAT SELF-SOW

While many perennials spread by crown division or by making runners, others multiply by setting and scattering seed after the manner of annuals. Occasionally the flower colors of your seedlings will vary from the hybrids that you originally planted. Surprises like this make gardening wonderfully exciting. One of my biggest thrills was watching a second generation of columbines spring into bloom in the shade of the extremely expensive hybrids planted the previous year. Not only did this quadruple the number of plants in the bed, but they were almost all entirely different from their parents, making for an even better display of color. I also had the satisfaction of knowing I had picked a good home for my columbines, a semi-shady spot by a small pond where they could happily raise their families. Seven years later, they are still there, having essentially naturalized themselves through continual reproduction.

Columbine (*Aquilegia*)	All
Cupid's dart (*Catananche caerulea*)	All
Red valerian (*Centranthus ruber*)	All
Cosmos (*Cosmos*)	All
Foxglove (*Digitalis purpurea*)	All
Purple coneflower (*Echinacea purpurea*)	All
Pride of Madeira (*Echium fastuosum*)	IV, NC, SC
Wild buckwheat (*Eriogonum*)	All
Blanket flower (*Gaillardia*)	All
Gaura (*Gaura lindheimeri*)	All
Hellebore (*Helleborus*)	SN, IV, NC, SC
Dame's rocket (*Hesperus matronalis*)	All
Sea lavender (*Limonium*)	SN, IV, HD, NC, SC
Rose campion (*Lychnis coronaria*)	SN, IV, NC, SC
Four o'clock (*Mirabilis jalapa*)	SN, IV, LD, NC, SC
Meadow sage (*Salvia pratensis*)	SN, IV, HD, NC, SC
Verbena (*Verbena*)	All

Carol Bornstein, director of horticulture at the Santa Barbara Botanic Garden, says that native plants for a natural look or meadow would include pink or white yarrow, seaside daisy, California fescue, red flowering buckwheat, Douglas iris, California goldenrod, deer grass, and blue-eyed grass. Carol notes, "Seaside daisy, *Erigeron glaucus*, is a good plant: reliable and pretty, for sun or part shade."

PERENNIALS THAT ATTRACT HUMMINGBIRDS

Hummingbird-watching is one of my favorite outdoor sports. These bright, tiny bundles of color are simply amazing as they hover in mid-air and perform their courtship dives. Perennials that provide nectar will bring them to your garden. They are most attracted to flowers that are red, orange, or hot pink.

Aloe (*Aloe*)	IV, LD, NC, SC
Alstroemeria (*Alstroemeria*)	IV, NC, SC
Columbine (*Aquilegia*)	All
Butterfly weed (*Asclepias tuberosa*)	All
Crocosmia, Montbretia (*Crocosmia*)	All
Foxglove (*Digitalis*)	All
Gladiolus (*Gladiolus*)	All
India lily (*Hedychium greenei*)	NC, SC
Coral bells (*Heuchera*)	SN, IV, HD, NC, SC
Iris (*Iris*)	All
Red-hot poker (*Kniphofia uvaria*)	SN, IV, NC, SC
Cardinal flower (*Lobelia cardinalis*)	SN, IV, LD, NC
Lupine (*Lupinus*)	All
Rose campion (*Lychnis coronaria*)	SN, IV, NC, SC
Bee balm (*Monarda*)	All
Geranium (*Pelargonium*)	IV, LD, NC, SC
Beard tongue (*Penstemon*)	All
Phlox (*Phlox*)	All
Sage (*Salvia*)	All
Bird of paradise (*Strelitzia*)	SC
Speedwell (*Veronica*)	SN, IV, NC, SC
California fuchsia (*Zauschneria, Epilobium*)	SN, IV, HD, NC, SC

To draw hummingbirds to your garden, plant montbretia (*Crocosmia crocrosmiiflora*), advises Lucy Tolmach, director of horticulture at the Filoli estate gardens in Woodside. This very drought-tolerant, summer-blooming bulb has bright orange and red flowers. "Hummingbirds love this plant, and montbretias make excellent cut flowers. Montbretias will naturalize in woodland areas, where they can unfortunately become invasive. This is a good choice for low water gardens where vivid warm colors are desired."

PERENNIALS WITH SEEDS FOR BIRDS TO EAT

To attract birds to your garden, plant seed-bearing perennials and don't remove the spent blossoms. The birds will glean the seeds for you and will provide hours of entertainment while they do so.

Aster (*Aster*)	All
Painted daisy, Pyrethrum (*Chrysanthemum coccineum*)	All
Marguerite (*Chrysanthemum frutescens*)	IV, NC, SC
Coreopsis (*Coreopsis*)	All
Cosmos (*Cosmos*)	All
Delphinium (*Delphinium*)	SN, IV, NC

Purple coneflower (*Echinacea purpurea*)	All
Globe thistle (*Echinops*)	All
Common fennel (*Foeniculum vulgare*)	All
Blanket flower (*Gaillardia*)	All
Sneezeweed (*Helenium autumnale*)	All
Oriental poppy (*Papaver orientale*)	SN, IV, HD, NC, SC
Rudbeckia, Yellow coneflower (*Rudbeckia*)	All
Goldenrod (*Solidago*)	All
Goldenrod aster (*Solidaster*)	All
Ironweed (*Vernonia noveboracensis*)	SN, IV, NC

PERENNIALS THAT CAN BE INVASIVE

The perennials below are what could be called "mixed blessings." They are vigorous, healthy, and good-looking, but in some regions they can quickly get out of hand in their eagerness to colonize your garden. Roof iris, for instance, is almost a pest along the North Coast, but in hotter, drier regions it is mannerly or even short-lived. Lamb's ears, which can take over a bed in no time if it receives mild winter weather, is more easy to manage when frost cuts it back to the ground or it grows in semi-shade.

If you have difficult areas or steep slopes, give these plants a try. They may succeed where others have failed.

Bear's breeches (*Acanthus mollis*)	All
Lady bells (*Adenophora*)	SN, IV, NC, SC
Bishop's weed (*Aegopodium podagraria*)	SN, IV, NC, SC
Perennial anchusa (*Anchusa azurea*)	All
Pampas grass (*Cortaderia selloana*)	All
Indian mock strawberry (*Duchesnea indica*)	All
Horsetail (*Equisetum hyemale*)	All
Spreading euphorbia (*Euphorbia cyparissias*)	All
Roof iris (*Iris tectorum*)	SN, IV, NC, SC
Dead nettle (*Lamium maculatum*)	All
Loosestrife (*Lysimachia*)	SN, IV, NC, SC
Creeping Jennie (*Lysimachia nummularia*)	SN, IV, NC, SC
Plume poppy (*Macleaya, Bocconia*)	All
Mints (*Mentha*)	All
Mexican evening primrose (*Oenothera speciosa*)	All
Fountain grass (*Pennisetum setaceum*)	All
Ribbon grass (*Phalaris arundinacea*)	SN, IV, NC, SC
Common reed (*Phragmites australis, P. communis*)	All
Obedient plant (*Physostegia virginiana*)	All
Creeping buttercup (*Ranunculus repens*)	All
Bog sage (*Salvia uliginosa*)	SN, IV, NC, SC
Lamb's ears (*Stachys byzantina*)	All

A serious warning about pampas grass: *Cortaderia jubata,* purple pampas grass, has become a serious pest along the North and South Coasts, driving out native grasses and reseeding madly. Do not collect seeds from any naturalized pampas grass—buy noninvasive plants from a nursery.

PERENNIALS THAT ATTRACT BUTTERFLIES

Here are some of the easiest to grow favorites of butterflies. You will find a group of nectar plants and a group of plants that the caterpillars will feed on, so you will be assured of future crops of butterflies.

Nectar Plants

Yarrow (*Achillea*)	All
Lily-of-the-Nile (*Agapanthus*)	SN, IV, LD, NC, SC
Columbine (*Aquilegia*)	All
Butterfly weed (*Asclepias tuberosa*)	All
Aster (*Aster*)	All
Astilbe, False spiraea (*Astilbe*)	SN, IV, NC
Borage (*Borago officinalis*)	All
Red valerian (*Centranthus ruber*)	All
Coreopsis (*Coreopsis*)	All
Purple coneflower (*Echinacea purpurea*)	All
Joe Pye weed (*Eupatorium maculatum, E. purpureum*)	SN, IV, NC
Blanket flower (*Gaillardia*)	All
Dame's rocket (*Hesperis matronalis*)	All
Gayfeather (*Liatris*)	SN, IV, NC, SC
Lobelia (*Lobelia*)	SN, IV, LD, NC
Bee balm (*Monarda*)	All
Catmint, Catnip (*Nepeta*)	All
Phlox (*Phlox*)	All
Rudbeckia, Yellow coneflower (*Rudbeckia*)	All
Sage (*Salvia*)	All
Pincushion flower (*Scabiosa columbaria*)	All
Showy sedum (*Sedum spectabile*)	All
Goldenrod (*Solidago*)	All
Verbena (*Verbena*)	All
California fuchsia (*Zauschneria californica, Epilobium*)	SN, IV, HD, NC, SC

Bee balm

Host Plants for Larvae

Butterfly weed (*Asclepias tuberosa*)	All
Aster (*Aster*)	All
Bleeding heart (*Dicentra*)	SN, IV, NC, SC
Foxglove (*Digitalis*)	All
Wild buckwheat (*Eriogonum*)	All
Common fennel (*Foeniculum vulgare*)	All
Geum (*Geum*)	All
Perennial sunflower (*Helianthus maximilianii*)	All
Toadflax (*Linaria purpurea*)	All
Lupine (*Lupinus*)	SN, IV, NC, SC
Beard tongue (*Penstemon*)	All
Miniature hollyhock (*Sidalcea*)	SN, IV, NC, SC
Speedwell (*Veronica*)	SN, IV, NC, SC

To attract butterflies and bees to your garden, Amacker Bullwinkle, a Palo Alto gardener, recommends butterfly bush, "which comes in purple, white, and pink, grows a lot larger than you are often led to believe, and is a beacon for butterflies and honey bees. Just make sure it has direct sun and plenty of room. Don't be afraid to cut it back in late fall. A thriving plant can top 10 feet." Another plant she recommends is lavender. "All three lavender varieties I grow—English, French, and Mexican—attract butterflies. Lavender, my favorite climber the Purple Vagabond, and the gregarious scarlet trumpet vines seem to cater to both monarchs and the large black butterflies."

A SAMPLER OF PERENNIAL BLOOM THROUGH THE SEASONS

Winter/Early Spring
Winter-blooming bergenia (*Bergenia crassifolia*)
Crocus (*Crocus*)
Winter cyclamen (*Cyclamen atkinsii, C. coum*)
Crown of thorns (*Euphorbia martinii*)
Snowdrops (*Galanthus*)
Lenten rose (*Helleborus orientalis*)
Reticulated iris (*Iris reticulata*)
Winter iris, Algerian iris (*Iris unguicularis*)
Ice plant (*Lampranthus*)
Early daffodils and narcissus (*Narcissus*)
Japanese coltsfoot (*Petasites japonicus*)
Fairy primrose (*Primula malacoides*)
English primrose (*Primula polyantha*)
Winter squill (*Scilla tubergeniana*)
Aztec lily (*Sprekelia formosissima*)
Lemon marigold (*Tagetes lemmonii*)
Wake robin (*Trillium ovatum*)
Violet (*Viola*)

Spring
Stonecress (*Aethionema*)
Peruvian lily (*Alstroemeria aurea*)
Wood anemone (*Anemone nemorosa*)
Snowdrop anemone (*Anemone sylvestris*)
Trailing aptenia (*Aptenia cordifolia*)
Columbine (*Aquilegia*)
Thrift, Sea pink (*Armeria*)
Bergenia (*Bergenia*)
Brodiaea lily (*Brodiaea*)
Bellflower (*Campanula*)
Coreopsis (*Coreopsis*)
Bleeding heart (*Dicentra*)
Pride of Madeira (*Echium fastuosum*)
Euryops, African daisy (*Euryops pectinatus*)
Freesia (*Freesia*)
Iris (*Iris*)

African corn lily (*Ixia*)
Poppy (*Papaver*)
Phlox (*Phlox*)
Goldmoss sedum (*Sedum acre*)
California Indian pink (*Silene californica*)
Harlequin flower (*Sparaxis tricolor*)

Summer
Bear's breeches (*Acanthus mollis*)
Lily-of-the-Nile (*Agapanthus*)
Belladonna lily (*Amaryllis belladonna*)
Trailing aptenia (*Aptenia cordifolia*)
Butterfly weed (*Asclepias tuberosa*)
Cigar plant (*Cuphea ignea*)
Dahlia (*Dahlia*)
Purple delosperma (*Delosperma cooperi*)
Purple coneflower (*Echinacea purpurea*)
Euryops, African daisy (*Euryops*)
Summer hyacinth (*Galtonia candicans*)
Gazania (*Gazania*)
Gladiolus (*Gladiolus*)
Curry plant (*Helichrysum italicum*)
Ox-eye (*Heliopsis helianthoides*)
Daylily (*Hemerocallis*)
Dame's rocket (*Hesperus matronalis*)
Coral bells (*Heuchera*)
Lily (*Lilium*)
Forget-me-not (*Myosotis scorpioides*)
Phlox (*Phlox*)
Tuberose (*Polianthes tuberosa*)
Rudbeckia, Yellow coneflower (*Rudbeckia*)
Sage, Salvia (*Salvia*)
Verbena (*Verbena*)
Watsonia (*Watsonia*)

Autumn
Anchusa (*Anchusa azurea*)
Florists' chrysanthemum (*Chrysanthemum morifolium*)
Golden aster (*Chrysopsis*)
Saffron crocus (*Crocus sativas*)
Autumn crocus (*Crocus speciosus*)
Florists' cyclamen (*Cyclamen persicum*)
Fortnight lily (*Dietes, Moraea*)
Euryops, African daisy (*Euryops*)
Perennial sunflower (*Helianthus maximilianii*)
Showy sedum (*Sedum spectabile*)
Moss campion (*Silene schafta*)
Goldenrod (*Solidago*)
Goldenrod aster (*Solidaster*)
Sternbergia (*Sternbergia lutea*)

TREES

California is a region of varied landscapes. A large part of it is—or was—forested with dominant species of conifers such as redwoods, firs, and pines. This native tree canopy is often cut down in landscaping and replaced with brighter, shorter, more rounded, non-native deciduous trees. These decidous trees are valued because they create shade in the hot summer but drop their leaves in the winter, allowing sunlight to warm the ground. In addition, they are generally more congenial to understory perennials and annuals than conifers are.

In desert, chapparal, and valley areas where native tree cover is sparse or non-existent, the sudden appearance of a new oasis of trees is usually a sign that a high-capacity local water system has been installed. The planting of trees in open areas is in a sense a mark of civilization, and their usefulness in moderating prevailing winds and mitigating summer heat cannot be overestimated.

When you plant trees, don't place them too close to house foundations, stone walls, concrete paths, or sidewalks. In time, their growing roots and widening trunks can break up the thickest masonry and you will be faced with having to cut down a valuable and beautiful part of your personal landscape to preserve the integrity of the concrete or stonework.

In the lists that follow, you will find everything from tall columnar evergreens to desert-hardy palms, from backyard fruit trees to sturdy windbreaks, from mighty redwoods to diminutive bonsai. There are trees for the oceanfront and for the patio, trees that can withstand stress from boron water or city smog, and trees that please because of their graceful weeping branches, fragrant flowers, or showy bark. We also include a few lists of trees you might want to avoid. Trees that litter the ground with messy spent flowers, for example, may demand more cleanup than you care to provide, and some trees have greedy surface roots that steal nutrients away from nearby plantings. For advice about what will work best for your particular needs and in your particular microclimate, talk to the folks at your local nursery or cooperative extension service.

At the end of this chapter are two samplers, one of flowering trees organized by the color of the flowers, and one organized by fall foliage color.

TREES FOR DRY CONDITIONS

California's climate is characterized by a long, rainless summer season that can wreak havoc on trees not adapted to dry soil conditions. The following trees are not much bothered by dry soil, but they will probably need at least a few soakings to get them through the long summer in good form and without leaf loss. (For a select few trees that can survive on groundwater alone, with no summer watering, see the list on page 40.)

Acacia (*Acacia*)	All
Norway maple (*Acer platanoides*)	SN, IV, NC
California buckeye (*Aesculus californica*)	SN, IV, NC, SC
Tree of heaven (*Ailanthus altissima*)	All
Silk tree (*Albizia julibrissin*)	All
Mexican blue palm (*Brahea armata*)	IV, HD, NC, SC
Lemon bottlebrush (*Callistemon citrinus*)	IV, LD, NC, SC
Beefwood, She-oak (*Casuarina*)	IV, LD, NC, SC
Deodar cedar (*Cedrus deodara*)	IV, LD, NC, SC
Hackberry (*Celtis*)	All
Western redbud (*Cercis occidentalis*)	All
Chitalpa (*Chitalpa tashkentensis*)	All
Loquat (*Eriobotrya japonica*)	All
Eucalyptus (*Eucalyptus*)	IV, HD, LD, NC, SC
Fig (*Ficus carica*)	SN, IV, LD, NC, SC
Oregon ash (*Fraxinus latifolia*)	All
Australian willow (*Geijera parviflora*)	IV, LD, NC, SC
Ginkgo (*Ginkgo biloba*)	SN, IV, NC, SC
Honey locust (*Gleditsia triacanthos*)	All
Walnut (*Juglans*)	All
Chinese flame tree (*Koelreuteria bipinnata*)	IV, HD, LD, NC, SC
Golden-rain tree (*Koelreuteria paniculata*)	All
Catalina ironwood (*Lyonothamnus floribundus*)	IV, NC, SC
Osage orange (*Maclura pomifera*)	All
Chinaberry (*Melia azedarach*)	IV, HD, LD, NC, SC
European olive (*Olea europaea*)	IV, LD, NC, SC
Jerusalem thorn (*Parkinsonia aculeata*)	IV, LD, NC, SC
Pines (*Pinus*)	All
Chinese pistache (*Pistacia chinensis*)	All
Sycamore (*Platanus occidentalis*)	All
Western cottonwood (*Populus fremontii*)	All
Hollyleaf cherry (*Prunus ilicifolia*)	SN, IV, LD, NC, SC
Oaks (*Quercus*)	All
African sumac (*Rhus lancea*)	IV, LD, NC, SC
Locusts (*Robinia*)	All
California pepper tree (*Schinus molle*)	IV, LD, NC, SC
Brazilian pepper tree (*Schinus terebinthifolius*)	IV, LD, NC, SC
Giant sequoia (*Sequoiadendron giganteum*)	All
Tamarisk (*Tamarix*)	SN, IV, NC, SC
Silver linden (*Tilia tomentosa*)	All
Brisbane box (*Tristania conferta*)	NC, SC

California buckeye

Siberian elm (*Ulmus pumila*)   All
Jujube (*Zizyphus jujuba*)   All

❧ "Palo verde (*Cercidium*) is a good tree for desert areas," advises Joe Clements, curator of the Desert Gardens at the Huntington Botanical Gardens in San Marino. "Trees that do well in the desert have small leaves and very deep roots." In spring, these tough trees are covered in so many small yellow flowers that you can hardly see their branches. Palo verdes attract birds, and they also have colorful bark. Blue palo verde has blue-green foliage.

TREES FOR POOR, SANDY SOIL

Coastal areas are notorious for thin, sandy soil that is poor in nutrients and lacks the capacity to hold water during the summer months. These soils can be upgraded by adding compost and other organic matter, but if you are working on a large-scale landscaping project with a limited budget, it is not feasible to amend every square yard of soil. Selecting trees that are naturally adapted to sandy soil is a sensible approach to the problem. Luckily many of these species are quite handsome. Some of the trees best suited to sandy soil are the ones naturally growing there. Although not commonly found through commercial nurseries, they may be worth a try if you can locate a source.

Beefwood, She-oak (*Casuarina*)	IV, LD, NC, SC
Catalpa (*Catalpa*)	All
Western hackberry (*Celtis reticulata*)	All
Redbud (*Cercis*)	All
Desert willow (*Chilopsis linearis*)	HD, LD, SC
Chitalpa (*Chitalpa tashkentensis*)	All
Italian cypress (*Cupressus sempervirens*)	All
Russian olive (*Elaeagnus angustifolia*)	All
Hardy rubber tree (*Eucommia ulmoides*)	SN, IV, NC, SC
Jacaranda (*Jacaranda mimosifolia*)	LD, NC, SC
Chinese flame tree (*Koelreuteria bipinnata*)	IV, HD, LD, NC, SC
Golden-rain tree (*Koelreuteria paniculata*)	All
Melaleuca (*Melaleuca*)	IV, LD, NC, SC
Mexican palo verde (*Parkinsonia aculeata*)	IV, HD, LD, NC, SC
Calabrian pine (*Pinus brutia*)	IV, LD, NC, SC
Aleppo pine (*Pinus halepensis*)	IV, LD, NC, SC
Chinese pistache (*Pistacia chinensis*)	All
Hollyleaf cherry (*Prunus ilicifolia*)	SN, IV, LD, NC, SC
Coast live oak (*Quercus agrifolia*)	All
Holly oak (*Quercus ilex*)	All
Japanese live oak (*Quercus myrsinifolia*)	SN, IV, NC, SC
Sumac (*Rhus*)	All
Locust (*Robinia*)	All
Chinese tallow tree (*Sapium sebiferum*)	IV, LD, NC, SC
Lacebark elm (*Ulmus parvifolia*)	All
Chinese jujube (*Ziziphus jujuba*)	IV, HD, LD, NC, SC

TREES THAT WILL SURVIVE ON GROUNDWATER ALONE

These trees are the toughest of the tough. They can survive on groundwater alone once they are established in your garden. According to Kitren Weis of the University of California at Davis, who supplied this list, although they are all super drought tolerant, you should give them a headstart in life. "Dig large holes, just as you would for transplanting any other tree, and water them as much as needed until they become established," she says. That may mean arranging for supplementary watering for the first year or two of their lives, but after they take hold, these trees will not need any water during the summer months.

California buckeye (*Aesculus californica*)	SN, IV, NC, SC
Western redbud (*Cercis occidentalis*)	All
Red ironbark (*Eucalyptus sideroxylon*)	IV, NC, SC
Toyon, California holly (*Heteromeles arbutifolia*)	All
California black walnut (*Juglans hindsii*)	SN, IV, NC, SC
Crape myrtle (*Lagerstroemia indica*)	SN, IV, LD, NC, SC
Hollyleaf cherry (*Prunus ilicifolia*)	SN, IV, LD, NC, SC
Blue oak (*Quercus douglasii*)	SN, IV, HD, NC, SC
California white oak (*Quercus lobata*)	SN, IV, NC, SC
Coffeeberry (*Rhamnus californica*)	All
California bay (*Umbellularia californica*)	SN, IV, LD, NC, SC

> Kitren Weis says that the drought-resistant red ironbark (*Eucalyptus sideroxylon*) deserves special mention. She points out that, "Unlike other members of its species, which can be messy and are not reliably hardy in Northern California, this one is non-shedding of bark and leaf litter and is frost tolerant to 10 degrees F."

TREES FOR WET SITES

The roots of the larger trees in this list can be vigorous water-seekers, so don't plant them near your septic tank—although it is a well-known fact that the largest weeping willows on historic California farmsteads grow in septic fields, and that these lovely old trees will die in short order if the farm is placed on city sewage lines and their source of moisture is removed. If you have an old weeping willow or other moisture-loving tree and plan to abandon the septic field that gave it life, consider installing a gray-water system to keep it thriving.

Red maple (*Acer rubrum*)	SN, IV, NC, SC
Alder (*Alnus*)	SN, IV, NC, SC
River birch (*Betula nigra*)	All
American hornbeam (*Carpinus caroliniana*)	SN, IV, NC, SC
Beefwood, She-oak (*Casuarina*)	IV, LD, NC, SC
Sugar hackberry (*Celtis laevigata*)	All
Lily-of-the-valley tree (*Clethra arborea*)	NC, SC
Oregon ash (*Fraxinus latifolia*)	All
American sweet gum (*Liquidambar styraciflua*)	SN, IV, NC, SC
Southern magnolia (*Magnolia grandiflora*)	SN, IV, HD, NC, SC
Sweet bay magnolia (*Magnolia virginiana*)	SN, IV, NC, SC

Cajeput tree (*Melaleuca quinquenervia*)	IV, LD, NC, SC
Myoporum (*Myoporum laetum*)	IV, NC, SC
Sour gum (*Nyssa sylvatica*)	SN, IV, NC, SC
Sitka spruce (*Picea sitchensis*)	SN
London plane tree (*Platanus acerifolia*)	All
Sycamore (*Platanus occidentalis*)	All
Poplar (*Populus*)	All
Chinese wingnut (*Pterocarya stenoptera*)	All
Pear (*Pyrus communis*)	SN, IV, HD, NC
Swamp white oak (*Quercus bicolor*)	SN, HD
Willow (*Salix*)	All
Weeping willow (*Salix babylonica*)	All
Blue elderberry (*Sambucus caerulea*)	All
Red elderberry (*Sambucus callicarpa*)	SN, IV, NC
Coast redwood (*Sequoia sempervirens*)	SN, IV, NC, SC
Cypress (*Taxodium*)	All
Bald cypress (*Taxodium distichum*)	SN, IV, LD, NC, SC
Arborvitae (*Thuja occidentalis*)	SN, IV, NC, SC
California bay (*Umbellularia californica*)	SN, IV, LD, NC, SC

TREES FOR HEAVY SOILS

Adobe clay soil is found in several areas of California. New housing developments, especially in areas such as the Silicon Valley and Santa Rosa plains, are notorious for their poor, heavy soil. This is not always the result of natural forces. Housing tract developers scrape off and sell the topsoil, leaving only the clay subsoil behind for new homeowners.

Anyone who has tried to garden in adobe knows that the small clay particles pack together in wet weather, leaving the plants' roots starved for oxygen. In the dry season, it bakes to the consistency of a piece of ceramic pottery. If you acquire property that is covered in "contractor's subsoil," you have two choices. Buy back the topsoil that was taken from the site, or adapt your gardening plans to the clay soil and slowly build topsoil through the application of biodegradable mulches and compost.

For fruit and nut trees that tolerate heavy soils (and high boron water), see the list on page 46.

American hornbeam

Maple (*Acer*)	All
American hornbeam (*Carpinus caroliniana*)	SN, IV, NC, SC
Sugar hackberry (*Celtis laevigata*)	All
Redbud (*Cercis*)	All
Mayhaw (*Crataegus aestivalis*)	IV, HD, LD, NC, SC
Chinese sweet gum (*Liquidambar formosana*)	SN, IV, NC, SC
London plane tree (*Platanus acerifolia*)	All
Ornamental pear (*Pyrus calleryana*)	SN, IV, NC, SC
Sawtooth oak (*Quercus accutissima*)	All
Sumac (*Rhus*)	All
Locust (*Robinia*)	All
Willow (*Salix*)	All

TREES FOR THE OCEANFRONT

Oceanfront property is some of the most desirable in California, but salt spray and wind limit the trees that can be grown in the coastal zone. Take advantage of the placement of buildings, fences, and other trees to provide protection for plants that are only moderately tolerant of wind and salt spray. The following trees should do well along the beaches and cliffs that make up our shoreline. They are appropriate for North and South Coasts.

Plume albizia (*Albizia distachya*)
Coast beefwood (*Casuarina stricta*)
Australian dracaena (*Cordyline australis*)
Blue dracaena (*Cordyline indivisa*)
Carrot wood (*Cupaniopsis anacardiodes*)
Leyland cypress (*Cupressocyparis leylandii*)
Dragon tree (*Dracaena draco*)
Russian olive (*Eleagnus angustifolia*)
Eucalyptus (*Eucalyptus*)
Wilson holly (*Ilex altaclarensis* 'Wilsonii')
Yaupon holly (*Ilex vomitoria*)
Eastern red cedar (*Juniperus virginiana*)
Primrose tree (*Lagunaria patersonii*)
Apples and crabapples (*Malus*)
Cajeput tree (*Melaleuca quinquenervia*)
New Zealand Christmas tree (*Metrosideros excelsus*)
Myoporum (*Myoporum laetum*)
Bishop pine (*Pinus muricata*)
French pine, Maritime pine (*Pinus pinaster*)
Monterey pine (*Pinus radiata*)
Japanese black pine (*Pinus thunbergiana*)
Holly oak (*Quercus ilex*)
Palmetto (*Sabal*)
Coast redwood (*Sequoia sempervirens*)
Tamarisk (*Tamarix*)
New Zealand chaste-tree (*Vitex lucens*)

Red cedar

Don Rodrigues of Pacific Horticulture Consultants in Ventura says, "It's hard to beat *Metrosideros excelsus*, the New Zealand Christmas tree, for coastal conditions. Excellent as a multitrunk and noted for its clusters of bright red flowers in the summer, it has gray-green foliage and forms a nice round-headed tree up to 25 to 30 feet tall." He adds, "I don't think anything grows as fast as *Myoporum laetum* along the coast. It has bright, shiny green leaves, grows rapidly to 30 feet by 30 feet, takes the wind and salt spray, and is very drought tolerant. It bears small white flowers in the summer that are followed by purplish berries, which are favored by birds. Plant it for a good multitrunk screen in mild coastal climates."

CITRUS TREES FOR THE GARDEN

For a list of citrus trees that will do well in California gardens, we need go no farther than Ottillia Bier, a researcher in botany and plant sciences with the University of California at Riverside, where she evaluates new citrus varieties for the California citrus industry. Ottillia works with the UCR Citrus Variety Collection, one of the most extensive collections of citrus in the world. She is also an avid home gardener, has been a Master Gardener since 1981, and writes a gardening column in the Riverside *Press-Enterprise*.

"Whether planted to provide fresh fruit for the table or to provide an attractive accent for the landscape, citrus trees are a welcome addition to many California gardens," Ottillia says. "As a garden subject, they are without parallel. Dressed in rich evergreen leaves, citrus trees are ornamented with fragrant white flowers followed by colorful delicious fruit." She notes that many citrus trees are available either as full-sized trees or as dwarfed specimens, making them adaptable to different garden uses. "The dwarfed trees are especially well-suited to container-growing. Many gardeners living in locations too cold for citrus successfully grow potted citrus trees indoors. Given bright light, the trees are attractive, produce fragrant flowers, and may even produce fruit if a self-fruitful cultivar has been selected." The following are her suggestions for Californians who like the idea of growing their own supply of fresh citrus, or who just want an attractive tree with fragrant blossoms.

Sweet Fruit

Washington navel orange	IV, LD, NC, SC
Cara Cara pink-fleshed navel orange	IV, LD, NC, SC
Midknight seedless Valencia orange	IV, LD, NC, SC
Moro blood orange	IV, LD, NC, SC
Owari Satsuma mandarin	IV, NC, SC
Pixie seedless mandarin	IV, NC, SC
Clementine mandarin	IV, LD, NC, SC
Minneola tangelo	IV, LD, NC, SC
Chandler pummelo	IV, LD, NC, SC
Rio Red grapefruit	IV, LD, NC, SC
Oroblanco grapefruit-pummelo hybrid	IV, LD, NC, SC

Acid Fruit

Variegated pink-fleshed Eureka lemon (Pink Lemonade lemon)	IV, LD, NC, SC
Meyer lemon hybrid	IV, LD, NC, SC
Bearss seedless lime	IV, LD, NC, SC
Chinotto sour orange	IV, LD, NC, SC
Nagami or Meiwa kumquat	IV, LD, NC, SC
Variegated calamondin	IV, LD, NC, SC

For those planning to raise citrus trees in Northern areas, Ken Adachi of Adachi Florist & Nursery in El Sobrante recommends the 'Provita Orange.' "The East Bay is difficult for citrus crops. Our cool summers can't encourage productivity, but this tree produces an early spring crop with a zesty fruit, a favorite with our long-term clients."

TREES FOR ALKALINE SOIL

Alkaline soil, which has a pH level above 7.0, is high in minerals such as lime and sodium. Some trees prefer alkaline soil and some trees just tolerate it. You can adjust the pH level of your soil by adding chemicals, or you can work in peat moss or fine mulch. The easiest solution to the problem is to find trees that don't mind growing in alkaline conditions.

Bailey acacia (*Acacia baileyana*)	SN, IV, LD, NC, SC
Catalpa (*Catalpa*)	All
Palo verde (*Cercidium*)	IV, HD, LD, NC, SC
Yellowwood (*Cladrastis lutea*)	SN, IV, NC
Hawthorn (*Crataegus*)	SN, IV, HD, NC
Chinese parasol tree (*Firmiana simplex*)	IV, LD, NC, SC
Oregon ash (*Fraxinus latifolia*)	All
Arizona ash (*Fraxinus velutina*)	IV, HD, LD, NC, SC
Ginkgo (*Ginkgo biloba*)	SN, IV, NC, SC
Honey locust (*Gleditsia triacanthos*)	All
Yaupon holly (*Ilex vomitoria*)	All
Chinese flame tree (*Koelreuteria bipinnata*)	IV, HD, LD, NC, SC
Golden-rain tree (*Koelreuteria paniculata*)	All
White mulberry (*Morus alba*)	All
Coast live oak (*Quercus agrifolia*)	All
California white oak (*Quercus lobata*)	SN, IV, NC, SC
Japanese tree lilac (*Syringa reticulata*)	SN, IV, HD, NC
Lacebark elm (*Ulmus parvifolia*)	All
California bay (*Umbellularia californica*)	SN, IV, LD, NC, SC

Alkaline soil doesn't deter Bailey acacias. These trees have blue-gray foliage. In winter, fragrant yellow flowers make the branches prized for cut arrangements. Also tolerant of alkalinity are slow-growing, shade-producing California bays, which bear small yellow flowers in spring, followed by ornamental fruit.

FAST-GROWING TREES

Silver maple

It is a daunting prospect to move into a tract of new homes that was built in a former cow pasture and to realize that you will be the one to plant the first tree on the block. The trees in this list will quickly provide shade or a screen. Some of these rapid-starters are not terribly long-lived, so it is a good idea to plant more permanent replacements at the same time, to have them waiting in the wings.

Acacia (*Acacia*)	All
Red maple (*Acer rubrum*)	SN, IV, NC, SC
Silver maple (*Acer saccharinum*)	SN, IV, NC, SC
Tree of heaven (*Ailanthus altissima*)	All
Plume albizia (*Albizia distachya*)	NC, SC
White alder (*Alnus rhombifolia*)	SN, IV, NC, SC

Lemon bottlebrush (*Callistemon citrinus*)	IV, LD, NC, SC
Crown of gold tree (*Cassia excelsa*)	LD, SC
Beefwood, She-oak (*Casuarina*)	IV, LD, NC, SC
Catalpa (*Catalpa*)	All
Deodar cedar (*Cedrus deodara*)	All
Palo verde (*Cercidium*)	IV, HD, LD, NC, SC
Desert willow (*Chilopsis linearis*)	HD, LD, SC
Tecate cypress (*Cupressus forbesii*)	IV, HD, LD, SC
Smooth Arizona cypress (*Cupressus glabra*)	IV, HD, LD, NC, SC
Eucalyptus (*Eucalyptus*)	IV, HD, LD, NC, SC
Ash (*Fraxinus*)	All
Silk oak (*Grevillea robusta*)	IV, LD, NC, SC
Tulip tree (*Liriodendron tulipifera*)	SN, IV, HD, NC, SC
Pink melaleuca (*Melaleuca nesophila*)	LD, NC, SC
Dawn redwood (*Metasequoia glyptostroboides*)	SN, IV, NC, SC
White mulberry (*Morus alba*)	All
Myoporum (*Myoporum laetum*)	IV, NC, SC
Guatemalan holly (*Olmediella betschlerana*)	IV, NC, SC
Jerusalem thorn (*Parkinsonia aculeata*)	IV, HD, LD, NC, SC
Empress tree (*Paulownia tomentosa*)	All
Pines (*Pinus*)	All
Lombardy poplar (*Populus nigra* 'Italica')	All
Quaking aspen (*Populus tremuloides*)	SN, IV, NC, SC
Black cottonwood (*Populus trichocarpa*)	SN, IV, NC, SC
Chinese wingnut (*Pterocarya stenoptera*)	All
Red oak (*Quercus rubra*)	SN, IV, HD, NC, SC
Locust (*Robinia*)	All
Willow (*Salix*)	All
Chinese tallow tree (*Sapium sebiferum*)	IV, LD, NC, SC
California pepper tree (*Schinus molle*)	IV, LD, NC, SC
Coast redwood (*Sequoia sempervirens*)	SN, IV, NC, SC
Montezuma cypress (*Taxodium mucronatum*)	SN, IV, LD, NC, SC
Tipu tree (*Tipuana tipu*)	IV, LD, NC, SC

If you want fast-growing, beautiful trees in your garden, Rick Yonkovich of Cameron Park Nursery in Rescue can't praise the maple enough. His favorite is the 'October Glory' variety, which can attain 50 feet in 20 years, growing at a pace of about 3 feet a year. The maple doesn't need much water, and Rick recommends, before you plant any bush, tree, or plant, that you check to see what drainage your soil offers. "If a maple begins to yellow at the edges, don't immediately water it; instead, allow the soil to dry naturally and see what response it makes." It may just have wet feet.

BEST BACKYARD FRUIT TREES

One of the ironies of our lovely climate is that California's generally warm winters keep some old favorites among the fruit trees from experiencing the proper amount of winter chill they need to thrive. To overcome the problem of few chill-hours and a short dormant season, California orchardists have developed warm-winter varieties here and imported varieties from regions with similar climates in Europe and Asia.

This list of backyard fruit trees is suited to the widest range of California conditions. It was developed by Kitren Weis, a pomologist at the University of California at Davis, with a few additions based on my own experience. Consult with your local nursery about cross-pollination requirements.

Apple: Granny Smith, Fuji, Gravenstein
Apricot: Patterson, Blenheim (Royal)
Citrus: Mineola tangelo, Washington navel orange, Meyer lemon
Sweet cherry: Bing, Rainier
Sour cherry: Montmorency
Fig: Mission, Brown Turkey
Nectarine: Red Jim
Peach: Fay Elberta, Indian Blood
Asian pear: Hosui
European pear: Bartlett, Bosc
Japanese persimmon: Fuyu
Plum: Greengage, Satsuma, Santa Rosa

> To conserve space in your mini-orchard, pomologist Kitren Weis with the University of California at Davis recommends that you order varieties from your nursery on semi-dwarf or dwarf rootstock. "You can also control size by high-density planting, placing them as close as 18 to 24 inches on center," she says. Not only that, if you are really pressed for space, many varieties are suitable for espalier, which means you can grow them along a fence or against a wall.

FRUIT AND NUT TREES THAT TOLERATE HEAVY SOILS AND HIGH BORON WATER

There are distinct patches of California's Inland Valleys and Low Deserts where dense, heavy clay soils or an unusually high boron content in the water make the going rather rough for fruit and nut trees, even though the climate itself is fine. Kitren Weis, a researcher with the University of California at Davis, lives on such property, and here is her tried-and-true short list of fruit and nut trees that will tolerate these hostile conditions. Consult with your local nursery about cross-pollination requirements.

Almond: Nonpareil, Mission (Texas)
Apple: Granny Smith, Fuji
Apricot: Patterson, Blenheim (Royal)
Fig: Mission, Brown Turkey
Asian pear: Hosui
European pear: Bartlett, Bosc

Pecan: Iroquois
Pistachio: Peters
Plum: Greengage, Satsuma, Santa Rosa
Walnut: Chandler

"During the early part of the 20th century," says Tom Spellman of La Verne Nursery in San Dimas, "many citrus growers planted avocados as windbreaks and orchard dividers." Now they are planted for their fruit. The Hass is "the most popular commercial variety," he notes. "The fruit has pebbly skin that turns black when ripe, a high oil content, and a buttery, nutty flavor." The Pinkerton variety originated as a chance seedling found growing on the Pinkerton Ranch in Santa Barbara, Tom says. "It has great flavor, a high oil content, and a very small seed. Pinkerton ripens October through February, before most of the Hass." The Bacon, a more cold-hardy variety, Tom calls "a very handsome tree with conical, upright growth, compact structure, and glossy dark-green foliage." For Northern California gardeners concerned about frost, Tom suggests Mexicola Grande, Newmex, or Stuart. Once established, these are cold-hardy down to the mid to low 20s.

TREES FOR TOUGH URBAN SITES

Heat reflected off buildings, soil compacted from pedestrians and traffic, and exhaust fumes from vehicles add up to a stressful situation for plants. The following trees are suitable for urban and suburban neighborhoods, wide median strips, and pocket-handkerchief parks. Give them water regularly for at least two years until their root systems become established.

Tree	Zones
Maple (*Acer*)	SN, IV, NC, SC
Paper mulberry (*Broussonetia papyrifera*)	All
Hackberry (*Celtis*)	All
Camphor tree (*Cinnamomum camphora*)	IV, LD, NC, SC
Hawthorn (*Crataegus*)	SN, IV, HD, NC, SC
Ginkgo (*Ginkgo biloba*)	SN, IV, NC, SC
Golden-rain tree (*Koelreuteria paniculata*)	All
Sweet gum (*Liquidambar*)	SN, IV, NC, SC
Chinese pistache (*Pistacia chinensis*)	All
Chinese wingnut (*Pterocarya stenoptera*)	All
California pepper tree (*Schinus molle*)	IV, LD, NC, SC
Montezuma cypress (*Taxodium mucronatum*)	SN, IV, LD, NC, SC
Silver linden (*Tilia tomentosa*)	All
Lacebark elm (*Ulmus parvifolia*)	All
Sawleaf zelkova (*Zelkova serrata*)	All

Western hackberry

ENERGY-SAVING TREES

When trees keep your house cool with shade, you reduce the amount of energy your air conditioner expends, and that reduces your energy bills. Greg McPherson of the Western Center for Urban Forest Research and Education says that shading the west and east sides of a 2,500 square foot house in Sacramento, for example, can reduce annual cooling costs by as much as 40 percent. He advises placing trees so that they shade west- and east-facing windows, but "Keep trees at least 5 to 10 feet from the home so the roots won't damage the foundation. Avoid planting evergreens to shade south-facing walls because they will block winter sunlight and increase heating costs." Greg also notes, "Shading paved areas like patios and driveways can make them cooler and more comfortable spaces." When you are doing your landscaping, however, be careful to keep trees away from overhead powerlines and underground utility lines or pipes.

The Western Center for Urban Forest Research and Education, located at the University of California at Davis, looks beyond the relationship of trees and houses and also examines the effects trees have on parking lots (they affect the microclimate, and evaporate hydrocarbon emissions from parked vehicles), and the impact of roots on sidewalks. They note that "the total cost of root-sidewalk conflicts in California alone is well over $62 million per year." All the more reason for a homeowner to think about a tree's behavior patterns when drawing up landscaping plans.

This is Greg's list of the best shade trees for California landscapes. He says that the best choice for a specific location depends on site-specific conditions such as microclimate and the amount of available space.

European hackberry (*Celtis australis*)	IV, HD, LD, NC, SC
Eastern redbud (*Cercis canadensis*)	All
Autumn Purple ash (*Fraxinus americana* 'Autumn Purple')	SN, IV, HD, NC
Chicago Regal ash (*Fraxinus americana* 'Chicago Regal')	SN, IV, HD, NC
Hybrid crape myrtle (*Lagerstroemia indica* x *L. fauriei*)	SN, IV, LD, NC, SC
Dawn redwood (*Metasequoia glyptostroboides*)	SN, IV, NC, SC
Keith Davey Chinese pistache (*Pistacia chinensis* 'Keith Davey')	All
Thundercloud flowering plum (*Prunus cerasifera* 'Thundercloud')	All
Chanticleer pear (*Pyrus calleryana* 'Chanticleer')	SN, IV, NC, SC
Trinity pear (*Pyrus calleryana* 'Trinity')	SN, IV, NC, SC
Chinese tallow tree (*Sapium sebiferum*)	IV, LD, NC, SC
Little-leaf linden (*Tilia cordata*)	All
Prospector elm (*Ulmus wilsoniana* 'Prospector')	SN, IV, HD, NC
Japanese zelkova (*Zelkova serrata*)	All

UNDERSTORY AND SHADE-TOLERANT TREES

Perhaps your property is bordered by a mature planting of tall evergreens—pines or redwoods, for instance—and you want to plant smaller, more ornamental trees under their shade. Maybe a north-facing wall casts a shadow on a portion of your garden. Perhaps a patio overhang blocks sunlight for part of the day. Or you may live on the shady side of the street. The trees in this list naturally tolerate or prefer the reduced light and slightly cooler temperatures provided by shade. Some of them will grow equally well in full sun, but in general these trees prefer dappled sunlight all day long or several hours per day of complete shadow.

Vine maple (*Acer circinatum*)	SN, IV, NC
Japanese maple (*Acer palmatum*)	SN, IV, NC, SC
American hornbeam (*Carpinus caroliniana*)	SN, IV, NC
Redbud (*Cercis*)	All
Mediterranean fan palm (*Chamaerops humilis*)	All
Flowering dogwood (*Cornus florida*)	SN, IV, NC
New Zealand laurel (*Corynocarpus laevigata*)	NC, SC
Snowdrop tree, Silver bell (*Halesia carolina*)	SN, IV, NC, SC
Holly (*Ilex*)	All
Sweet bay, Grecian laurel (*Laurus nobilis*)	SN, IV, LD, NC, SC
Chinese fountain palm (*Livistona chinensis*)	IV, LD, NC, SC
Fern pine (*Podocarpus gracilior*)	IV, LD, NC, SC
Lancewood (*Pseudopanax lessonii*)	NC, SC
Firewheel tree (*Stenocarpus sinuatus*)	NC, SC
Stewartia (*Stewartia*)	IV, NC, SC
Japanese snowbell (*Styrax japonicus*)	SN, IV, NC, SC
California bay (*Umbellularia californica*)	SN, IV, LD, NC, SC

SOME TREES FOR ESPALIER

When garden space is at a premium, espaliered trees can be used to create an eye-catching area of interest. Some nurseries now carry young trees—especially fruit trees—that have already received their first pruning cuts to shape them, but you can do just as well yourself if you study the subject, decide on what form you want the tree to take, and keep up a regular program of maintenance.

Espaliered trees planted against a reflective wall in full sun will be subjected to a great deal of heat stress. Lacking a complete leaf canopy, they may fail to thrive under such conditions, so place them where they will have some protection from mid-day heat. They also need plenty of root space.

Serviceberry (*Amelanchier*)	SN, IV
Citrus (*Citrus*)	IV, LD, NC, SC
Japanese persimmon (*Diospyros kaki*)	SN, IV, NC, SC
Loquat (*Eriobotrya*)	All
Fig (*Ficus*)	SN, IV, LD, NC, SC
Laburnum, Goldenchain (*Laburnum*)	SN, IV, NC
Southern magnolia (*Magnolia grandiflora*)	SN, IV, HD, NC, SC
Apple (*Malus*)	IV, NC, SC
Crabapple (*Malus*)	All
Redtip (*Photinia fraseri*)	All
Pear (*Pyrus*)	SN, IV, NC, SC

HEAT-RESISTANT TREES FOR BRIGHT, SUNNY PLACES

These trees will withstand intense reflected light and heat. They are naturals to place beside a light-colored south or west-facing stone wall or a stucco wall that is painted white. Be sure to water them sufficiently while they are getting established.

Silk tree (*Albizia julibrissin*)	All
Bird of paradise tree (*Caesalpinia gilliesii*)	All
Camphor tree (*Cinnamomum camphora*)	IV, LD, NC, SC
Citrus (*Citrus*)	IV, LD, NC, SC
Fig (*Ficus*)	SN, IV, LD, NC, SC
Juniper (*Juniperus*)	All
Southern magnolia (*Magnolia grandiflora*)	SN, IV, HD, NC, SC
Crabapple (*Malus*)	All
Olive (*Olea europaea*)	IV, HD, LD, NC, SC
Carolina cherry laurel (*Prunus caroliniana*)	All
Hollyleaf cherry (*Prunus ilicifolia*)	SN, IV, LD, NC, SC

FIRE-RESISTANT TREES

No tree is entirely immune to fire, but the ones in this list do resist burning better than most, and their low fuel volume may slow down a fire around your house.

Lemon bottlebrush (*Callistemon citrinus*)	IV, LD, NC, SC
Toyon, California holly (*Heteromeles arbutifolia*)	All
Myoporum (*Myoporum laetum*)	IV, NC, SC
Catalina cherry (*Prunus lyonii*)	SN, IV, LD, NC, SC
Italian buckthorn (*Rhamnus alaternus*)	All
California pepper tree (*Schinus molle*)	IV, LD, NC, SC
Brazilian pepper tree (*Schinus terebinthifolius*)	IV, LD, NC, SC

PALMS FOR DESERT AREAS

This list comes from Don Hodel, a palm expert who is a nursery and landscape advisor in Los Angeles County for the University of California Cooperative Extension. He has written articles about quite a few aspects of ornamental horticulture, including irrigation, pest control, plant nutrition, and tree selection. He's also author of a book about *Chamaedorea* palms and one about trees in the greater Los Angeles area. "I'm currently working on several other books about palms and cycads," Don notes. "One is on the culture of palms, and another is a general pictorial reference book to palms of the world. While I do research and education in a variety of subject areas, palms are a favorite of mine and a subject where I feel very comfortable and knowledgeable. I have a fondness for palms because they capture that so-sought-after, lush, tropical motif like no other plant."

Most of the palms in this list will do well in both the High Desert and Low Desert areas. Don advises, however, that some of these palms are not as hardy as others. The needle palm, lady palm, palmetto, dwarf palmetto, and saw palmetto will need protection from sun and wind.

Mexican blue palm (*Brahea armata*)	HD, LD
Pindo palm (*Butia capitata*)	HD, LD

Mediterranean fan palm (*Chamaerops humilis*)	HD, LD
Australian fountain palm (*Livistona australis*)	HD, LD
Chinese fountain palm (*Livistona chinensis*)	HD, LD
Canary Island date palm (*Phoenix canariensis*)	HD, LD
Date palm (*Phoenix dactylifera*)	HD, LD
Senegal date palm (*Phoenix reclinata*)	LD
Cliff date palm (*Phoenix rupicola*)	LD
Needle palm (*Rhapidophyllum hystrix*)	HD, LD
Lady palm (*Rhapis excelsa*)	HD, LD
Slender lady palm (*Rhapis humilis*)	HD, LD
Dwarf palmetto (*Sabal minor*)	HD, LD
Palmetto (*Sabal palmetto*)	HD, LD
Saw palmetto (*Serenoa repens*)	HD, LD
Windmill palm (*Trachycarpus fortunei*)	HD, LD
Brazilian needle palm (*Trithrinax acanthocoma*)	HD, LD
California fan palm (*Washingtonia filifera*)	HD, LD
Mexican fan palm (*Washingtonia robusta*)	HD, LD

According to Michael Letzring, lead gardener of the San Diego Zoo, the queen palm (*Arecastrum romanzoffianum*) does very well in the San Diego area. "Some queen palms at the Zoo have been here for 40 years or more," he notes. This fast-growing palm with gray-brown trunk and feathery fronds can reach a height of 40 to 50 feet, while its arching fronds can grow to at least 15 feet. Similar but not quite as tall is the king palm (*Archontophoenix cunninghamiana*). "One thing people like about the king palm," Michael advises, "is that it sheds its own leaves, so you don't have to trim it." For those palms that you do have to trim, Michael suggests not cutting off the leaves until they are dead. "Green tissue allows pests to enter. They can't enter dead tissue."

TREES TO USE NEAR SWIMMING POOLS

Because people walk barefoot around swimming pools, trees with prickly or thorny leaves or twigs should never be planted near them. Also, when you landscape a swimming pool with trees, you will not be able to avoid some leaf-fall into the water, so the trees in this list were selected for the large size of their leaves, making them easy to fish out before they pass into the pool's filtration system.

Mediterranean fan palm (*Chamaerops humilis*)	All
Australian dracaena (*Cordyline australis*)	IV, HD, NC, SC
Blue dracaena (*Cordyline indivisa*)	NC, SC
Carrot wood (*Cupaniopsis anacardioides*)	NC, SC
Dragon tree (*Dracaena draco*)	NC, SC
Fig (*Ficus*)	SN, IV, LD, NC, SC
Chinese parasol tree (*Firmiana simplex*)	IV, LD, NC, SC
Daisy tree (*Montanoa arborescens*)	NC, SC
Umbrella tree (*Schefflera*)	SC
Firewheel tree (*Stenocarpus sinuatus*)	NC, SC

TREES FOR SMALL LOTS, PATIOS, AND UNDER UTILITY LINES

If your garden is small but you still want the effect of a tree, choose from this list. These trees are ornamental, have character, and will fit in a patio, courtyard, or townhouse backyard. Since they stay small, they can be planted under power lines. But don't think of these small trees as useful only in tight quarters; most of them will interplant well in front of larger trees.

Any small tree that will look beautiful in a patio planting will look great in a regular garden bed, but not all trees suitable for garden beds will do equally well in a patio setting. To earn a spot on a patio, a tree should not only be small but should have some point of seasonal interest, such as showy flowers, highly textured bark, bright fall foliage, or a striking crop of fruit. It must not crack pavement or steal water from smaller neighboring plants. Messy litter and fruit drop disqualify a tree from the patio or courtyard too, because of the extra work involved in clean-up.

Maple (*Acer*)	SN, IV, NC, SC
Silk tree (*Albizia julibrissin*)	All
Serviceberry (*Amelanchier*)	SN, IV
Strawberry tree (*Arbutus unedo*)	All
Orchid tree (*Bauhinia*)	IV, LD, NC, SC
Lemon bottlebrush (*Callistemon citrinus*)	IV, LD, NC, SC
Palo verde (*Cercidium*)	IV, HD, LD, NC, SC
Redbud (*Cercis*)	All
Desert willow (*Chilopsis linearis*)	HD, LD, SC
Citrus (*Citrus*)	IV, LD, NC, SC
Flowering dogwood (*Cornus florida*)	SN, IV, NC
Hawthorn (*Crataegus*)	SN, IV, HD, NC
Loquat (*Eriobotrya*)	All
Coral tree (*Erythrina*)	IV, LD, NC, SC
Eucalyptus, Gum (*Eucalyptus*)	IV, HD, LD, NC, SC
Gordonia, Franklin tree (*Franklinia alatamaha, Gordonia alatamaha*)	SN, IV, NC
Australian willow, Wilga (*Geijera parviflora*)	IV, LD, NC, SC
Snowdrop tree, Silver bell (*Halesia carolina*)	SN, IV, NC, SC
Flamegold (*Koelreuteria elegans*)	IV, NC, SC
Crabapple (*Malus*)	All
Fruitless olive (*Olea europaea*)	IV, HD, LD, NC, SC
Pittosporum (*Pittosporum*)	IV, LD, NC, SC
Fern pine (*Podocarpus gracilior*)	IV, LD, NC, SC
Hollyleaf cherry (*Prunus ilicifolia*)	SN, IV, LD, NC, SC
Pear (*Pyrus*)	SN, IV, NC, SC
Locust (*Robinia*)	All
Mescal bean (*Sophora secundiflora*)	IV, HD, LD, NC, SC
Stewartia (*Stewartia*)	SN, IV, NC, SC
Snowbell (*Styrax*)	SN, IV, NC, SC
Tipu tree (*Tipuana tipu*)	IV, LD, NC, SC

TREES TO USE FOR WINDBREAKS

In many parts of California the wind blows predictably from one quarter, day after day, and a windbreak provides grateful relief for garden plants—and people. Don't put in just a single row of trees for a windbreak, though; they will be vulnerable to storm damage, and as they mature the wind will whistle through their trunks. Instead, create an "airflow" shape that will lift the wind up gently over the trees. To do this, lay out an array of up to five rows of shrubs and trees of progressive height, spaced 15 to 16 feet apart. If you don't have that much space, plant at least one row of shrubs on the windward side of the trees. If space is even more limited, use bushy, multitrunked trees rather than columnar ones.

Because eucalyptus trees are not native to California, may lose large limbs during wind storms, can inhibit the growth of other species, and are considered hazardous fuel plants in areas where wildfires occur, these beautiful trees have fallen out of favor in recent years. However, there is nothing quite so characteristic of our older highways and county roads as the long, bordering windbreaks of massive gum trees, the trunks white-washed up to chest level. No matter what has been learned about the trouble caused by indiscriminate planting of eucalyptus, it is sad to see their gray-green leaves and picturesquely shredded bark slowly vanish from our rural landscape.

Evergreen

Blackwood acacia (*Acacia melanoxylon*)	IV, LD, NC, SC
Bottle tree (*Brachychiton populneus*)	IV, LD, NC, SC
Incense cedar (*Calocedrus decurrens*)	SN, IV, HD, NC, SC
Beefwood, She-oak (*Casuarina*)	IV, LD, NC, SC
Leyland cypress (*Cupressocyparis leylandii*)	All
Smooth Arizona cypress (*Cupressus glabra*)	IV, HD, LD, NC, SC
Monterey cypress (*Cupressus macrocarpa*)	NC
Eucalyptus, Gum (*Eucalyptus*)	IV, HD, LD, NC, SC
Glossy privet (*Ligustrum lucidum*)	IV, HD, LD, NC, SC
Pine (*Pinus*)	All
Pittosporum (*Pittosporum*)	IV, LD, NC, SC
Douglas fir (*Pseudotsuga menziesii*)	SN, IV, NC, SC
California pepper tree (*Schinus molle*)	IV, LD, NC, SC
Western red cedar (*Thuja plicata*)	SN, IV, NC, SC

Deciduous

Paper mulberry (*Broussonetia papyrifera*)	All
Russian olive (*Elaeagnus angustifolia*)	All
Osage orange (*Maclura pomifera*)	All
White poplar (*Populus alba* 'Pyramidalis')	All
Lombardy poplar (*Populus nigra* 'Italica')	All
Mesquite (*Prosopis glandulosa*)	HD, LD
Siberian elm (*Ulmus pumila*)	All

COLUMNAR EVERGREENS

Evergreen trees that are tall and narrow are perfect for creating privacy screens and for emphasizing the vertical architectural thrust of townhouse facades. If you want to recreate a formal European garden, they are indispensible, either as accent trees or to line a long driveway. In California, the classic columnar evergreen is the Italian cypress, which was widely planted in Italianate estate gardens of the 1910s and 1920s and can reach a height of 60 feet when mature.

One thing to consider before you line your estate driveway with these dramatic trees: While a quarter-mile-long, double-row of 60-foot tall columnar cypresses is a thing of great beauty, it is not maintenance free. Despite careful selection for uniformity of habit, both the Italian and Arizona cypress will produce an occasional wild branch that pops out at right angles to the trunk and mars the tree's perfect form. You can't lop the maverick branch off, because that would create a bald spot in the greenery. Instead you must hire a tree service with a cherry-picker rig to climb up and tie the misplaced branch back to the trunk and train it upright. Expensive? Yes. Worth it? Well, if you have the where-with-all to plant a quarter-mile-long driveway double-lined with Italian cypresses, the answer is probably yes.

Arizona cypress (*Cupressus arizonica*)	IV, HD, LD, NC, SC
Smooth Arizona cypress (*Cupressus glabra*)	IV, HD, LD, NC, SC
Italian cypress (*Cupressus sempervirens*)	All
Spartan juniper (*Juniperus chinensis* 'Spartan')	All
Irish juniper (*Juniperus chinensis* 'Stricta')	All
Torulosa juniper (*Juniperus chinensis* 'Torulosa')	All
Rocky Mountain juniper (*Juniperus scopulorum*)	All
Eastern red cedar (*Juniperus virginiana*)	All
Engelmann spruce (*Picea engelmannii*)	SN, IV, NC
Irish yew (*Taxus baccata* 'Stricta')	SN, IV, NC, SC
Hogan cedar (*Thuja plicata* 'Fastigiata')	SN, IV, NC, SC

> Popular varieties of Italian cypress include 'Glauca,' with blue-green foliage; 'Indica,' with bright green foliage; and 'Fastigiata' or 'Stricta,' the columnar form most commonly seen.

THE MOST COLD-HARDY PALMS

As the old pop song of the 1920s has it, California is the land "Where the Redwood Kissed the Palm." Newcomers to our state are often disconcerted by the sight of palms growing side by side with redwoods, but to a native Californian—at least one born after the great palm-planting craze of the early 1900s—nothing could be more natural. Southern California avenues lined with washingtonia palms have become a Hollywood cliche, but just as characteristic of our landscape are the beautifully aged, stout-trunked Canary Island date palms planted in pairs or quartets at the entrances to 19th-century North Coast farmhouses.

Palms take a lot more cold than people think, and the older they get, the more likely they are to withstand a freakish cold snap or even prolonged freezing temperatures. I am sure that someone with an interest in botanical record-keeping has made a note of the individual palm tree that is growing at the highest elevation in the Sierra Nevadas. It would be reasonable to assume that this hypothetical record-holder is a low-growing species, perhaps a needle palm, that has been planted in a sheltered garden spot—but I can personally vouch for the existence of elderly Canary Island date palms on the uphill side of the Gold Rush town of Auburn.

Pindo palm (*Butia capitata*)	IV, HD, LD, NC, SC
Mediterranean fan palm (*Chamaerops humilis*)	All
Australian dracaena (*Cordyline australis*)	IV, HD, NC, SC
Blue dracaena (*Cordyline indivisa*)	NC, SC
Sago palm (*Cycas revoluta*)	IV, HD, LD, NC, SC
Chilean wine palm (*Jubaea chilensis*)	IV, LD, NC, SC
Canary Island date palm (*Phoenix canariensis*)	IV, HD, LD, NC, SC
Date palm (*Phoenix dactylifera*)	IV, HD, LD, NC, SC
Needle palm (*Rhapidophylum hystrix*)	IV, HD, LD, NC, SC
Palmetto (*Sabal palmetto*)	IV, HD, LD, NC, SC
Windmill palm (*Trachycarpus fortunei*)	All
California fan palm (*Washingtonia filifera*)	IV, HD, LD, NC, SC

> The Mexican fan palm (*Washingtonia robusta*), a fairly cold-hardy plant, is usually seen at heights of 40 to 50 feet, but it can reach 100 feet or more. Its dark-green fronds form a compact head, and you will find spines close to the shaggy trunk, advises Michael Letzring, lead gardener of the San Diego Zoo. "Most palms are slow growing, reaching their full height in 20 to 25 years, but the Mexican fan palm is fairly fast growing."

TREES THAT MAKE BEAUTIFUL BONSAI

Bonsai's popularity as a garden art in California is no doubt due to the long presence of Asian Americans in the state, but it has spread far beyond its cultural origins. Many rural county fairs offer prizes for the most beautiful bonsai, and most large cities have at least one nursery that stocks bonsai trees and can put you in touch with a local bonsai club. Although evergreens have the richest history as subjects for bonsai, many other trees adapt to the dwarfing regimen and make lovely and unusual miniatures.

Trident maple (*Acer buergeranum*)
Japanese maple (*Acer palmatum*)
Red maple (*Acer rubrum*)
Hornbeam (*Carpinus*)
Deodar cedar (*Cedrus deodara*)
Katsura tree (*Cercidiphyllum japonicum*)
Redbud (*Cercis*)
False cypress (*Chamaecyparis*)
Japanese cryptomeria (*Cryptomeria japonica*)
Beech (*Fagus*)
Juniper (*Juniperus*)
Crabapple (*Malus*)
Pine (*Pinus*)
Bald cypress (*Taxodium distichum*)
Zelkova (*Zelkova*)

> Osamu Hiroyama of Hida Bonsai Garden & Tools in Berkeley notes that bonsai is popular with many gardeners. "After you select the variety you want, you will have to work with it," he advises, and the right tool is integral to your success. At Hida, they suggest you don't splurge on fancy equipment, but instead "buy a steel tool of median price range. You'll get good quality at the fairest price, and a tool which can be used for many different types of bonsai gardening styles."

TREES RESISTANT TO OAK ROOT FUNGUS

Oak root fungus (*Armillaria mellea*) is a problem in many parts of California. Although it grows all over the the world, it seems to be especially harmful in our state. The fungus lives on dead roots and buried wood; in time it can infect the living roots of trees and kill them. If you are in an area where oak root fungus is known to be a problem or you want to replace a tree that was killed by the disease, try selecting one from the list of resistant species below.

White fir (*Abies concolor*)	SN, IV, NC, SC
Sydney golden wattle (*Acacia longifolia*)	IV, HD, NC, SC
Bigleaf maple (*Acer macrophyllum*)	SN, IV, HD, LD, NC
Japanese maple (*Acer palmatum*)	SN, IV, NC, SC
Tree of heaven (*Ailanthus altissima*)	All
Madrone (*Arbutus menziesii*)	SN, IV, NC, SC
Bottle tree (*Brachychiton populneus*)	IV, LD, NC, SC
Paper mulberry (*Broussonetia papyrifera*)	All
Incense cedar (*Calocedrus decurrens*)	All
Pecan (*Carya illinoensis*)	SN, IV, LD, NC, SC
Spanish chestnut (*Castanea sativa*)	SN, IV, NC
Catalpa, Indian bean (*Catalpa bignonioides*)	All
Common hackberry (*Celtis occidentalis*)	All
Carob (*Ceratonia siliqua*)	IV, LD, NC, SC
Redbud (*Cercis*)	All
Japanese cryptomeria (*Cryptomeria japonica*)	SN, IV, NC, SC
Persimmon (*Diospyros*)	SN, IV, NC, SC
Russian olive (*Elaeagnus angustifolia*)	All
Red gum (*Eucalyptus camaldulensis*)	IV, LD, NC, SC
Kadota and Mission fig (*Ficus carica*)	SN, IV, LD, NC, SC
Evergreen ash (*Fraxinus uhdei*)	IV, LD, NC, SC
Modesto ash (*Fraxinus velutina* 'Modesto')	All
Ginkgo (*Ginkgo biloba*)	SN, IV, NC, SC
English holly (*Ilex aquifolium*)	SN, IV, NC
American holly (*Ilex opaca*)	SN, IV, NC, SC
Jacaranda (*Jacaranda mimosifolia*)	LD, NC, SC
California black walnut (*Juglans hindsii*)	SN, IV, NC, SC
Oriental sweet gum (*Liquidambar orientalis*)	SN, IV, NC, SC
American sweet gum (*Liquidambar styraciflua*)	SN, IV, NC, SC
Tulip tree (*Liriodendron tulipifera*)	SN, IV, HD, NC, SC
Osage orange (*Maclura pomifera*)	All
Magnolia (*Magnolia*)	All
Mayten tree (*Maytenus boaria*)	IV, NC, SC
Melaleuca, Cajeput tree (*Melaleuca*)	IV, LD, NC, SC
Dawn redwood (*Metasequoia glyptostroboides*)	SN, IV, NC, SC
Canary Island pine (*Pinus canariensis*)	IV, LD, NC, SC
Austrian black pine (*Pinus nigra*)	SN, IV, HD, NC, SC
Jelecote pine (*Pinus patula*)	All
Monterey pine (*Pinus radiata*)	IV, NC, SC
Torrey pine (*Pinus torreyana*)	SC
Chinese pistache (*Pistacia chinensis*)	All

Douglas fir (*Pseudotsuga menziesii*)	SN, IV, NC
Pear (*Pyrus*)	SN, IV, HD, NC
Soapbark tree (*Quillaja saponaria*)	SN, IV, NC, SC
Chinese tallow tree (*Sapium sebiferum*)	IV, LD, NC, SC
Coast redwood (*Sequoia sempervirens*)	SN, IV, NC, SC
Japanese pagoda tree (*Sophora japonica*)	All
Chinese elm (*Ulmus parvifolia*)	All

TREES TO HIDE UGLY VIEWS

You say your neighbor's garage is an eyesore? You say that the folks next door have a backyard filled with rusting cars? The utility company put in a power line that ruins your view of pristine hills and grazing sheep? Most of the trees in this list have low branches to screen out unattractive sights at eye level. The taller trees will screen out ugly views from an upper-level window or balcony.

Also check page 100 and consider the option of planting a shrub. Shrubs tend to be denser than trees at ground level or when viewed from a seated position.

Bailey acacia (*Acacia baileyana*)	SN, IV, LD, NC, SC
Incense cedar (*Calocedrus decurrens*)	SN, IV, HD, NC, SC
European hornbeam (*Carpinus betulus*)	SN, IV, NC
Cedar (*Cedrus*)	All
Camphor tree (*Cinnamomum camphora*)	IV, LD, NC, SC
Japanese cryptomeria (*Cryptomeria japonica*)	SN, IV, NC, SC
Leyland cypress (*Cupressocyparis leylandii*)	All
European beech (*Fagus sylvatica*)	SN, IV, NC, SC
Holly (*Ilex*)	All
Rocky Mountain juniper (*Juniperus scopulorum*)	All
Eastern red cedar (*Juniperus virginiana*)	All
Sweet bay (*Laurus nobilis*)	SN, IV, LD, NC, SC
Southern magnolia (*Magnolia grandiflora*)	SN, IV, HD, NC, SC
Norway spruce (*Picea abies*)	SN, NC
Scotch pine (*Pinus sylvestris*)	SN, IV, NC, SC
Japanese black pine (*Pinus thunbergiana*)	SN, IV, HD, NC, SC
Yew pine (*Podocarpus macrophyllus*)	IV, HD, LD, NC, SC
Holly oak (*Quercus ilex*)	All
Western red cedar (*Thuja plicata*)	SN, IV, NC, SC
California bay (*Umbellularia californica*)	SN, IV, LD, NC, SC

The camphor tree is superbly evergreen, for it changes colors with the seasons, showing rusty-red new growth in spring and intriguing shades of chartreuse and yellow-green at other times. It is a mannerly subject for city plantings and can be clipped to a formal globe shape with very little trouble. The trunk will hide nothing at ground level, but the dense ball of leaves is perfect for blocking the sight of parked cars from a second-story balcony or breaking up a monotonous row of rooflines across the street.

EXTREMELY LONG-LIVED TREES

I f you want to plant trees for your grandchildren to enjoy, try the following—but be aware that not every one of these species will succeed in every environment. Some of the oaks are fussy about water (too much or too little will shorten their lives, depending on the species), and the coast redwood, while without a doubt one of nature's noblest trees, is highly sensitive to excessive traffic around its base and resents hard-packed or paved-over soil.

Giant
sequoia

Cedar (*Cedrus*)	All
European beech (*Fagus sylvatica*)	SN, IV, NC, SC
Ginkgo (*Ginkgo biloba*)	SN, IV, NC, SC
Tulip tree (*Liriodendron tulipifera*)	SN, IV, HD, NC, SC
Dawn redwood (*Metasequoia glyptostroboides*)	SN, IV, NC, SC
Olive (*Olea europaea*)	IV, LD, NC, SC
Douglas fir (*Pseudotsuga menziesii*)	SN, IV, NC, SC
Oak (*Quercus*)	All
Coast redwood (*Sequoia sempervirens*)	SN, IV, NC, SC
Giant sequoia (*Sequoiadendron giganteum*)	All
Bald cypress (*Taxodium distichum*)	SN, IV, LD, NC, SC
Yew (*Taxus*)	SN, IV, NC, SC

GREAT TREES WITH MULTIPLE TRUNKS

S pecimen trees with multiple trunks are extremely desirable in small environments where their bark and branch structure can be admired close up. In a sense, they are living sculptures, and as such they can make an impact in backyards where seating is arranged to show them off to best advantage.

In California, some of the prettiest multitrunked trees are the large-flowered *Magnolia soulangiana* hybrids, sometimes called "tulip trees," whose maroon buds open to silvery-pink within. (They should not be confused with that other "tulip tree," *Liriodendron tulipifera*, which is a forest giant.) In neighborhoods built during the 1920s, it is common to see multitrunked magnolias or flowering dogwoods placed near the front of the house, where their annual bloom can be admired by passersby. In neighborhoods developed during the 1950s, multitrunked clumps of birch have the position of honor.

Amur maple (*Acer ginnala*)	SN, IV, NC
Japanese maple (*Acer palmatum*)	SN, IV, NC, SC
Willow myrtle, Peppermint tree (*Agonis flexuosa*)	NC, SC
River birch, Red birch (*Betula nigra*)	All
Whitespire birch (*Betula platyphylla japonica* 'Whitespire')	SN, IV, HD, NC, SC
Katsura tree (*Cercidiphyllum japonicum*)	SN, IV, NC, SC
Palo verde (*Cercidium*)	IV, HD, LD, NC, SC
Flowering dogwood (*Cornus florida*)	SN, IV, NC
Pacific dogwood (*Cornus nuttallii*)	SN, IV, NC, SC
Filbert, Hazelnut (*Corylus*)	SN, IV, NC, SC
Silver bell (*Halesia*)	SN, IV, NC, SC
Southern magnolia (*Magnolia grandiflora*)	SN, IV, HD, NC, SC
Saucer magnolia (*Magnolia soulangiana*)	SN, IV, LD, NC, SC
Pacific wax myrtle (*Myrica californica*)	SN, IV, NC, SC

Olive (*Olea europaea*)	IV, HD, LD, NC, SC
Persian parrotia (*Parrotia persica*)	SN, IV, NC
Lacebark pine (*Pinus bungeana*)	SN, IV, NC, SC
Mesquite (*Prosopis*)	HD, LD
Portugal laurel (*Prunus lusitanica*)	SN, IV, NC, SC
Chinese quince (*Pseudocydonia sinensis*)	SN, IV, NC, SC
Guava (*Psidium*)	IV, NC, SC
African sumac (*Rhus lancea*)	IV, LD, NC, SC
Brazilian pepper tree (*Schinus terebinthifolius*)	IV, LD, NC, SC
California bay (*Umbellularia californica*)	SN, IV, LD, NC, SC
Chaste tree (*Vitex agnus-castus*)	All

Here is the good word from Don Rodrigues of Pacific Horticulture Consultants on some unusual multitrunked trees: "*Rhus lancea*, African sumac, is often overlooked as one of the best drought-tolerant desert trees. It is a beautiful specimen with weeping branches and shiny evergreen, willow-like leaves. The bark is a dark red-brown. It is very hardy and takes summer heat. Train it as a multitrunk. *Agonis flexuosa*, or peppermint tree, is an excellent multitrunked coastal evergreen tree noted for its weeping branches and reddish-brown trunk. This willow myrtle from Australia grows 25 to 30 feet tall and bears small white flowers all along the branches in the spring."

Here's an interesting idea for a multitrunk tree. Plant two or three avocado trees in the same hole. Tom Spellman, of La Verne Nursery in San Dimas, says they can be grown this way as a double or multitrunk clump. This works well if space is a problem in your garden.

TREES TO TRY IN CONTAINERS

Trees that live outdoors in containers will have a rough life, despite your best intentions. Irregular watering can make them alternate between drought and drowning. Wind tends to stress them more than ground-planted trees because they often are made to stand alone, without mutual protection from a clump of other plants. Not every tree will survive in a container, but here are some traditional favorites.

Wurtz avocado (*Avocado 'Wurtz'*)	IV, NC, SC
Old man cactus (*Cephalocereus senilis*)	SC
Apple cactus (*Cereus peruvianus*)	NC, SC
Parlor palm (*Chamaedorea elegans*)	NC, SC
Mediterranean fan palm (*Chamaerops humilis*)	All
Citrus (*Citrus*)	IV, LD, NC, SC
Goldenchain tree (*Laburnum watereri 'Vossii'*)	SN, IV, NC
New Zealand tea tree (*Leptospermum scoparium*)	IV, NC, SC
Little Gem magnolia (*Magnolia grandiflora 'Little Gem'*)	SN, IV, HD, NC, SC
Crabapple (*Malus*)	All
Pomegranate (*Punica granatum*)	SN, IV, NC, SC
Umbrella tree (*Schefflera*)	NC, SC

TREES WITH MANY SURFACE ROOTS

Some trees seem to lay their roots practically at the surface of the soil rather than underground. While this is picturesque in certain cases, it can also lead to troubles when mowing lawns, and to the invasion of flower beds by water-stealing tree roots. The trees in this list tend to form shallow roots, but almost any tree will do so if the topsoil is shallow and a heavy layer of hardpan prevents the roots from reaching lower.

Two of the species in this list deserve special mention. The redwood is a valuable tree that can be effectively planted in groves or clumps where its surface roots are rarely a problem—but it needs those roots to remain undisturbed if it is to thrive. Mature redwoods on college campuses have been killed by paving over their root zone and some fine specimens have been stressed to the point of visible damage by the presence of regular foot traffic over their roots. The black walnut is not generally suited to garden planting, but not only because its surface roots invade planting beds; the roots secrete a toxic substance called juglone that inhibits the growth of other plants in the walnut's vicinity.

Maple (*Acer*)	SN, IV, NC, SC
Beech (*Fagus*)	SN, IV, NC, SC
California walnut (*Juglans californica*)	SN, IV, NC, SC
Hinds walnut (*Juglans hindsii*)	SN, IV, NC, SC
Black walnut (*Juglans nigra*)	SN, IV, NC, SC
Southern magnolia (*Magnolia grandiflora*)	SN, IV, HD, NC, SC
Poplar, Cottonwood (*Populus*)	All
Chinese wingnut (*Pterocarya stenoptera*)	All
Oak (*Quercus*)	All
Chinese tallow tree (*Sapium sebiferum*)	IV, LD, NC, SC
California pepper tree (*Schinus molle*)	IV, LD, NC, SC
Coast redwood (*Sequoia sempervirens*)	SN, IV, NC, SC
Bald cypress (*Taxodium distichum*)	SN, IV, LD, NC, SC
Linden (*Tilia*)	All
Canada hemlock (*Tsuga canadensis*)	SN, IV, NC
Elm (*Ulmus*)	All

TREES UNDER WHICH IT IS IMPOSSIBLE
TO GROW ANYTHING

There are many reasons that grass and other plants won't grow under some trees, and not all of them are the trees' fault. Planting trees with a light canopy that allows sunlight in, selecting shade-tolerant plants, and keeping branches from sweeping down to the ground will help, but there are still some trees that resist the gardener's urge to grow something beneath them. There's nothing wrong with these trees—for one reason or another, they just don't coexist with other plants.

Tulip
tree

Japanese cryptomeria (*Cryptomeria japonica*)	SN, IV, NC, SC
China fir (*Cunninghamia lanceolata*)	SN, IV, NC, SC
Eucalyptus, Gum (*Eucalyptus*)	IV, HD, LD, NC, SC
Beech (*Fagus*)	SN, IV, NC, SC
Holly (*Ilex*)	All

Tulip tree (*Liriodendron tulipifera*)	SN, IV, HD, NC, SC
Southern magnolia (*Magnolia grandiflora*)	SN, IV, HD, NC, SC
Japanese blue oak (*Quercus glauca*)	IV, HD, LD, NC, SC
Japanese live oak (*Quercus myrsinifolia*)	SN, IV, NC, SC
Poplar, Cottonwood, Aspen (*Populus*)	All
English laurel (*Prunus laurocerasus*)	SN, IV, NC, SC
Redwood (*Sequoia*)	SN, IV, NC, SC
Elm (*Ulmus*)	All
California bay (*Umbellularia californica*)	SN, IV, LD, NC, SC

"Growing grass in the shade of trees is a challenging task for gardeners," says Vic Gibeault, a cooperative extension specialist at the University of California, Riverside, who specializes in turf grasses. "Not only is light restricted, which results in a reduction of photosynthesis and carbohydrate production, but also air movement is curtailed, and shallow feeder tree roots compete for water and nutrients." If you still want to give it a try, Vic recommends the cool-season fine-leaved fescues and tall fescue, and the warm-season St. Augustine grass and zoysia. To give grass some help, Vic says to "give it more light by selectively pruning tree branches. Thin surrounding underbrush and shrubs to open the landscape, which increases air movement. Raising mowing heights one-half-inch above normal will provide greater leaf area for light absorption. In shady areas, fertilization with nitrogen should be about one-half of full-sun conditions. However, increase potassium amounts above normal for the fall and spring fertilization programs. The amount of water needed by grass in shade is less than in sun, so reduce irrigation amounts and frequency to shaded turf. Also, try to reduce traffic on lawns growing in shade."

TREES WITH WEAK WOOD OR STRUCTURAL PROBLEMS

These trees are most likely to shed limbs during high winds or—if you live above the snow line—to break under the accumulated weight of snow and ice. Avoid planting them where their branches will grow over sheds, carports, or other low structures. They are fine trees in many ways, but there is no sense in asking for trouble.

Box elder (*Acer negundo*)	SN, IV, LD, NC, SC
Silver maple (*Acer saccharinum*)	SN, IV, NC, SC
Tree of heaven (*Ailanthus altissima*)	All
River birch (*Betula nigra*)	All
Eucalyptus (*Eucalyptus*)	IV, HD, LD, NC, SC
Golden-rain tree (*Koelreuteria paniculata*)	All
Tulip tree (*Liriodendron tulipifera*)	SN, IV, HD, NC, SC
Chinaberry (*Melia azedarach*)	All
Pine (*Pinus*)	All
Cottonwood (*Populus*)	All
White poplar (*Populus alba*)	All
Pear (*Pyrus*)	SN, IV, NC, SC
Scarlet oak (*Quercus coccinea*)	All
Brazilian pepper tree (*Schinus terebinthifolius*)	IV, LD, NC, SC

TREES THAT RESEED TOO WELL

Unless you are considering the establishment of a tree nursery, or can plant these trees in a lawn that is regularly mowed, you will need to check the beds beneath them to rid yourself of "sprouts." In the case of plums, the parent trees may not even be on your property—friendly, helpful birds will deposit the seeds for you!

Tree of heaven (*Ailanthus altissima*)	All
Silk tree, Mimosa (*Albizia julibrissin*)	All
Walnut (*Juglans*)	SN, IV, NC, SC
Golden-rain tree (*Koelreuteria paniculata*)	All
Chinaberry (*Melia azedarach*)	All
Mulberry (*Morus*)	All
Plums, Prunes (*Prunus*)	All
Chinese tallow tree (*Sapium sebiferum*)	IV, LD, NC, SC

TREES WITH INCONVENIENT LITTER

Stately trees make for beautiful neighborhoods, but every year, especially in autumn, one hears homeowners complain about how much work it is to clean up their "messes." If you already have a grand but messy tree, please don't cut it down; just think of cleaning beneath it as another household chore, like mopping the kitchen floor. However, if you are starting with a lot devoid of trees, you might consider avoiding the following species, unless you really like mopping the kitchen floor and want to perform such duties outdoors as well.

Leaves, Twigs, or Flowers

Silk tree (*Albizia julibrissin*)	All
River birch (*Betula nigra*)	All
Pindo palm (*Butia capitata*)	IV, LD, NC, SC
Pecan (*Carya illinoensis*)	SN, IV, LD, NC, SC
Mediterranean fan palm (*Chamaerops humilis*)	All
Australian dracaena (*Cordyline australis*)	IV, HD, NC, SC
Blue dracaena (*Cordyline indivisa*)	NC, SC
Sago palm (*Cycas revoluta*)	IV, HD, LD, NC, SC
Dragon tree (*Dracaena draco*)	NC, SC
Chinese parasol tree (*Firmiana simplex*)	IV, LD, NC, SC
Saucer magnolia (*Magnolia soulangiana*)	SN, IV, LD, NC, SC
Empress tree (*Paulownia tomentosa*)	All
Canary Island date palm (*Phoenix canariensis*)	IV, LD, NC, SC
Date palm (*Phoenix dactylifera*)	IV, LD, NC, SC
Sycamore (*Platanus occidentalis*)	All
Blackjack oak (*Quercus marilandica*)	All
Needle palm (*Rhapidophylum hystrix*)	IV, HD, LD, NC, SC
Palmetto (*Sabal*)	IV, HD, LD, NC, SC
Weeping willow (*Salix babylonica*)	All
Windmill palm (*Trachycarpus fortunei*)	All
California fan palm (*Washingtonia filifera*)	IV, HD, LD, NC, SC

Messy Seeds and Pods

Pecan, Hickory (*Carya*)	SN, IV, LD, NC, SC
Honey locust (*Gleditsia triacanthos*)	All

Kentucky coffee tree (*Gymnocladus dioica*)	SN, IV, LD, NC, SC
Walnut (*Juglans*)	SN, IV, NC, SC
Sweet gum (*Liquidambar styraciflua*)	SN, IV, NC, SC
Empress tree (*Paulownia tomentosa*)	All
Pine (*Pinus*)	All
Cottonwood (*Populus*)	All
Locust (*Robinia*)	All
California pepper tree (*Schinus molle*)	IV, LD, NC, SC

Fruit Drop

Ginkgo (*Ginkgo biloba*)	SN, IV, NC, SC
Glossy privet (*Ligustrum lucidum*)	IV, HD, LD, NC, SC
Crabapple (*Malus*)	All
Chinaberry (*Melia azedarach*)	All
Mulberry (*Morus*)	All
Olive (*Olea europaea*)	IV, HD, LD, NC, SC
Carolina cherry laurel (*Prunus caroliniana*)	All
Hollyleaf cherry (*Prunus ilicifolia*)	SN, IV, LD, NC, SC

If a tree's fruit drop would create a mess, try planting a fruitless variety or a male tree. Buy a male ginkgo or male cottonwood, for example, or the fruitless 'Swan Hill' variety of olive. Problems with seedpods can be avoided if you buy the seedless 'Imperial' variety of honey locust, or the fruitless 'Rotundiloba' variety of sweet gum.

TREES WITH WEEPING BRANCHES

The trees in this list have branches that, like the weeping willow's, droop gracefully toward the ground.

Cutleaf weeping birch (*Betula pendula* 'Laciniata')	SN, IV, HD, NC, SC
Weeping bottlebrush (*Callistemon viminalis*)	IV, LD, NC, SC
Weeping atlas cedar (*Cedrus atlantica* 'Pendula')	All
Weeping beech (*Fagus sylvatica* 'Pendula')	SN, IV, NC, SC
Weeping copper beech (*Fagus sylvatica* 'Purpurea Pendula')	SN, IV, NC, SC
Weeping European ash (*Fraxinus excelsior* 'Pendula')	SN, IV, HD, NC
Weeping yaupon (*Ilex vomitoria* 'Pendula')	All
Tolleson weeping juniper (*Juniperus scopulorum* 'Tolleson's Weeping')	All
Weeping Scotch laburnum (*Laburnum alpinum* 'Pendulum')	SN, IV, NC
Weeping crabapple (*Malus* 'Pink Weeper')	All
Willow pittosporum (*Pittosporum phillyraeoides*)	IV, LD, NC, SC
White Fountain flowering cherry (*Prunus serrulata* 'White Fountain')	SN, IV, NC, SC
Weeping higan cherry (*Prunus subhirtella* 'Pendula')	SN, IV, NC, SC
Weeping willow-leaf pear (*Pyrus salicifolia* 'Pendula')	SN, IV, NC, SC
African sumac (*Rhus lancea*)	IV, LD, NC, SC
Weeping willow (*Salix babylonica*)	All
Weeping pagoda tree (*Sophora japonica* 'Pendula')	All
Montezuma cypress (*Taxodium mucronatum*)	SN, IV, LD, NC, SC

TREES WITH PERFECT FORM

Perfection is in the eye of the landscape designer, but the trees in this list tend to develop symmetrical tops, whether conical, globular, or columnar. This makes them well-suited for planting in repeated patterns or as single specimen trees. For other trees with symmetrical form, see the sections on columnar evergreens and the section on cold-hardy palms on page 54 and palms for desert areas on page 50.

Spanish fir (*Abies pinsapo*)	SN, IV, HD, NC, SC
Incense cedar (*Calocedrus decurrens*)	SN, IV, HD, NC, SC
Camphor tree (*Cinnamomum camphora*)	IV, LD, NC, SC
Japanese cryptomeria (*Cryptomeria japonica*)	SN, IV, NC, SC
Leyland cypress (*Cupressocyparis leylandii*)	All
American sweet gum (*Liquidambar styraciflua*)	SN, IV, NC, SC
Tulip tree (*Liriodendron tulipifera*)	SN, IV, HD, NC, SC
Dawn redwood (*Metasequoia glyptostroboides*)	SN, IV, NC, SC
Canary Island date palm (*Phoenix canariensis*)	IV, LD, NC, SC
Date palm (*Phoenix dactylifera*)	IV, LD, NC, SC
Golden larch (*Pseudolarix kaempferi*)	SN, IV, NC
Palmetto (*Sabal*)	IV, HD, LD, NC, SC
Cypress (*Taxodium*)	SN, IV, LD, NC, SC
Western red cedar (*Thuja plicata*)	SN, IV, NC, SC

Michael Letzring, lead gardener of the San Diego Zoo, recommends the triangle palm (*Neodypsis decaryi*) for its interesting shape and the color of its leaves. Its gray-green, feathery fronds arch up and out for 15 feet or more to create an inverted pyramid shape, or peacock fan, at the top of the trunk.

TREES WITH ORNAMENTAL FRUIT, BERRIES, OR SEEDPODS

To get the most out of your garden trees, select for variety of interest throughout the seasons, not just spring or fall. Some trees produce especially colorful fruit or interesting seedpods. Winter berries or seeds will attract birds, a bonus in the landscape. Because some hollies require both a male and a female plant to set fruit, ask your local nursery staff for help in selecting them.

Amur maple (*Acer ginnala*)	SN, IV, NC
Lilly-pilly (*Acmena smithii*)	IV, NC, SC
Downy serviceberry (*Amelanchier arborea*)	SN, IV, HD
Strawberry tree (*Arbutus unedo*)	All
Deodar cedar (*Cedrus deodara*)	All
Citrus (*Citrus*)	IV, LD, NC, SC
Dogwood (*Cornus*)	SN, IV, NC, SC
Hawthorn (*Crataegus*)	SN, IV, HD, NC
Persimmon (*Diospyros*)	SN, IV, NC, SC
Loquat (*Eriobotrya japonica*)	All
Holly (*Ilex*)	All
Chinese flame tree (*Koelreuteria bipinnata*)	IV, HD, LD, NC, SC
Golden-rain tree (*Koelreuteria paniculata*)	All
Southern magnolia (*Magnolia grandiflora*)	SN, IV, HD, NC, SC
Crabapple (*Malus*)	All
Sumac (*Rhus*)	All

Blue elderberry (*Sambucus mexicana, S. glauca*)	SN, IV, NC, SC
Chinese tallow tree (*Sapium sebiferum*)	IV, LD, NC, SC
Brazilian pepper tree (*Schinus terebinthifolius*)	IV, LD, NC, SC
Mountain ash (*Sorbus*)	SN, IV, NC
Brush cherry (*Syzygium paniculatum*)	IV, NC, SC

Michael A. Parten of Orchard Nursery & Florist in Lafayette notes that eastern dogwoods (*Cornus florida*), Washington thorns (*Crataegus phaenopyrum*), and European mountain ash (*Sorbus aucuparia*) all have red berries that add color to the landscape and are appreciated by wildlife as food. All have attractive fall foliage as well.

TREES WITH SHOWY BARK

Tree bark can have interesting color, texture, or pattern. To appreciate the true beauty of bark patterns, perhaps one must live in a snowy area. With all the leaves fallen and a backdrop of sparkling white to set them off, the trunks of many trees assume a rare showiness that is underappreciated at other times. However, even in our warm-winter areas, outstanding bark color, texture, or pattern is an asset in any tree that will be viewed up close, as from a ground-floor window, along a path or sidewalk, or on a patio.

Paperbark maple (*Acer griseum*)	SN, IV, NC, SC
Pacific madrone (*Arbutus menziesii*)	SN, IV, NC, SC
Strawberry tree (*Arbutus unedo*)	All
Birch (*Betula*)	All
Flame tree (*Brachychiton acerifolius*)	IV, NC, SC
Shagbark hickory (*Carya ovata*)	SN, IV
Hackberry (*Celtis*)	All
Katsura tree (*Cercidiphyllum japonicum*)	SN, IV, NC, SC
Camphor tree (*Cinnamomum camphora*)	IV, LD, NC, SC
Eucalyptus, Gum (*Eucalyptus*)	IV, HD, LD, NC, SC
Franklin tree, Gordonia (*Franklinia alatamaha, Gordonia alatamaha*)	All
Crape myrtle (*Lagerstroemia*)	SN, IV, LD, NC, SC
Sweet gum (*Liquidambar styraciflua*)	SN, IV, NC, SC
Melaleuca (*Melaleuca*)	IV, LD, NC, SC
Jerusalem thorn (*Parkinsonia aculeata*)	IV, HD, LD, NC, SC
Lacebark pine (*Pinus bungeana*)	SN, IV, NC, SC
London plane tree (*Platanus acerifolia*)	All
California sycamore (*Platanus racemosa*)	All
Yoshino flowering cherry (*Prunus yedoensis*)	SN, IV, NC, SC
California white oak (*Quercus lobata*)	SN, IV, NC, SC
California pepper tree (*Schinus molle*)	IV, LD, NC, SC
Japanese stewartia (*Stewartia pseudocamellia*)	IV, NC, SC
Lacebark elm (*Ulmus parvifolia*)	All

California sycamore

Pacific madrone not only has showy, reddish, peeling bark, but it also offers an interesting twisted shape and lightly fragrant, white spring flowers followed by reddish-orange berries. This evergreen does well in sun or shade and in poor, dry soil.

TREES WITH COLORED FOLIAGE

While colored flowers and fruit are always of interest in the garden, it takes a sophisticated eye to appreciate the variety of leaf colors available in trees. Use these unusually foliaged varieties to break up the monotony of a green canopy, to complement the hues of the flowers or lawn at their feet, and—if you are daring—to contrast with each other.

Blue

Mexican blue palm (*Brahea, Erythea*)	IV, LD, NC, SC
Lawson cedar, False cypress (*Chamaecyparis lawsoniana*)	NC
China fir (*Cunninghamia lanceolata* 'Glauca')	SN, IV, NC, SC
Snow gum (*Eucalyptus niphophila*)	IV, HD, LD, NC, SC
Blue juniper (*Juniperus deppeana pachyphlaea*)	All

Gray

Smooth Arizona cypress (*Cupressus glabra*)	IV, HD, LD, NC, SC
Blue box (*Eucalyptus baueriana*)	IV, LD, NC, SC
Bluish-gray gum (*Eucalyptus caesia*)	IV, NC, SC
Dwarf blue gum (*Eucalyptus globulus* 'Compacta')	IV, NC, SC
Kruse's eucalyptus (*Eucalyptus kruseana*)	IV, NC, SC
White ironbark (*Eucalyptus leucoxylon*)	IV, LD, NC, SC
Big-fruited gum (*Eucalyptus macrocarpa*)	IV, LD, NC, SC
Silver mountain gum (*Eucalyptus pulverulenta*)	IV, LD, NC, SC
Rose gum (*Eucalyptus rhodantha*)	IV, LD, NC, SC
Gray gleam juniper (*Juniperus scopulorum* 'Gray Gleam')	All
Pendula weeping juniper (*Juniperus scopulorum* 'Pendula')	All
Olive (*Olea europaea*)	IV, HD, LD, NC, SC

Bronze, Red, Maroon

Red Japanese maple (*Acer palmatum*)	SN, IV, NC, SC
Crimson King maple (*Acer platanoides* 'Crimson King')	SN, IV, NC
Bronze dracaena (*Cordyline australis* 'Atropurpurea')	IV, HD, NC, SC
Purple filbert (*Corylus maxima* 'Purpurea')	SN, IV, NC
Velvet Cloak smoke tree (*Cotinus coggygria* 'Velvet Cloak')	SN, IV, HD, NC, SC
Purple beech (*Fagus sylvatica* 'Purpurea')	SN, IV, NC, SC
Flowering plum (*Prunus blireiana*)	All
Purple-leaf plum (*Prunus cerasifera* 'Atropurpurea')	All

Yellow-Green, Golden

Golden maple (*Acer japonicum* 'Aureum')	SN, IV, NC
Golden King cedar (*Chamaecyparis lawsoniana* 'Golden King')	SN, IV, NC
Camphor tree (*Cinnamomum camphora*)	IV, LD, NC, SC
Sunburst honey locust (*Gleditsia triacanthos* 'Sunburst')	All
Frisia black locust (*Robinia pseudoacacia* 'Frisia')	All
Aurea cedar (*Thuja plicata* 'Aurea')	SN, IV, NC, SC

Variegated

Variegated box elder (*Acer negundo* 'Variegatum')	SN, IV, LD, NC, SC
Tricolor dogwood (*Cornus florida* 'Welchii')	SN, IV, NC
Goldspot dogwood (*Cornus nuttallii* 'Goldspot')	SN, IV, NC, SC

Tricolor beech (*Fagus sylvatica* 'Tricolor')	SN, IV, NC, SC
Silver Queen holly (*Ilex aquifolium* 'Silver Queen')	All
Variegated arborvitae (*Thuja plicata* 'Aurea Variegata')	SN, IV, NC, SC

 Many varieties of juniper, false cypress, and Japanese maple with colored foliage are available. Check with your local nursery for the species that do best in your area. Be aware that the amount of sunlight a Japanese maple receives can influence its leaf color, so act on the recommendation of the nursery when it comes to placing it in your garden.

TREES WITH FRAGRANT BLOSSOMS OR FOLIAGE

Because trees bloom above nose level, visitors to your garden might not know what is responsible for the delicate aroma they perceive as they stroll your grounds, but half the fun of growing fragrant trees is convincing friends that it is the trees, not the flowers, that they are smelling. All of these trees will perfume the air, but to reap the full effect of their aroma, plant them uphill from where you will be sniffing, because scent flows downward. Most will be at their best in the morning, when the air is still.

Included in this list are a few trees like eucalyptus and cypress, whose primary fragrance comes from their leaves, especially when they are bruised or crushed.

Bailey acacia (*Acacia baileyana*)	SN, IV, LD, NC, SC
Amur maple (*Acer ginnala*)	SN, IV, NC
Incense cedar (*Calocedrus decurrens*)	All
Siberian pea shrub (*Caragana arborescens*)	SN, IV, HD
Camphor tree (*Cinnamomum camphora*)	IV, LD, NC, SC
Citrus (*Citrus*)	SN, IV, LD, NC, SC
Yellowwood (*Cladrastis lutea*)	SN, IV, NC
Cypress (*Cupressus*)	All
Smokethorn (*Dalea spinosa*)	HD, LD
Winter's bark (*Drimys winteri*)	IV, NC, SC
Loquat (*Eriobotrya japonica*)	All
Eucalyptus, Gum (*Eucalyptus*)	IV, HD, LD, NC, SC
Franklin tree, Gordonia (*Franklinia alatamaha, Gordonia alatamaha*)	SN, IV, NC
Kentucky coffee tree (*Gymnocladus dioica*)	SN, IV, LD, NC, SC
Sweetshade (*Hymenosporum flavum*)	IV, NC, SC
Sweet bay (*Laurus nobilis*)	SN, IV, LD, NC, SC
Southern magnolia (*Magnolia grandiflora*)	SN, IV, HD, NC, SC
Chinaberry (*Melia azedarach*)	All
Michelia (*Michelia*)	IV, NC, SC
Sweet olive (*Osmanthus fragrans*)	IV, LD, NC, SC
Alma Stultz nectarine (*Prunus* 'Alma Stultz')	All
Flowering plum (*Prunus blireiana*)	All
Yoshino flowering cherry (*Prunus yedoensis*)	SN, IV, NC, SC
Black locust (*Robinia pseudoacacia*)	All
Arborvitae (*Thuja*)	All
Little-leaf linden (*Tilia cordata*)	All
California bay (*Umbellularia californica*)	SN, IV, LD, NC, SC
Chaste tree (*Vitex agnus-castus*)	All

TREES WITH CHARACTER

Trees with crooked trunks, twisted branches, spreading but irregular canopies, and odd limb placement can give a garden spot wonderful character. The following trees are anything but perfect when mature. They can be used with great effect as single specimen trees to offset the all-too-regular lines of plain, box-like houses.

California white oak

Silk tree, Mimosa (*Albizia julibrissin*)	All
Monkey puzzle tree (*Araucaria araucana*)	SN, IV, NC, SC
Bunya-bunya (*Araucaria bidwillii*)	SN, IV, LD, NC, SC
Bottle palm, Ponytail (*Beaucarnea recurvata*)	LD, NC, SC
Desert willow (*Chilopsis linearis*)	HD, LD, SC
Australian dracaena (*Cordyline australis*)	IV, HD, NC, SC
Russian olive (*Elaeagnus angustifolia*)	All
Coral tree (*Erythrina*)	IV, LD, NC, SC
Silver dollar tree (*Eucalyptus cinerea*)	IV, LD, NC, SC
Chinese flame tree (*Koelreuteria bipinnata*)	IV, HD, LD, NC, SC
Golden-rain tree (*Koelreuteria paniculata*)	All
Australian tea tree (*Leptospermum laevigatum*)	IV, NC, SC
Pink melaleuca (*Melaleuca nesophila*)	LD, NC, SC
Mulberry (*Morus*)	All
Olive (*Olea europaea*)	IV, HD, LD, NC, SC
Sourwood (*Oxydendrum arboreum*)	SN, IV, NC, SC
Empress tree (*Paulownia tomentosa*)	All
Mesquite (*Prosopis*)	HD, LD
Chinese quince (*Pseudocydonia sinensis*)	SN, IV, NC, SC
California white oak (*Quercus lobata*)	SN, IV, NC, SC
Dragon-claw willow (*Salix matsudana* 'Tortuosa')	All
Japanese fantail willow (*Salix udensis* 'Sekka')	All
California pepper tree (*Schinus molle*)	IV, LD, NC, SC

> **Don Rodrigues of Pacific Horticultural Consultants in Ventura says, "The Australian tea tree, *Leptospermum laevigatum*, generates one of the most interesting twisting branch forms with gray to reddish-brown bark. Branching low to the ground, the gnarling limbs are a sculpture all their own. This tree makes a great tub or bonsai specimen if regularly pruned."**

TREES THAT ATTRACT BIRDS

If you like to have birds in your garden, you can include some of these plants in your landscaping. Remember, though, that if your attempt to lure birds succeeds, you probably won't get full enjoyment from plants that produce enticing fruit; birds will eat the fruit just when they become colorful.

Many of the trees whose flowers are listed as attractants are visited by hummingbirds. For trees listed by genus only, check with a local nursery for the species appropriate to your zone.

Fruit

Serviceberry (*Amelanchier*)	SN, IV
Strawberry tree (*Arbutus unedo*)	All
Hackberry (*Celtis*)	All

Dogwood (*Cornus*)	SN, IV, NC, SC
Hawthorn (*Crataegus*)	SN, IV, HD, NC, SC
Persimmon (*Diospyrus*)	SN, IV, NC, SC
Loquat (*Eriobotrya*)	All
Fig (*Ficus*)	SN, IV, LD, NC, SC
Apple (*Malus*)	IV, NC, SC
Crabapple (*Malus*)	All
Mulberry (*Morus*)	All
Plum, Prune, Apricot, Peach (*Prunus*)	SN, IV, NC, SC
Elderberry (*Sambucus*)	SN, IV, NC, SC
California pepper tree (*Schinus molle*)	IV, LD, NC, SC
Mountain ash (*Sorbus*)	SN, IV, NC

Seeds

Fir (*Abies*)	SN, IV, HD, NC, SC
Maple (*Acer*)	SN, IV, NC, SC
Alder (*Alnus*)	SN, IV, NC, SC
Birch (*Betula*)	All
Beech (*Fagus*)	SN, IV, NC, SC
Larch (*Larix*)	SN, IV, NC, SC
Spruce (*Picea*)	SN, IV, NC
Pine (*Pinus*)	All
Oak (*Quercus*)	All
Elm (*Ulmus*)	All

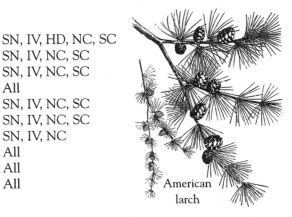

American larch

Flowers

Acacia (*Acacia*)	All
Maple (*Acer*)	SN, IV, LD, NC, SC
Horsechestnut (*Aesculus*)	SN, IV, NC, SC
Silk tree (*Albizia*)	All
Bird of paradise tree (*Caesalpinia*)	All
Hawthorn (*Crataegus*)	SN, IV, HD, NC, SC
Loquat (*Eriobotrya*)	All
Snowdrop tree, Silver bell (*Halesia*)	SN, IV, NC, SC
Tulip tree (*Liriodendron*)	SN, IV, HD, NC, SC
Flowering crabapple (*Malus*)	All
Chinaberry (*Melia*)	All

Most humans think the fruit of the strawberry tree (**Arbutus unedo**) is tasteless, but the 'Marina' hybrid has better flavor than most. 'Marina' does well in the landscape or a large container. It has pink blossoms in spring, followed by the fruit. Fine for sun or light shade, this tree needs little water after established.

TREES WITH LAYERED HORIZONTAL BRANCHES

Some trees put out many horizontal branches, layering them one atop the other so that their leaves are uniformly exposed to sunlight. When they are seen against a backdrop of vertical, spiky trees, the contrast is quite charming.

Fir (*Abies*)	SN, IV, HD, NC, SC
Japanese maple (*Acer palmatum*)	SN, IV, NC, SC
Silk tree, Mimosa (*Albizia julibrissin*)	All
Catalpa (*Catalpa*)	All
Dogwood (*Cornus*)	SN, IV, NC, SC
Hawthorn (*Crataegus*)	SN, IV, HD, NC, SC
European beech (*Fagus sylvatica*)	SN, IV, NC, SC
Japanese larch (*Larix kaempferi*)	SN, IV, NC, SC
Mt. Fuji flowering cherry (*Prunus serrulata* 'Mt. Fuji')	SN, IV, NC, SC
Yoshino flowering cherry (*Prunus yedoensis*)	SN, IV, NC, SC
Ornamental pear (*Pyrus calleryana*)	SN, IV, NC, SC
Japanese snowdrop tree (*Styrax japonicus*)	SN, IV, NC, SC
Hemlock (*Tsuga*)	SN, IV, NC

TREES WITH BRANCHES PRIZED FOR ARRANGEMENTS

Almost everyone loves cut flowers in the home, but how many people regularly cut and display tree branches? If you have your own trees, it is no trouble at all to cut a few branches for spectacular arrangements. Don't limit yourself to springtime blossoms, either: a sweet gum branch in fall color or a branch of Fuyu persimmon in fruit can make an amazing table centerpiece or entry hall display.

Bailey acacia (*Acacia baileyana*)	SN, IV, LD, NC, SC
Flowering quince (*Chaenomeles*)	All
Citrus (*Citrus*)	IV, LD, NC, SC
Persimmon (*Diospyros*)	SN, IV, NC, SC
Loquat (*Eriobotrya japonica*)	All
Eucalyptus (*Eucalyptus*)	IV, HD, LD, NC, SC
Holly (*Ilex*)	All
Chinese flame tree (*Koelreuteria bipinnata*)	IV, HD, LD, NC, SC
Golden-rain tree (*Koelreuteria paniculata*)	All
Contorted mulberry (*Morus australis* 'Unryu')	All
Jerusalem thorn (*Parkinsonia aculeata*)	IV, HD, LD, NC, SC
Pussy willow (*Salix caprea, S. discolor*)	All
Dragon-claw willow (*Salix matsudana* 'Tortuosa')	All

A SAMPLER OF TREES BY THE COLOR OF THEIR FLOWERS

Flowering trees are among the most impressive landscape plants. There are few sights as uplifting as orchards in the spring, when the plums or apricots or apples are in bloom, or a stand of blossoming roadside acacias in late winter (unless you are allergic to their pollen). You can bring beauty on a grand scale to your own garden by planting trees from the following list, keeping in mind that the backdrop they appear against will improve the impact of their floral display. Trees with white or yellow flowers will show to best advantage against dark walls or green lawns; those with pink flowers need either a dark or a white backdrop but will lose their effectiveness against tan or khaki walls.

Chinese fringe tree

White	Season	Region
Downy serviceberry (*Amelanchier arborea*)	Early spring	SN, IV
Pacific madrone (*Arbutus menziesii*)	Spring	SN, IV, NC, SC
Catalpa (*Catalpa*)	Late spring	All
Chinese fringe tree (*Chionanthus retusus*)	Late spring	SN, IV, NC, SC
Flowering dogwood (*Cornus florida*)	Spring	SN, IV, NC
Kousa dogwood (*Cornus kousa*)	Summer	SN, IV, NC, SC
Smoke tree (*Cotinus coggygria*)	Summer	All
Washington thorn (*Crataegus phaenopyrum*)	Spring	SN, IV, HD, NC, SC
Silver bell (*Halesia carolina*)	Spring	SN, IV, NC, SC
Crape myrtle (*Lagerstroemia*)	Summer	SN, IV, LD, NC, SC
Southern magnolia (*Magnolia grandiflora*)	Summer	SN, IV, HD, NC, SC
Yoshino cherry (*Prunus yedoensis*)	Early spring	SN, IV, NC, SC
Ornamental pear (*Pyrus calleryana*)	Early spring	SN, IV, NC, SC
Japanese pagoda tree (*Sophora japonica*)	Summer	All
Japanese snowdrop (*Styrax japonicus*)	Spring	SN, IV, NC, SC

Blue, Purple		
Redbud (*Cercis*)	Spring	All
Desert willow (*Chilopsis linearis*)	Spring	HD, LD, SC
Jacaranda (*Jacaranda mimosifolia*)	Spring	LD, NC, SC
Crape myrtle (*Lagerstroemia*)	Summer	IV, LD, NC, SC
Saucer magnolia (*Magnolia soulangiana*)	Early spring	SN, IV, LD, NC, SC
Lilac melaleuca (*Melaleuca decussata*)	Spring	IV, LD, NC, SC
Empress tree (*Paulownia tomentosa*)	Early spring	All
Chaste tree (*Vitex agnus-castus*)	Summer	All

Yellow, Orange		
Acacia (*Acacia*)	Winter	All
Senna (*Cassia*)	Summer	IV, LD, SC
Coral tree (*Erythrina*)	Spring	IV, LD, NC, SC
Chinese flame tree (*Koelreuteria bipinnata*)	Summer	IV, HD, LD, NC, SC
Goldenchain tree (*Laburnum*)	Spring	SN, IV, NC
Jerusalem thorn (*Parkinsonia aculeata*)	Late spring	IV, HD, LD, NC, SC

Pink, Red

Silk tree (*Albizia*)	Summer	All
Redbud (*Cercis*)	Spring	All
Flowering dogwood (*Cornus florida*)	Spring	SN, IV, NC
Hawthorn (*Crataegus*)	Spring	SN, IV, HD, NC
Chinese quince (*Cydonia sinensis*)	Mid-spring	SN, IV, NC, SC
Coral tree (*Erythrina*)	Spring	IV, LD, NC, SC
Crape myrtle (*Lagerstroemia*)	Summer	SN, IV, LD, NC, SC
Crabapple (*Malus*)	Spring	All
Flowering plum (*Prunus blireiana*)	Winter	All
Flowering apricot (*Prunus mume*)	Winter	SN, IV, LD, NC, SC
Tamarisk (*Tamarix*)	Spring	All

A SAMPLER OF TREES FOR FALL COLOR

Yellow, Gold, Orange

Bigleaf maple (*Acer macrophyllum*)	SN, IV, HD, LD, NC
Box elder (*Acer negundo*)	SN, IV, LD, NC, SC
Birch (*Betula*)	All
Catalpa (*Catalpa*)	All
Hackberry (*Celtis*)	All
Katsura tree (*Cercidiphyllum japonicum*)	SN, IV, NC, SC
Eastern redbud (*Cercis candensis*)	All
Yellowwood (*Cladrastis lutea*)	SN, IV, NC
Arizona ash (*Fraxinus velutina*)	All
Ginkgo (*Ginkgo biloba*)	SN, IV, NC, SC
Japanese crape myrtle (*Lagerstroemia fauriei*)	SN, IV, LD, NC, SC
Larch (*Larix*)	SN, IV, NC, SC
Tulip tree (*Liriodendron tulipifera*)	SN, IV, HD, NC, SC
Osage orange (*Maclura pomifera*)	All
Western cottonwood (*Populus fremontii*)	All
Bald cypress (*Taxodium distichum*)	SN, IV, LD, NC, SC

Red

Amur maple (*Acer ginnala*)	SN, IV, NC
Paperbark maple (*Acer griseum*)	SN, IV, NC, SC
Red maple (*Acer rubrum*)	SN, IV, NC
Dogwood (*Cornus*)	SN, IV, NC, SC
Washington thorn (*Crataegus phaenopyrum*)	SN, IV, HD, NC, SC
Japanese persimmon (*Diospyros kaki*)	SN, IV, NC, SC
Franklin tree, Gordonia (*Franklinia alatamaha, Gordonia alatamaha*)	All
Crape myrtle (*Lagerstroemia indica*)	SN, IV, LD, NC, SC
Sweet gum (*Liquidambar styraciflua*)	SN, IV, NC, SC
Sour gum (*Nyssa sylvatica*)	SN, IV, NC, SC
Sourwood (*Oxydendrum arboreum*)	SN, IV, NC, SC
Chinese pistache (*Pistacia chinensis*)	All
Ornamental pear (*Pyrus calleryana*)	SN, IV, NC, SC
Sumac (*Rhus*)	All

Chinese tallow tree (*Sapium sebiferum*)	IV, LD, NC, SC
Sawleaf zelkova (*Zelkova serrata*)	All

Purple, Burgundy, Bronze

Japanese maple (*Acer palmatum*)	SN, IV, NC, SC
Spanish chestnut (*Castanea sativa*)	SN, IV, NC
Dogwood (*Cornus*)	SN, IV, NC, SC
Beech (*Fagus*)	SN, IV, NC, SC
White ash (*Fraxinus americana*)	SN, IV, HD, NC
Claret ash (*Fraxinus angustifolia*)	SN, IV, LD, NC, SC
Acoma crape myrtle (*Lagerstroemia* 'Acoma')	SN, IV, LD, NC, SC
Oriental sweet gum (*Liquidambar orientalis*)	SN, IV, NC, SC
Purple-leaf plum (*Prunus cerasifera* 'Atropurpurea')	All
Red oak (*Quercus rubra*)	SN, IV, HD, NC, SC
Korean stewartia (*Stewartia koreana*)	SN, IV, NC, SC
Japanese stewartia (*Stewartia pseudocamellia*)	SN, IV, NC, SC

SHRUBS

Shrubs are often the most important element in the small garden, and in fact on a small urban lot, they may be the largest form of vegetation found, especially if trees are positioned well in neighboring yards or in the parking strip maintained by the city. A garden can look good without trees, but it is unlikely to present a beautiful picture in the complete absence of shrubs. Because these versatile plants range from knee-high to the size of small trees, they can be put to many uses. Evergreen shrubs are the standard choice for creating privacy screens, while flowering deciduous shrubs such as lilacs and snowball bushes are not only ornamental but find a warm, nostalgic place in almost everyone's heart. Shrubs that combine the best of these characteristics, such as the evergreen flowering oleanders and azaleas, arc among the most popular species grown in California and, in some neighborhoods, can almost be said to define our regional gardening styles.

Japanese spiraea

When choosing a shrub for a particular place in your garden, don't just go by what the young plant looks like in a nursery. Try to locate a mature example of the same variety growing near your home. Notice how large it is and try to figure out whether it is that size because it has been regularly clipped to maintain its form. This is especially important if you are considering foundation plantings, which will be placed near the house. Nothing is more discouraging than finding out, five years down the road, that the mannerly little shrub you planted beneath your picture window is now blocking the view!

Another reason not to judge the ultimate size and form of a shrub in the nursery is that some of our grandest shrubs are very gawky as babies. The mock orange, for instance, is spindly, awkward, and uncomfortable when young, but given a decade, it will develop into a magnificent, scene-stealing monster, especially if it is never pruned and the new growth is allowed to build on the framework of the dead branches beneath its green exterior. When treated in this manner, the mock orange becomes a mound of flowering fragrance, 10 feet tall and 15 feet in diameter, far too large for most city gardens, yet exceptionally fine in an old farmyard such as mine, where every year its bloom-time is heralded by passersby who stop to smell its fragrance and marvel at its girth.

SHRUBS FOR HILLSIDES AND
EROSION CONTROL

Hillsides generally offer a less hospitable plant environment than do level gardens. Soil may be shallow, poor, or—where the bank is the result of a grading cut—virtually nonexistent. Hillsides also are more difficult to water thoroughly unless you form watering basins around each new plant so that water will soak in rather than run off. Fortunately, numerous plants cope successfully with less than ideal conditions and provide good-looking cover for slopes. In addition, the roots of these plants hold the soil in place to help prevent erosion. Most of these shrubs reach medium height (4 to 6 feet) or taller. For shorter plants that offer similar protection, see the list of low-growing shrubs for ground cover on page 84.

Vine hill manzanita (*Arctostaphylos densiflora*)	SN, IV, NC, SC
Monterey manzanita (*Arctostaphylos hookeri*)	SN, IV, NC, SC
Saltbush (*Atriplex*)	All
Fiery bottlebrush (*Callistemon phoenicius*)	IV, LD, NC, SC
Ceanothus, Wild lilac (*Ceanothus*)	SN, IV, NC, SC
Flowering quince (*Chaenomeles*)	All
Geraldton waxflower (*Chamelaucium uncinatum*)	IV, LD, NC, SC
Rockrose (*Cistus*)	SN, IV, NC, SC
Breath of heaven (*Coleonema*)	SN, IV, NC, SC
Australian fuchsia (*Correa*)	IV, NC, SC
Cotoneaster (*Cotoneaster*)	All
Broom (*Cytisus, Genista*)	SN, IV, LD, NC, SC
Bush poppy (*Dendromecon*)	SN, IV, NC, SC
Apache plume (*Fallugia paradoxa*)	All
Weeping forsythia (*Forsythia suspensa*)	All
Flannel bush (*Fremontodendron*)	All
Salal (*Gaultheria shallon*)	SN, IV, NC
Lavender starflower (*Grewia occidentalis, G. caffra*)	IV, NC, SC
Toyon, California holly (*Heteromeles arbutifolia*)	All
Savin juniper (*Juniperus sabina*)	All
Blue Carpet juniper (*Juniperus squamata* 'Blue Carpet')	All
Crape myrtle (*Lagerstroemia indica*)	SN, IV, LD, NC, SC
Trailing myoporum (*Myoporum debile*)	IV, NC, SC
Evergreen mock orange (*Philadelphus mexicanus*)	IV, NC, SC
Cape plumbago (*Plumbago auriculata*)	IV, LD, NC, SC
Zabel laurel (*Prunus laurocerasus* 'Zabeliana')	SN, IV, NC, SC
Victory pyracantha (*Pyracantha koidzumii* 'Victory')	All
Holly-leaf redberry (*Rhamnus crocea ilicifolia*)	All
Lemonade berry (*Rhus integrifolia*)	NC, SC
Laurel sumac (*Rhus laurina*)	SC
Sugar bush (*Rhus ovata*)	All
Rosemary (*Rosmarinus officinalis*)	All
Santolina (*Santolina*)	All
Mescal bean (*Sophora secundiflora*)	IV, HD, LD, NC, SC
Snowberry (*Symphoricarpos albus, S. racemosus*)	SN, IV, HD, NC, SC
Coralberry (*Symphoricarpos orbiculatus*)	SN, IV, HD, NC, SC
Spreading English yew (*Taxus baccata* 'Repandens')	SN, IV, NC, SC
Woolly blue curls (*Trichostema lanatum*)	IV, NC, SC
Dwarf xylosma (*Xylosma congestum* 'Compacta')	IV, HD, LD, NC, SC

SHRUBS FOR DRY SITES

California's dry summers lead us to favor shrubs that require little water. Drought-tolerant shrubs mean less work watering during hot spells. If you live in an area where water is in short supply or rationed, they may be the only varieties you can grow.

The shrubs in this list require less water than most other plants of their size and form, but if you want them to really thrive, help them out by covering the soil with a deep mulch of organic matter to retain moisture, and supply water to their roots with a drip system or a hose, rather than using sprinklers that only wet the surface of the mulch. The major exception to this rule is the ubiquitous oleander, which actually seems to prefer the glare of gravel or concrete paving to soft, organic mulch, and has therefore become the most popular freeway shrub in California.

Acacia (*Acacia*)	IV, HD, LD, NC, SC
White thorn, Mescat acacia (*Acacia constricta*)	HD, LD, NC, SC
Cape mallow (*Anisodontea*)	IV, NC, SC
Manzanita (*Arctostaphylos*)	SN, IV, NC, SC
Japanese aucuba (*Aucuba japonica*)	All
Japanese barberry (*Berberis thunbergii*)	All
Butterfly bush (*Buddleia*)	All
Fairy duster (*Calliandra eriophylla*)	HD, LD, NC, SC
Beautyberry (*Callicarpa*)	SN, IV, NC, SC
Bush anemone (*Carpenteria californica*)	SN, IV, NC, SC
Flowering quince (*Chaenomeles*)	All
Mediterranean fan palm (*Chamaerops humilis*)	All
Texas olive (*Cordia boissieri*)	IV, HD, LD, NC, SC
Cotoneaster (*Cotoneaster*)	SN, IV, NC, SC
Sago palm (*Cycas revoluta*)	IV, HD, LD, NC, SC
Scotch broom (*Cytisus scoparius*)	SN, IV, NC, SC
Silverberry (*Elaeagnus pungens*)	All
Apache plume (*Fallugia paradoxa*)	All
Japanese aralia (*Fatsia japonica*)	SN, IV, LD, NC, SC
Forsythia (*Forsythia*)	All
Dyer's greenweed (*Genista tinctoria*)	All
Rose of Sharon (*Hibiscus syriacus*)	All
Chinese holly (*Ilex cornuta*)	SN, IV, NC, SC
Yaupon (*Ilex vomitoria*)	All
Juniper (*Juniperus*)	All
Shrub mallow (*Lavatera thuringiaca*)	SN, IV, NC, SC
Violet silverleaf (*Leucophyllum candidum*)	All
Heavenly bamboo, Nandina (*Nandina domestica*)	All
Oleander (*Nerium oleander*)	IV, HD, LD, NC, SC
Delavay osmanthus (*Osmanthus delavayi*)	SN, IV, NC, SC
Tobira (*Pittosporum tobira*)	IV, HD, LD, NC, SC
Pomegranate, nonfruiting varieties (*Punica granatum*)	All
Firethorn (*Pyracantha coccinea*)	All
Coffeeberry (*Rhamnus californica*)	All
India hawthorn (*Rhaphiolepis*)	IV, LD, NC, SC
Sumac (*Rhus*)	All
Autumn sage (*Salvia greggii*)	All

Spiraea (*Spiraea*)	All
Laurel tristania (*Tristania laurina*)	NC, SC

 The common creosote bush, *Larrea*, which is native to the South California desert, notably the Mohave, makes an attractive shrub, advises Joe Clements, curator of the Desert Gardens at the Huntington Botanical Gardens in San Marino. "It is bright green all year, has bright yellow flowers, and is a very handsome plant." But he notes that not all native plants work out in all areas of California. Joshua trees, for example, do not grow well at the Huntington, or in the coastal areas in general, "but out in the desert, they are fine. They like the high elevations of the High Desert. I would recommend them for areas like Palmdale and Victorville."

"When planting, find out as much as you can about plants who hate to have wet feet. Azalea and camellia are two such shrubs," offers Nancy Scanlon of Sloat Garden Center in San Francisco. "They prefer to be planted in a mound 1 to 2 inches above the soil line, and must be mulched with a high acid content neutral mulch."

HEAT-TOLERANT SHRUBS

These tough shrubs can take the heat and sun on a south-facing wall painted white, if that's what you have to offer. Like any plant placed in a somewhat stressful environment, they need a good start in life, so pay attention to their first two years of growth and provide extra water if they seem to need it. After their root systems are developed, they'll have adapted to their environment and will need no further coddling. Some of these shrubs, such as the not-quite-hardy lantanas, will prefer all the extra heat you can give them if you are trying to grow them at the cooler limits of their range. Others, such as the ever popular oleanders, actually do better with brightly reflective gravel at their base than with a cooling organic mulch tucked up around their roots.

Red bauhinia (*Bauhinia punctata*)	HD, NC, SC
Lemon bottlebrush (*Callistemon citrinus*)	IV, LD, NC, SC
Mirror plant (*Coprosma repens*)	NC, SC
Cotoneaster (*Cotoneaster*)	All
Silverberry, Russian olive (*Elaeagnus*)	All
Evergreen euonymus (*Euonymus japonica*)	All
Pearl bush (*Exochorda macrantha*)	SN, IV, NC
Grevillea (*Grevillea*)	IV, LD, NC, SC
Chinese hibiscus (*Hibiscus rosa-sinensis*)	IV, LD, NC, SC
Junipers (*Juniperus*)	All
Lantana (*Lantana montevidensis*)	IV, LD, NC, SC
California privet (*Ligustrum ovalifolium*)	All
Oleander (*Nerium oleander*)	IV, HD, LD, NC, SC
Photinia (*Photinia fraseri*)	All
Pittosporum (*Pittosporum*)	All
Carolina laurel cherry (*Prunus caroliniana*)	All
Firethorn, Pyracantha (*Pyracantha coccinea*)	All
Sage (*Salvia*)	All
Xylosma (*Xylosma congestum*)	IV, HD, LD, NC, SC

SHRUBS FOR WET SOIL

The boggy, poorly drained soils that deprive plant roots of oxygen and foster root rot are not common in California, due to our dry summers. But if you have a wet or boggy area in your garden, here is a list of shrubs that will endure wet feet.

Red chokeberry (*Aronia arbutifolia*)	SN, HD
Spice bush (*Calycanthus occidentalis*)	SN, IV, NC, SC
Button willow (*Cephalanthus occidentalis*)	SN, IV, NC, SC
Japanese sweetshrub (*Clethra barbinervis*)	SN, IV, NC, SC
Redtwig dogwood, Red-osier dogwood (*Cornus stolonifera, C. sericea*)	SN, IV, NC, SC
Salal (*Gaultheria shallon*)	SN, IV, NC, SC
Winterberry, Black alder (*Ilex verticillata*)	SN, IV
Western laurel (*Kalmia microphylla*)	SN, IV, NC
Sierra laurel (*Leucothoe davisiae*)	SN, IV, NC
Pussy willow (*Salix discolor*)	All
Rose-gold pussy willow (*Salix gracilistyla*)	SN, IV, NC, SC
American arborvitae (*Thuja occidentalis*)	SN, IV, NC, SC
Highbush blueberry (*Vaccinium corymbosum*)	All SN, IV, NC
Cowberry, Foxberry (*Vaccinium vitis-idaea*)	SN, IV, NC
Arrow-wood viburnum (*Viburnum dentatum*)	SN, IV, HD, NC, SC
European cranberry bush (*Viburnum opulus*)	SN, IV, NC, SC

SHRUBS FOR ALKALINE SOIL

If your soil is alkaline, you have two choices: either spend a lot of time and money altering the pH of your soil, or grow shrubs that are adapted to alkaline conditions. Luckily for your time budget and your pocketbook, numerous shrubs either tolerate or prefer "limey" soil. The list below can be expanded by shrubs native to areas with alkaline soil, such as shrubs native to California's desert areas and to the Southwest. Native plants may be difficult to find in large, commercial nurseries, but if you can locate a local native plant society, they may have some good leads for you.

Acanthopanax (*Acanthopanax sieboldianus*)	SN, IV, NC, SC
Monterey manzanita (*Arctostaphylos hookeri*)	SN, IV, NC, SC
Barberry (*Berberis*)	All
Japanese boxwood, Korean boxwood (*Buxus microphylla japonica, B.m. koreana*)	All
Fountain butterfly bush (*Buddleia alternifolia*)	All
Flame bush (*Calliandra tweedii*)	IV, LD, NC, SC
Western redbud (*Cercis occidentalis*)	All
Flowering quince (*Chaenomeles*)	All
Scotch broom (*Cytisus scoparius*)	SN, IV, NC, SC
Deutzia (*Deutzia*)	SN, IV, HD, NC, SC
Pineapple guava (*Feijoa sellowiana*)	IV, LD, NC, SC
Evergreen broom (*Genista fragrans, G. racemosa*)	SN, IV, NC, SC
Golden-flowered broom (*Genista sagittalis*)	All
Rose of Sharon (*Hibiscus syriacus*)	All
Yaupon (*Ilex vomitoria*)	All

Japanese kerria (*Kerria japonica*)	All
Violet silverleaf (*Leucophyllum candidum*)	All
Texas sage, Chihuahua sage	All
(*Leucophyllum frutescens, L. laevigatum*)	
Privet (*Ligustrum*)	All
Winter honeysuckle (*Lonicera fragrantissima*)	SN, IV, NC, SC
Mahonia, Oregon grape (*Mahonia*)	All
Mock orange (*Philadelphus*)	All
Firethorn, Pyracantha (*Pyracantha*)	All
India hawthorn (*Rhaphiolepis*)	IV, LD, NC, SC
Sumac (*Rhus*)	All
Spiraea, Bridal wreath (*Spiraea*)	SN, IV, HD, NC, SC
Chinese lilac (*Syringa chinensis*)	SN, IV, HD, NC, SC
Wayfaring tree (*Viburnum lantana*)	SN, IV, NC

❧ According to Michael A. Parten, an advanced certified nursery professional with Orchard Nursery & Florist in Lafayette, several shrub varieties that tolerate alkaline soil are 'Howard McMinn' manzanita, 'Joyce Coulter' ceanothus, 'Jet Trail' flowering quince, 'Early Wonderful' pomegranate, 'Eve Case' coffeeberry, and 'Pink Lady' India hawthorn.

❧ "Salinity can be a problem in some areas of California," notes Warren Roberts of the UC Davis Arboretum. "In Sacramento, camellias and azaleas grow well, but across the river, in Davis, we have lots of bicarbonate and boron. Boron is vital for all plants, but too much causes dead areas on leaves along the edges (necrosis) and in the Davis area, violets are prettily edged in beige in the summer. Rhododendrons have a difficult time. I don't know of any here that are older than five years."

NARROW, UPRIGHT SHRUBS FOR TIGHT PLACES

Tight places—such as the space between a driveway and the house, or a corner spot where a fence meets garden gate—call for narrow shrubs that grow upright and stay out of the faces of passersby. Some of the shrubs in this list are just naturally skinny; others are narrow cultivars of broader shrubs. Some are shrubs with an erect growth habit that are easily pruned to keep a narrow, upright shape. If you are in doubt about the final form a shrub will take, ask your local nursery owner for help.

Redvein enkianthus (*Enkianthus campanulatus*)	SN, IV, NC, SC
Heath, tall tubular forms (*Erica*)	SN, IV, NC, SC
Irish juniper (*Juniperus chinensis* 'Stricta')	All
Cologreen juniper (*Juniperus scopulorum* 'Cologreen')	All
Welch juniper (*Juniperus scopulorum* 'Welchii')	All
Skyrocket juniper (*Juniperus virginiana* 'Skyrocket')	All
Oregon grape (*Mahonia aquifolium*)	SN, IV, HD, NC, SC
African boxwood (*Myrsine africana*)	IV, NC, SC
Nandina, Heavenly bamboo (*Nandina domestica*)	All
Lily-of-the-valley shrub (*Pieris japonica*)	SN, IV, NC
Teton pyracantha (*Pyracantha* 'Teton')	All
Rose-gold pussy willow (*Salix gracilistyla*)	All

DROUGHT-TOLERANT SHRUBS

Much of the West is characterized by a short annual rainy season followed by many dry months in which plants receive no water unless you deliberately apply it. In periodically recurring drought years, in which rainfall is far below normal, water available for gardens may be severely limited or completely nonexistent. Fortunately, there are numerous fine plants that will thrive with little or no water during the normal dry season once they are established in the garden. Here are some proven performers.

Manzanita (*Arctostaphylos*)	All
Coyote brush (*Baccharis pilularis*)	SN, IV, HD, NC, SC
Bird of paradise bush (*Caesalpinia gilliesii*)	IV, HD, LD, NC, SC
Lemon bottlebrush (*Callistemon citrinus*)	IV, LD, NC, SC
Siberian pea shrub (*Caragana arborescens*)	SN, IV, HD
Feathery cassia, Feathery senna (*Cassia artemisioides, Senna artemisioides*)	IV, LD, NC, SC
Khat (*Catha edulis*)	IV, HD, NC, SC
Western redbud (*Cercis occidentalis*)	All
Mountain mahogany (*Cercocarpus*)	All
Mediterranean fan palm (*Chamaerops humilis*)	All
Geraldton waxflower (*Chamelaucium uncinatum*)	IV, LD, NC, SC
Rockrose (*Cistus*)	SN, IV, LD, NC, SC
Kirk's coprosma (*Coprosma kirkii*)	IV, NC, SC
Smoke tree (*Cotinus coggygria*)	All
Cotoneaster (*Cotoneaster*)	All
Broom (*Cytisus, Genista*)	All
Smoke tree (*Dalea spinosa*)	HD, LD
Hop bush (*Dodonaea viscosa*)	SN, IV, LD, NC, SC
Russian olive, Silverberry (*Elaeagnus*)	All
Escallonia (*Escallonia*)	SN, IV, NC, SC
Apache plume (*Fallugia paradoxa*)	All
Ocotillo (*Fouquieria splendens*)	HD, LD, SC
Flannel bush, California glory (*Fremontodendron*)	All
Silktassel (*Garrya*)	SN, IV, NC, SC
Grevillea (*Grevillea*)	All
Toyon, California holly (*Heteromeles arbutifolia*)	All
Crape myrtle (*Lagerstroemia*)	SN, IV, LD, NC, SC
Lantana (*Lantana montevidensis*)	IV, LD, NC, SC
Lavender (*Lavandula*)	All
Feather bush (*Lysiloma thornberi*)	IV, HD, LD, NC, SC
Oregon grape (*Mahonia aquifolium*)	SN, IV, HD, NC, SC
Creeping mahonia (*Mahonia repens*)	All
Oleander (*Nerium oleander*)	IV, HD, LD, NC, SC
Osmanthus, Sweet olive (*Osmanthus*)	All
Cape plumbago (*Plumbago auriculata*)	IV, LD, NC, SC
Mesquite (*Prosopis*)	HD, LD
Carolina laurel cherry (*Prunus caroliniana*)	All
Hollyleaf cherry (*Prunus ilicifolia*)	SN, IV, LD, NC, SC
Catalina cherry (*Prunus lyonii*)	SN, IV, LD, NC, SC
Coffeeberry (*Rhamnus californica*)	All

Sugar bush (*Rhus ovata*)	All
Rosemary (*Rosmarinus officinalis*)	All
Sage (*Salvia*)	All
Santolina (*Santolina*)	All
Lavender cotton (*Santolina chamaecyparissus*)	All
Jojoba (*Simmondsia chinensis*)	IV, HD, LD, NC, SC
Spanish broom (*Spartium junceum*)	All
Tamarisk (*Tamarix*)	All
Woolly blue curls (*Trichostema lanatum*)	IV, NC, SC

Cindy Milroy of Red Bluffs Garden Center recommends osmanthus "for a fragrant, hedge-type shrub. The tiny, bell-shaped flowers are hard to see, but they cover the plant, and in the spring and summer months osmanthus perfumes the whole yard." Cindy likes to think of that fragrance magnified by planting a hedge of osmanthus. This evergreen shrub is fairly drought tolerant once established, and tolerant of different soils as well. Cindy, who says she has loved gardening ever since she was born, describes the Red Bluffs area as cold in winter, reaching 30 degrees or lower, while summers can get up to 115 degrees.

SHRUBS RESISTANT TO OAK ROOT FUNGUS

Oak root fungus (*Armillaria mellea*) is a problem in low-elevation, nondesert areas of California. It grows primarily on buried wood and dead roots, but it can infest living plants and eventually kill them. If trees or shrubs in your garden are known to have died of oak root fungus, try replanting with species that are known to be resistant to the disease, such as those listed below. Some of these plants can be grown either as trees or shrubs, depending on how they are pruned.

Acacia verticillata (*Acacia verticillata*)	IV, NC, SC
Angels' trumpet (*Brugmansia suaveolens*)	NC, SC
Common boxwood (*Buxus sempervirens*)	SN, IV, NC
Spice bush (*Calycanthus occidentalis*)	SN, IV, NC, SC
Bush anemone (*Carpenteria californica*)	SN, IV, NC, SC
Cashmere bouquet (*Clerodendrum bungei*)	SN, IV, LD, NC, SC
Smoke tree (*Cotinus coggygria*)	All
Common pearl bush (*Exochorda racemosa*)	SN, IV, NC
Rose of Sharon (*Hibiscus syriacus*)	All
Brilliant holly (*Ilex aquipernyi* 'Brilliant')	SN, IV, NC, SC
Box honeysuckle (*Lonicera nitida*)	SN, IV, NC, SC
Mahonia, Oregon grape (*Mahonia*)	All
Bayberry (*Myrica pensylvanica*)	SN, IV
Nandina, Heavenly bamboo (*Nandina domestica*)	All
Jerusalem sage (*Phlomis fruticosa*)	All
Carolina laurel cherry (*Prunus caroliniana*)	All
Hollyleaf cherry (*Prunus ilicifolia*)	SN, IV, LD, NC, SC
Catalina cherry (*Prunus lyonii*)	SN, IV, LD, NC, SC
Lemon guava, Strawberry guava (*Psidium cattleianum, P. littorale*)	IV, NC, SC
Chaste tree (*Vitex agnus-castus*)	All

SHRUBS FOR THE OCEANFRONT

No matter whether you live in the cool North Coast region or the subtropical South Coast, any shrubs you plant will have to contend with salt spray, summer fog, and strong winds. The following plants will endure direct exposure to seashore winds and can provide shelter to perennials, ground covers, and annuals, but they will appreciate a bit of windbreak help from the oceanfront trees listed on page 42. If placed on the lee side of a structure, they will grow more rapidly and may attain a more symmetrical form. All should do well in either a North Coast or South Coast garden.

Saltbush (*Atriplex*)
Dwarf coyote brush (*Baccharis pilularis*)
Lemon bottlebrush (*Callistemon citrinus*)
Netbush (*Calothamnus*)
Rockrose (*Cistus*)
Cotoneaster (*Cotoneaster*)
Scotch broom (*Cytisus scoparius*)
Hop bush (*Dodonaea viscosa*)
Echium (*Echium*)
Silverberry (*Elaeagnus pungens*)
Escallonia (*Escallonia*)
Euonymus (*Euonymus japonica*)
Juniper (*Juniperus*)
Box honeysuckle (*Lonicera nitida*)
Privet honeysuckle (*Lonicera pileata*)
Melaleuca (*Melaleuca*)
Myoporum (*Myoporum*)
Pacific wax myrtle (*Myrica californica*)
Oleander (*Nerium oleander*)
Tobira (*Pittosporum tobira*)
Italian buckthorn (*Rhamnus alaternus*)
Rhaphiolepis, India hawthorn (*Rhaphiolepis*)
Lemonade berry (*Rhus integrifolia*)
Rugosa rose (*Rosa rugosa*)
Rosemary (*Rosmarinus officinalis*)
Spanish broom (*Spartium junceum*)
Tamarisk (*Tamarix*)
Laurustinus (*Viburnum tinus*)
Westringia (*Westringia fruticosa*)

Lemonade berry

Sidney Hilburn, who helps caretake the Community Garden at Pt. San Pablo Yacht Harbor, says that for the oceanfront, "Nandina, also called heavenly bamboo, is wonderfully low maintenance. Its gorgeous red leaves in the wintertime can make any garden spectacular. Unlike real bamboos, nandinas will not grow excessively tall or bushy. Also, in warm-winter areas, blue-flowered felicia is a perennial shrub with wonderful aromatic green foliage that may be exactly what you're looking for." Don't try it in cold-winter coastal areas, though, where it is too tender to survive.

FIRE-RESISTANT SHRUBS

As people spread out into what were formerly rural and wilderness areas, the need to plant fire-resistant plants increases. No shrub is immune to wildfire, but some are more resistant to burning than others. These shrubs and small trees are recommended for planting on hills in semirural areas were wildfires are a danger.

Lemon bottlebrush (*Callistemon citrinus*)	IV, LD, NC, SC
Toyon, California holly (*Heteromeles arbutifolia*)	All
Myoporum (*Myoporum*)	IV, LD, NC, SC
Oleander (*Nerium oleander*)	IV, HD, LD, NC, SC
Catalina cherry (*Prunus lyonii*)	SN, IV, LD, NC, SC
Italian buckthorn (*Rhamnus alaternus*)	All
Evergreen sumacs (*Rhus*)	All
Rosemary (*Rosmarinus officinalis*)	All

SHRUBS THAT DO WELL IN FULL SHADE

When buying shrubs for a garden spot in full shade, it is a good idea to get the largest size available (5-gallon or 15-gallon shrubs) even if the cost is higher than you would normally consider spending. Because plants grow very slowly in the shade, it takes longer for 1-gallon sized shrubs to fill in and make the kind of display you are envisioning than it takes for the larger plants. You can amortize the extra cost over five years, if it makes you feel better!

Acanthopanax (*Acanthopanax sieboldianus*)	SN, IV, NC
Marlberry (*Ardisia japonica*)	IV, NC
Japanese aucuba (*Aucuba japonica*)	All
Boxwood (*Buxus*)	All
Chamaedorea palm (*Chamaedorea*)	NC, SC
Japanese aralia (*Fatsia japonica*)	SN, IV, LD, NC, SC
Western laurel (*Kalmia microphylla*)	SN, IV, NC
Oregon grape (*Mahonia aquifolium*)	SN, IV, HD, NC, SC
Longleaf mahonia (*Mahonia nervosa*)	SN, IV, NC
Heavenly bamboo, Nandina (*Nandina domestica*)	All
Lily-of-the-valley shrub (*Pieris japonica*)	SN, IV, NC
Lady palm (*Rhapis excelsa*)	IV, LD, NC, SC
Sweet box (*Sarcococca*)	SN, IV, NC, SC
Skimmia (*Skimmia*)	SN, IV, NC, SC
Snowberry (*Symphoricarpos chenaultii*)	SN, IV, HD, NC, SC
Ternstroemia (*Ternstroemia gymnanthera*)	SN, IV, LD, NC, SC
Cowberry, Foxberry (*Vaccinium vitis-idaea*)	SN, IV, NC
Leatherleaf viburnum (*Viburnum rhytidophyllum*)	SN, IV, NC, SC

LOW-GROWING SHRUBS FOR GROUND COVER

Some shrubs are so low-growing (under 3 feet) and spreading, they can be used for ground cover and erosion control, especially on hills, slopes, or in wild-looking areas where there is no foot traffic. California's native chaparral shrubs adapt well to the needs of a formally designed shrub-covered expanse, and they can be supplemented by low-growing flowering shrubs from other regions of the world. See also the entire chapter on ground covers, and the chapters on roses, perennials, and vines for other plants that make good ground covers.

Prostrate abelia (*Abelia grandiflora* 'Prostrata')	All
Little Sur manzanita (*Arctostaphylos edmundsii*)	SN, IV, NC, SC
Monterey Carpet manzanita (*Arctostaphylos hookeri* 'Monterey Carpet')	SN, IV, NC, SC
Bearberry (*Arctostaphylos uva-ursi*)	SN, IV, NC, SC
Marlberry (*Ardisia japonica*)	IV, NC
California saltbush (*Atriplex californica*)	IV, LD, NC, SC
Dwarf coyote brush (*Baccharis pilularis*)	SN, IV, HD, NC, SC
Crimson Pygmy barberry (*Berberis thunbergii* 'Crimson Pygmy')	All
Scotch heather, dwarf ground cover forms (*Calluna*)	SN, IV, NC
Sasanqua camellia, low spreading forms (*Camellia sasanqua*)	SN, IV, NC, SC
Point Reyes ceanothus (*Ceanothus gloriosus*)	IV, NC
Carmel creeper (*Ceanothus griseus horizontalis*)	IV, NC, SC
Flame pea (*Chorizema ilicifolium*)	IV, NC, SC
Sageleaf rockrose (*Cistus salvifolius, C. villosus*)	SN, IV, NC, SC
Kirk's coprosma (*Coprosma kirkii*)	IV, NC, SC
Bunchberry (*Cornus canadensis*)	SN, IV
Bearberry cotoneaster (*Cotoneaster dammeri*)	All
Emerald Carpet cotoneaster (*Cotoneaster salicifolius* 'Emerald Carpet')	All
Kew broom (*Cytisus kewensis*)	IV, NC
Irish heath (*Daboecia*)	SN, IV, NC, SC
Heath, low spreading forms (*Erica*)	SN, IV, NC, SC
Purple-leaf winter creeper (*Euonymus fortunei* 'Colorata')	SN, IV, HD, LD, NC
Dwarf gardenia (*Gardenia jasminoides* 'Radicans')	SN, IV, LD, NC, SC
Wintergreen (*Gaultheria procumbens*)	SN, IV, NC
Broom, low spreading forms (*Genista*)	All
Sunrose (*Helianthemum nummularium*)	SN, IV, NC, SC
Creeping St. Johnswort (*Hypericum calycinum*)	All
Lantana (*Lantana montevidensis, L. sellowiana*)	IV, LD, NC, SC
Hall's honeysuckle (*Lonicera japonica* 'Halliana')	All
Privet honeysuckle (*Lonicera pileata*)	SN, IV, NC, SC
Longleaf mahonia (*Mahonia nervosa*)	SN, IV, NC
Creeping mahonia (*Mahonia repens*)	All
Harbour Dwarf nandina (*Nandina domestica* 'Harbour Dwarf')	All
Santa Cruz firethorn (*Pyracantha koidzumii* 'Santa Cruz')	All
Evergreen currant (*Ribes viburnifolium*)	IV, NC, SC
Collingwood Ingram rosemary (*Rosmarinus officinalis* 'Collingwood Ingram')	All
Spreading sweet box (*Sarcococca hookerana humilis*)	SN, IV, NC, SC
Snowberry (*Symphoricarpos chenaultii*)	SN, IV, HD, NC, SC

Bearberry

| Prostrate germander (*Teucrium chamaedrys* 'Prostratum') | All |
| Cowberry, Foxberry (*Vaccinium vitis-idaea*) | SN, IV, NC |

SHRUBS THAT BLOOM FOR A MONTH OR LONGER

The shrubs on this list are heavy producers, staying in bloom for a month or longer. In cool coastal areas, some may flower for 8 weeks or more. Some of these shrubs are just the thing for a flowering roadside hedge. To keep interest up throughout the year, cross-check this list with the seasonal sampler on page 108 and select something for each season. Then add a few reblooming roses from the list on page 127.

Most of these shrubs are very low-maintenance, but butterfly bush will look its best and rebloom for a longer period if old blossoms are deadheaded when they fade, and many remontant (reblooming) roses require the same treatment to produce a good second crop of flowers.

Abelia (*Abelia*)	All
Butterfly bush (*Buddleia*)	All
Camellia (*Camellia*)	SN, IV, NC, SC
Blue mist (*Caryopteris clandonensis*)	SN, IV, NC
Blue spiraea, Common bluebeard (*Caryopteris incana*)	SN, IV, NC
Mexican orange (*Choisya ternata*)	SN, IV, NC, SC
Glory bower (*Clerodendrum trichotomum*)	IV, LD, NC, SC
Texas olive (*Cordia boissieri*)	IV, HD, LD, NC, SC
Irish heath (*Daboecia cantabrica*)	SN, IV, NC, SC
Daphne (*Daphne*)	SN, IV, NC, SC
Bidwill coral tree (*Erythrina bidwillii*)	IV, LD, NC, SC
Escallonia (*Escallonia*)	SN, IV, NC, SC
Gardenia (*Gardenia jasminoides*)	SN, IV, LD, NC, SC
Chinese hibiscus (*Hibiscus rosa-sinensis*)	IV, LD, NC, SC
Rose of Sharon (*Hibiscus syriacus*)	All
Hydrangea (*Hydrangea*)	All
St. Johnswort (*Hypericum*)	All
Italian jasmine (*Jasminum humile*)	SN, IV, LD, NC, SC
Lantana (*Lantana montevidensis, L. sellowiana*)	IV, LD, NC, SC
Shrub mallow (*Lavatera thuringiaca*)	SN, IV, NC, SC
Oleander (*Nerium oleander*)	IV, HD, LD, NC, SC
Sweet olive (*Osmanthus fragrans*)	IV, HD, LD, NC
Mock orange (*Philadelphus*)	All
Dwarf carnation-flowered pomegranate (*Punica granatum* 'Chico')	All
India hawthorn (*Rhaphiolepis indica*)	IV, LD, NC, SC
Magic Beauty rhaphiolepis (*Rhaphiolepis* 'Magic Beauty')	IV, LD, NC, SC
Yeddo hawthorn (*Rhaphiolepis umbellata, R. ovata*)	IV, LD, NC, SC
Chaste tree (*Vitex agnus-castus*)	All
Weigela (*Weigela florida*)	SN, IV, HD, NC, SC

Abelia

> "A beautiful flowering shrub, perfect for growing faux walls, is the 'Nuccio's Pearl' camellia," says Jim Mehdy of Green Thumb Nursery, Petaluma. "The blossom is pearl white with pink on the outside, and the shape is a formal double. When offered afternoon shade, this variety will produce long-lasting blooms February until May."

SHRUBS THAT TOLERATE MODERATE SHADE

Shady areas, whether the shadows are cast by tall trees, walls, or a patio overhang, provide plants with less light and cooler average temperatures than nearby sunny locations. Many sun and heat loving shrubs will not prosper under these conditions, but luckily for people with semi-shady areas, many plants tolerate or prefer partial or moderate shade.

Flowering maple (*Abutilon megapotamicum*)	IV, LD, NC, SC
Japanese aucuba (*Aucuba japonica*)	All
Boxwood (*Buxus*)	All
Camellia (*Camellia*)	SN, IV, NC, SC
Magic flower (*Cantua buxifolia*)	IV, NC, SC
Bush anemone (*Carpenteria californica*)	SN, IV, NC, SC
Cleyera (*Cleyera japonica, Eurya ochnacea*)	SN, IV, NC, SC
Cocculus (*Cocculus laurifolius*)	IV, LD, NC, SC
Coffee (*Coffea arabica*)	SC
Mirror plant (*Coprosma repens*)	IV, NC, SC
Dogwood (*Cornus*)	SN, IV, NC, SC
Winter daphne (*Daphne odora*)	SN, IV, NC, SC
Enkianthus (*Enkianthus campanulatus*)	SN, IV, NC, SC
Euonymus (*Euonymus*)	All
Japanese aralia (*Fatsia japonica*)	SN, IV, LD, NC, SC
Fuchsia (*Fuchsia*)	All
Gardenia (*Gardenia jasminoides*)	IV, LD, NC, SC
Checkerberry, Wintergreen, Teaberry (*Gaultheria*)	SN, IV, NC
Salal (*Gaultheria shallon*)	SN, IV, NC, SC
Griselinia (*Griselinia lucida*)	IV, NC, SC
Hydrangea (*Hydrangea*)	All
Holly (*Ilex*)	All
Hollyleaf sweetspire (*Itea ilicifolia*)	All
Juniper (*Juniperus*)	All
Kalmiopsis (*Kalmiopsis leachiana*)	IV, NC
Sweet bay (*Laurus nobilis*)	SN, IV, LD, NC, SC
Sierra laurel (*Leucothoe davisiae*)	SN, IV, NC
Loropetalum (*Loropetalum chinense*)	SN, IV, NC, SC
Longleaf mahonia (*Mahonia nervosa*)	SN, IV, NC
Costa Rican holly (*Olmediella betschlerana*)	IV, NC, SC
Osmanthus, Sweet olive (*Osmanthus*)	All
Pernettya, Gaultheria	SN, IV, NC
(*Pernettya mucronata, Gaultheria mucronata*)	
Chinese pieris (*Pieris forrestii*)	SN, IV, NC
Lily-of-the-valley shrub (*Pieris japonica*)	SN, IV, NC
Pittosporum (*Pittosporum*)	IV, LD, NC, SC
Cascara sagrada (*Rhamnus purshiana*)	SN, IV, HD, NC
Rhododendron, Azalea (*Rhododendron*)	SN, IV, NC, SC
Sweet box (*Sarcococca*)	SN, IV, NC, SC
Threadleaf schefflera (*Schefflera elegantissima*)	NC, SC
Skimmia (*Skimmia*)	SN, IV, NC, SC
Stachyurus (*Stachyurus praecox*)	SN, IV, NC

Creeping snowberry (*Symphoricarpos mollis*) — SN, IV, NC, SC
Yew (*Taxus*) — SN, IV, NC, SC
Evergreen huckleberry (*Vaccinium ovatum*) — SN, IV, NC
David's viburnum (*Viburnum davidii*) — SN, IV, NC, SC
Sandankwa viburnum (*Viburnum suspensum*) — IV, LD, NC, SC

FASTEST-GROWING SHRUBS

The shrubs in this list will begin to reach their mature form, both in height and width, within four years of transplanting into your garden. Rapid maturation sometimes carries hidden costs, though—some of these shrubs may not look good in old age, and others, such as the much-loved ceanothus, have relatively short life spans. Not all of the plants on this list, however, are short-lived, by any means. A buddleia in my garden, for instance, is at least 40 years old. No one would call this tangle of odd angles and ungainly sprouts graceful at this stage in its life, but it cloaks itself in such a wealth of purple bloom every summer that it would be unthinkable to remove it from the garden.

When you need a quick effect—on a new lot, for example—interplant fast-growing shrubs with those that take longer to mature but live longer. Then, as the long-term shrubs begin to fill out, you can remove the place-marker shrubs—unless they are buddleias, in which case you may end up loving them despite their ungainly tangles.

Flowering maple (*Abutilon megapotamicum*) — IV, LD, NC, SC
Dwarf coyote brush (*Baccharis pilularis*) — SN, IV, HD, NC, SC
Butterfly bush (*Buddleia*) — All
Bird of paradise bush (*Caesalpinia*) — IV, HD, LD, NC, SC
Lemon bottlebrush (*Callistemon citrinus*) — IV, LD, NC, SC
Ceanothus, Wild lilac (*Ceanothus*) — All
Geraldton waxflower (*Chamelaucium uncinatum*) — IV, LD, NC, SC
Mexican orange (*Choisya ternata*) — SN, IV, NC, SC
Flame pea (*Chorizema*) — IV, NC, SC
Rockrose (*Cistus*) — SN, IV, NC, SC
Parney cotoneaster (*Cotoneaster lacteus*) — All
Canary bird bush (*Crotalaria agatiflora*) — IV, HD, NC, SC
Escallonia (*Escallonia*) — SN, IV, NC, SC
Forsythia (*Forsythia*) — All
Lavender starflower (*Grewia occidentalis*) — IV, LD, NC, SC
Griselinia (*Griselinia littoralis*) — IV, NC, SC
Sweet hakea (*Hakea suaveolens*) — IV, LD, NC, SC
Hibiscus (*Hibiscus*) — All
Lantana (*Lantana montevidensis*) — IV, LD, NC, SC
Honey bush (*Melianthus major*) — IV, LD, NC, SC
Mock orange (*Philadelphus*) — All
Italian buckthorn (*Rhamnus alaternus*) — All
Pussy willow (*Salix caprea, S. discolor, S. gracilistyla*) — All
African linden (*Sparmannia africana*) — NC, SC
Spanish broom (*Spartium junceum*) — All
Yellow oleander (*Thevetia peruviana*) — HD, SC
Princess flower (*Tibouchina urvilleana*) — NC, SC
Weigela (*Weigela florida*) — SN, IV, HD, NC

SHRUBS THAT ADAPT TO EITHER SUN OR PARTIAL SHADE

Suppose you want a continuous line of matching shrubs along the front of your garden, but half of that expanse is sunny and the other half in partial shade. Or you may want to repeat clusters of a shrub to esthetically tie together several areas of your garden, but the amount of sun isn't uniform throughout your landscape. The shrubs in this list will cooperate with such landscaping goals and do well in partial shade or in sun.

Glossy abelia (*Abelia grandiflora*)	All
Manzanita (*Arctostaphylos*)	SN, IV, NC, SC
Chokeberry (*Aronia*)	SN, IV
Barberry (*Berberis*)	All
Angel's trumpet (*Brugmansia, Datura*)	NC, SC
Boxwood (*Buxus*)	All
Beautyberry (*Callicarpa*)	SN, IV, NC, SC
Spice bush (*Calycanthus occidentalis*)	SN, IV, NC, SC
Blue blossom (*Ceanothus thyrsiflorus*)	SN, IV, NC, SC
Mediterranean fan palm (*Chamaerops humilis*)	All
Wintersweet (*Chimonanthus praecox*)	SN, IV, NC
Areca palm, Cane palm (*Chrysalidocarpus lutescens*)	SC
Dogwood (*Cornus*)	SN, IV, NC, SC
European filbert (*Corylus avellana*)	SN, IV, NC, SC
Silverberry (*Elaeagnus pungens*)	All
Euonymus (*Euonymus*)	All
Griselinia (*Griselinia lucida*)	IV, NC, SC
Witch hazel (*Hamamelis*)	SN, IV, NC, SC
Toyon, California holly (*Heteromeles arbutifolia*)	All
Holly (*Ilex*)	All
Italian jasmine (*Jasminum humile*)	SN, IV, LD, NC, SC
Arabian jasmine (*Jasminum sambac*)	HD, SC
Sweet bay (*Laurus nobilis*)	SN, IV, LD, NC, SC
Loropetalum (*Loropetalum chinense*)	SN, IV, NC, SC
Lily magnolia (*Magnolia liliiflora*)	SN, IV, NC, SC
Pacific wax myrtle (*Myrica californica*)	SN, IV, NC, SC
Myrtle (*Myrtus communis*)	IV, HD, LD, NC, SC
Nandina, Heavenly bamboo (*Nandina domestica*)	All
Osmanthus (*Osmanthus*)	SN, IV, NC, SC
Sweet olive (*Osmanthus fragrans*)	IV, LD, NC, SC
Hardy philodendron (*Philodendron selloum*)	IV, LD, NC, SC
Pittosporum (*Pittosporum*)	IV, NC, SC
Tobira (*Pittosporum tobira*)	IV, HD, LD, NC, SC
Oriental arborvitae (*Platycladus orientalis, Thuja orientalis*)	All
Strawberry guava (*Psidium cattleianum, P. littorale*)	IV, NC, SC
Coffeeberry (*Rhamnus californica*)	All
Rhaphiolepis, India hawthorn (*Rhaphiolepis indica*)	SN, IV, LD, NC, SC
Evergreen currant, Catalina perfume (*Ribes viburnifolium*)	IV, NC, SC
Blue elderberry (*Sambucus caerulea, S. neomexicana*)	SN, IV, NC, SC
Windmill palm (*Trachycarpus fortunei*)	All

| Evergreen huckleberry (*Vaccinium ovatum*) | SN, IV, NC |
| Viburnum (*Viburnum*) | All |

> Rhododendrons and azaleas generally do well at the Filoli estate gardens in Woodside, but horticulture director Lucy Tolmach advises that the rhododendrons need sufficient light. "In the shadier areas of the garden they tend to stretch upward and bloom only at the tops of the plant. Azaleas do better for us in the shadier areas."

SHRUBS THAT WORK NEAR SWIMMING POOLS

It seems like common sense, but here's a reminder. Plants near swimming pools must not be thorny or shed sharp-edged, prickly leaves, and the litter they shed ought to be large enough to be removed from the pool by hand rather than clogging up the filter system. Here are some good choices that meet these needs.

Camellia (*Camellia japonica*)	SN, IV, NC, SC
Sasanqua camellia (*Camellia sasanqua*)	SN, IV, NC, SC
Jade plant (*Crassula argentea, C. ovata*)	SN, IV, LD, NC, SC
Japanese aralia (*Fatsia japonica*)	SN, IV, LD, NC, SC
Griselinia (*Griselinia littoralis, G. lucida*)	IV, NC, SC
Wheeler's Dwarf pittosporum (*Pittosporum tobira* 'Wheeler's Dwarf')	IV, HD, LD, NC, SC
Rhaphiolepis, India hawthorn (*Rhaphiolepis*)	IV, LD, NC, SC
African linden (*Sparmannia africana*)	NC, SC
Ternstroemia (*Ternstroemia gymnanthera*)	SN, IV, LD, NC, SC
David's viburnum (*Viburnum davidii*)	SN, IV, NC, SC

SHRUBS THAT CAN BECOME INVASIVE

Everyone wants foolproof, vigorous, carefree plants, the kind that seem to take care of themselves—but the shrubs in this list can be too much of a good thing, especially in smaller gardens. These plants may spread by seeding, root suckers, or runners. Although they may be just what you want to fill a large space, in smaller areas you may have to be aggressive to keep them in bounds.

Barberry (*Berberis*)	All
Glory bower (*Clerodendrum*)	SN, IV, LD, NC, SC
Willowleaf cotoneaster (*Cotoneaster salicifolius*)	All
Scotch broom (*Cytisus scoparius*)	SN, IV, NC, SC
Privet honeysuckle (*Lonicera pileata*)	SN, IV, NC, SC
Mahonia, Oregon grape (*Mahonia*)	All
Sumac (*Rhus*)	All
Bramble (*Rubus*)	SN, IV, HD, NC
False spiraea (*Sorbaria*)	SN, IV, NC, SC
Spanish broom (*Spartium junceum*)	All
Tamarisk (*Tamarix*)	All
Rice paper plant (*Tetrapanax papyriferus*)	NC, SC

SHRUBS THAT BLOOM IN MODERATE SHADE

Because plants that must contend with shade don't get as much solar energy as those growing in full sun, only those varieties adapted to low light conditions will bloom really well in the darker corners of your garden. The shrubs in this list will bloom very well in moderate shade. Perhaps the classic California shade shrub is the French hydrangea, at one time the pride and joy of every home located on the shady side of a street, especially in Italian neighborhoods. However, there are many more choices available than that sturdy standby, and some of them are better suited to today's smaller urban gardens.

A few of the plants listed below don't have really showy flowers, but their flowers are fragrant. If you are dealing with areas of very dense shade, such as that found under decks, the plants in this list will probably not work for you and you'd be better off with ferns or other low-growing greenery.

Flowering maple, Chinese lantern (*Abutilon*)	IV, LD, NC, SC
Brunfelsia (*Brunfelsia pauciflora*)	IV, LD, NC, SC
Butterfly bush (*Buddleia*)	All
Camellia (*Camellia*)	SN, IV, NC, SC
Winter hazel (*Corylopsis*)	SN, IV, NC
Burkwood daphne (*Daphne burkwoodii*)	SN, IV, NC
Fuchsia (*Fuchsia*)	SN, IV, NC, SC
Gardenia (*Gardenia jasminoides*)	SN, IV, LD, NC, SC
Hydrangea (*Hydrangea*)	All
European St. Johnswort (*Hypericum androsaemum*)	All
Italian jasmine (*Jasminum humile*)	SN, IV, LD, NC, SC
Arabian jasmine (*Jasminum sambac*)	LD, SC
Western laurel (*Kalmia microphylla*)	SN, IV, NC
Kerria (*Kerria japonica*)	All
Beauty bush (*Kolkwitzia amabilis*)	SN, IV, HD, NC, SC
Sierra laurel (*Leucothoe davisiae*)	SN, IV
Drooping leucothoe (*Leucothoe fontanesiana*)	SN, IV, NC
Winter honeysuckle (*Lonicera fragrantissima*)	SN, IV, NC, SC
Maxim's honeysuckle (*Lonicera maximowiczii sachalinensis*)	SN, IV, NC, SC
Oregon grape (*Mahonia aquifolium*)	SN, IV, HD, NC, SC
Leatherleaf mahonia (*Mahonia bealei*)	SN, IV, HD, NC, SC
Heavenly bamboo, Nandina (*Nandina domestica*)	All
Sweet olive (*Osmanthus fragrans*)	IV, HD, LD, NC, SC
Pieris (*Pieris*)	SN, IV, NC
Rhododendron (*Rhododendron*)	SN, IV, NC, SC
Azalea (*Rhododendron*)	SN, IV, NC, SC
Golden currant (*Ribes aureum*)	SN, IV, HD, NC, SC
Red flowering currant (*Ribes sanguineum*)	SN, IV, NC, SC
Spiraea (*Spiraea*)	SN, IV, HD, NC, SC
Viburnum (*Viburnum*)	All

Livermore is renowned for its kindly weather and soil conditions, so "Obviously any rose will flourish," notes Jacqueline Williams-Courtright of Alden Lane Nursery. She also recommends the smaller deciduous magnolias, advising "Provide afternoon shade and talk to your professional about specific pruning and fertilization techniques."

SHRUBS WITH ORNAMENTAL FRUIT
OR BERRIES

The shrubs in this list develop highly ornamental fruits and berries in a variety of colors, from orange and red to purple and black, and even white. This fruit may attract birds to your garden, which is an added benefit, although a flock of birds can strip the shrubs of berries in short order.

If you are looking for a particular color effect, shop for these shrubs when you can see the berries on them at the nursery.

Elfin King strawberry tree (*Arbutus unedo* 'Elfin King')	All
Manzanita (*Arctostaphylos*)	SN, IV, NC, SC
Bearberry (*Arctostaphylos uva-ursi*)	SN, IV, NC, SC
Chokeberry (*Aronia*)	SN, IV
Japanese aucuba (*Aucuba japonica*)	All
Darwin barberry (*Berberis darwinii*)	SN, IV, NC, SC
Japanese barberry (*Berberis thunbergii*)	All
Wilson barberry (*Berberis wilsoniae*)	All
American beautyberry (*Callicarpa americana*)	SN, IV, NC, SC
Purple beautyberry (*Callicarpa dichotoma*)	SN, IV, NC, SC
Natal plum (*Carissa grandiflora, C. macrocarpa*)	SC
Harlequin gloryblower (*Clerodendrum trichotomum*)	SN, IV, NC, SC
Kousa dogwood (*Cornus kousa*)	SN, IV, NC, SC
Cornelian cherry (*Cornus mas*)	SN, IV
Hazelnut, Filbert (*Corylus*)	SN, IV, NC, SC
Cotoneaster (*Cotoneaster*)	All
Winged euonymus (*Euonymus alata*)	SN, IV, NC
Toyon, California holly (*Heteromeles arbutifolia*)	All
Burford holly (*Ilex cornuta* 'Burfordii')	SN, IV, NC, SC
Nellie R. Stevens holly (*Ilex* 'Nellie R. Stevens')	SN, IV, NC, SC
Beauty bush (*Kolkwitzia amabilis*)	SN, IV, HD, NC, SC
Crabapple (*Malus*)	SN, IV, HD, NC, SC
Pernettya, Gaultheria	SN, IV, NC
(*Pernettya mucronata, Gaultheria mucronata*)	
Chinese photinia (*Photinia serrulata*)	All
Photinia (*Photinia villosa*)	SN, IV
Pomegranate (*Punica granatum*)	All
Firethorn, Pyracantha (*Pyracantha*)	All
Rhaphiolepis, India hawthorn (*Rhaphiolepis*)	IV, LD, NC, SC
Sweet box (*Sarcococca*)	SN, IV, NC, SC
Skimmia (*Skimmia*)	SN, IV, NC, SC
Snowberry, Coralberry (*Symphoricarpos*)	SN, IV, HD, NC, SC
Yew (*Taxus*)	SN, IV, NC, SC
Arrow-wood viburnum	SN, IV, HD, NC, SC
(*Viburnum dentatum*)	
European cranberry bush	SN, IV, NC, SC
(*Viburnum opulus*)	
Tea viburnum (*Viburnum setigerum*)	All
Laurustinus (*Viburnum tinus*)	SN, IV, LD, NC, SC

Viburnum

PALMS THAT ARE GREAT SHRUBS

Not all palms have mammoth fronds on tree-stature trunks. Some stay in the medium-height range, anywhere from 3 to 10 feet, while others take a very long time getting to a mature height of 20 feet or so. Many of these shorter palms are suitable for container growing. Consult with your local nursery about cold hardiness.

Pindo palm (*Butia capitata*)	IV, HD, LD, NC, SC
Chamaedorea palm (*Chamaedorea cataractarum, C. radicalis*)	NC, SC
Mediterranean fan palm (*Chamaerops humilis*)	All
Areca palm (*Chrysalidocarpus lutescens*)	SC
Sago palm (*Cycas revoluta*)	IV, HD, LD, NC, SC
Chinese fountain palm (*Livistona chinensis*)	IV, HD, LD, NC, SC
Triangle palm (*Neodypsis decaryi*)	SC
Pygmy date palm (*Phoenix roebellenii*)	SC
Cliff date palm (*Phoenix rupicola*)	LD, NC, SC
Macarthur palm (*Ptychosperma macarthuri*)	SC
Lady palm (*Rhapis excelsa*)	IV, HD, LD, NC, SC
Rattan palm, Slender lady palm (*Rhapis humilis*)	IV, HD, LD, NC, SC
Dwarf palmetto (*Sabal minor*)	IV, HD, LD, NC, SC
Dwarf fan palm (*Trachycarpus takil*)	NC, SC

Pygmy date palm

"The pygmy date palm, *Phoenix roebellenii*, is a good understory palm," says Michael Letzring, lead gardener of the San Diego Zoo. "It does well in shade, has very feathery, fine-textured leaves, and fairly long spines. All the *Phoenix* family of palms do." Pygmy date palms grow mostly to a range of 5 to 10 feet. Michael notes that most palms are slow growing, reaching their mature height in 20 to 25 years.

SHRUBS WITH FOLIAGE IN COLORS OTHER THAN GREEN

Planting shrubs is an art when you select the color of the foliage the way an artist selects colors on a palette. Use the shrubs in this list to draw attention to certain areas, as foundation shrubs, or as a backdrop for flowering plants. The blue- and gray-leafed shrubs are especially nice as a setting for pink-flowered roses of small stature. If you are really daring, you can paint an entire landscape with little more than the contrasting colors of showily foliaged shrubs. To surprise visitors with a time-lapse color-change effect in your garden, interplant these colorful shrubs with those in the list of shrubs for autumn foliage, on page 94.

Gray

Saltbush, Desert holly (*Atriplex*)	All
Pfitzer juniper (*Juniperus chinensis* 'Pfitzerana')	All
Gray Gleam juniper (*Juniperus scopulorum* 'Gray Gleam')	All
Violet silverleaf (*Leucophyllum candidum*)	All
Texas ranger (*Leucophyllum frutescens*)	All
Nevin mahonia (*Mahonia nevinii*)	IV, HD, LD, NC, SC
White sage (*Salvia apiana*)	All

Bronze, Red

Copper leaf (*Acalypha wilkesiana*)	SC
Japanese maple (*Acer palmatum*)	SN, IV, NC, SC
Bronze-leaf European filbert (*Corylus avellana* 'Fusco-Rubra')	SN, IV, NC
Purple-leaf hazelnut (*Corylus maxima* 'Purpurea')	SN, IV, NC
Purple hop bush (*Dodonaea viscosa* 'Purpurea')	SN, IV, LD, NC, SC
Saratoga hop bush (*Dodonaea viscosa* 'Saratoga')	SN, IV, LD, NC, SC
Dwarf red-leaf plum (*Prunus cistena*)	All

Yellow, Golden

Lutea false cypress (*Chamaecyparis lawsoniana* 'Lutea')	NC
Variegated Hollywood juniper (*Juniperus chinensis* 'Corymbosa Variegata')	All
Golden Armstrong juniper (*Juniperus chinensis* 'Golden Armstrong')	All
Vicary Golden privet (*Ligustrum vicaryi*)	All
Dwarf Golden arborvitae (*Platycladus orientalis* 'Aureus')	All
Golden English yew (*Taxus baccata* 'Aurea')	SN, IV, NC, SC
Rheingold arborvitae (*Thuja occidentalis* 'Rheingold')	SN, IV, HD, NC, SC

Blue

Ellwood false cypress (*Chamaecyparis lawsoniana* 'Ellwoodii')	NC
Big-fruited gum (*Eucalyptus macrocarpa*)	IV, HD, LD, NC, SC
Roselike gum (*Eucalyptus rhodantha*)	IV, HD, LD, NC, SC
Blaauw's juniper (*Juniperus chinensis* 'Blaauw')	All
Hetz blue juniper (*Juniperus chinensis* 'Hetzii')	All

Variegated

Gold Dust aucuba (*Aucuba japonica* 'Variegata')	All
Variegated boxwood (*Buxus sempervirens* 'Aureo-Variegata')	SN, IV, NC
Variegated mirror plant (*Coprosma repens* 'Variegata')	IV, NC, SC
Variegated cotoneaster (*Cotoneaster horizontalis* 'Variegatus')	SN, IV, HD, NC, SC
Variegated winter daphne (*Daphne odora* 'Marginata')	SN, IV, NC, SC
Rainbow leucothoe (*Leucothoe fontanesiana* 'Rainbow')	SN, IV, NC
Golden privet (*Ligustrum ovalifolium* 'Aureum')	All

Salvia apiana, a California native, was revered by Native Americans for its healing and spiritual values, says Betsy Clebsch, author of *A Book of Salvias* (Timber Press). "This spectacularly beautiful plant is easy to grow and requires no summer water. Picture long, graceful, pearl-gray leaves in rosettes that can measure over 1 foot in width." In late spring these rosettes send up a flowering stalk that can reach 3 to 4 feet. "Called white sage because of its splendid leaves," Betsy notes, "it makes a prominent structural plant in the garden throughout the year. On a moonlight night, this sage is indeed elegant."

SHRUBS FOR AUTUMN FOLIAGE

In California we have such a great choice of evergreen shrubs, some gardeners think it pointless to plant deciduous ones, even if they do provide a fall display. But to tell the truth, a garden completely filled with evergreens, even those that bloom well in spring, can become pretty boring after a long summer. Used as accents, the shrubs in this list really spark up the autumn landscape.

Much of California is too mild for the startling displays of fall color that make autumn such a garden event in the East. Of course, if you live in the Sierras or the northern part of the state, you will see the most showy change of foliage color. However, even those in warmer regions will find something to love in this list of shrubs that produce vivid foliage in autumn. *Fothergilla major* in particular will produce reliable fall color with no chilling.

Red, Orange

Japanese maple (*Acer palmatum*)	SN, IV, NC, SC
Serviceberry (*Amelanchier*)	SN, IV
Red chokeberry (*Aronia arbutifolia*)	SN, IV
Smoke tree (*Cotinus coggygria*)	All
Spreading cotoneaster (*Cotoneaster divaricatus*)	All
Rock cotoneaster (*Cotoneaster horizontalis*)	SN, IV, HD, NC, SC
Enkianthus (*Enkianthus*)	SN, IV, NC, SC
Winged euonymus (*Euonymus alata*)	SN, IV, NC
Persian parrotia (*Parrotia persica*)	IV, NC, SC
Photinia (*Photinia villosa*)	SN
Royal azalea (*Rhododendron schlippenbachii*)	NC
Smooth sumac (*Rhus glabra*)	SN, IV, HD, NC
Staghorn sumac (*Rhus typhina*)	SN, IV, HD, NC
Goldflame spiraea (*Spiraea bumalda* 'Goldflame')	SN, IV, HD, NC, SC
Stachyurus (*Stachyurus praecox*)	IV, NC
Stewartia (*Stewartia*)	IV, NC, SC

Purple, Maroon, Bronze

Black chokeberry (*Aronia melanocarpa*)	SN, IV
Dogwood (*Cornus*)	SN, IV, NC, SC
Japanese deutzia (*Deutzia crenata*)	SN, IV, HD, NC
Fothergilla (*Fothergilla major*)	SN, NC
Oakleaf hydrangea (*Hydrangea quercifolia*)	All
Anise magnolia (*Magnolia salicifolia*)	SN, IV, NC, SC
Heavenly bamboo, Nandina (*Nandina domestica*)	All
Highbush blueberry (*Vaccinium corymbosum*)	SN, IV, NC
Fragrant snowball (*Viburnum carlcephalum*)	SN, IV, HD, NC, SC

Yellow, Gold

Yellow laceleaf maple (*Acer palmatum* 'Dissectum Viridis')	SN, IV, NC, SC
Japanese barberry (*Berberis thunbergii*)	All
Smoke tree (*Cotinus coggygria*)	All
Enkianthus (*Enkianthus*)	SN, IV, NC, SC
Dwarf fothergilla (*Fothergilla gardenii*)	SN, IV, NC
Witch hazel (*Hamamelis virginiana*)	SN, IV, NC, SC
Kerria (*Kerria japonica*)	All

Maxim's honeysuckle (*Lonicera maximowiczii sachalinensis*)	SN, IV, NC, SC
Photinia (*Photinia villosa*)	SN
Pomegranate (*Punica granatum*)	All
Cascara sagrada (*Rhamnus purshiana*)	SN, IV, HD, NC
Mollis hybrid azalea (*Rhododendron* mollis hybrids)	SN, IV, NC
Flame willow (*Salix* 'Flame')	All

FRUIT TREES THAT MAKE GOOD SHRUBS

Dwarf fruit trees or species that are genetically predisposed to remain small can be used as shrubs in your garden, and many are easy to grow in containers. This list of fruit trees combines suggestions from Tom Spellman, general manager of La Verne Nursery in San Dimas, and Ottillia Bier, a researcher in botany and plant sciences with the University of California at Riverside, where she evaluates new citrus varieties for the California citrus industry.

Tom especially recommends dwarf varieties of avocado if you live in the Southern California coastal and inland valleys, where the climate is ideal. "Littlecado and Whitsell can be easily grown in containers for several years," Tom says, and recommends half whiskey barrels or large redwood tubs. "These two varieties complement each other's fruiting season, with Littlecado producing in the summer and Whitsell during the winter months." During an avocado's first years, Tom advises, you have to fight the temptation to let the first fruits grow. "If your young tree flowers and begins to set fruit, keep it picked off for the first year, and thin the fruit by two-thirds the second year. This allows the young tree to stabilize and grow vigorously during the first critical years."

Ottillia notes that dwarf specimens of many citrus can be used as shrubs. "Commercial growers produce a number of citrus varieties on dwarfing rootstocks that may reduce the ultimate height of the tree to less than 6 feet." Besides the dwarf varieties, she says, "Many citrus cultivars—such as the Satsuma mandarin, Meyer lemon, kumquat, and Chinotto sour orange—tend to be small by nature. Also, a number of cultivars such as calamondin, kumquat and its hybrids, and Chinotto sour orange can be pruned to maintain small formal or informal shapes." Ottillia notes that their evergreen leaves, fragrant white flowers, and colorful fruit make citrus excellent foundation plants or garden shrubs.

Because the plants in this list vary in cold hardiness, consult with your local nursery to determine which may be best suited for your area. Ask them, too, about any cross-pollination needs.

Babaco papaya
Calamondin sour mandarin
Chinotto sour orange
Dwarf Cavendish banana
Dwarf kumquat
Flory peach
Garden Beauty nectarine
Littlecado avocado
Meyer lemon
Red strawberry guava
Satsuma mandarin
Whitsell avocado

SHRUBS THAT PROVIDE WINTER INTEREST

The plants in this list are especially desirable in winter when their color, foliage, flowers, or berries please the eye. From the flowers of the camellia and winter daphne, to the gnarled branches of Harry Lauder's walking stick, to the purple-bronze leaves of Oregon grape, you will find something on this list that will add interest to your landscape in winter.

Shrub	Interest	Zones
Japanese aucuba (*Aucuba japonica*)	foliage, berries	All
Green Beauty boxwood (*Buxus microphylla japonica* 'Green Beauty')	green color	All
Camellia (*Camellia*)	flowers	IV, HD, LD, NC, SC
Wintersweet (*Chimonanthus praecox*)	flowers	SN, IV, NC
Tatarian dogwood (*Cornus alba*)	red twigs	SN, IV, NC, SC
Red-osier dogwood (*Cornus sericea*)	red twigs	SN, IV, NC, SC
Red-twig dogwood (*Cornus stolonifera*)	red twigs	SN, IV, NC, SC
Harry Lauder's walking stick (*Corylus avellana* 'Contorta')	gnarled branches	SN, IV, NC, SC
Cotoneaster (*Cotoneaster*)	berries	All
Quince (*Cydonia oblonga*)	gnarled branches	SN, IV, NC, SC
Winter daphne (*Daphne odora*)	flowers	SN, IV, NC, SC
Holly (*Ilex*)	foliage, berries	All
Blaauw's juniper (*Juniperus chinensis* 'Blaauw')	blue color	All
Golden Pfitzer juniper (*Juniperus chinensis* 'Pfitzerana Aurea')	gold new growth	All
Cologreen juniper (*Juniperus scopulorum* 'Cologreen')	bright green color	All
Kerria (*Kerria japonica*)	yellow-green stems	All
Japanese crape myrtle (*Lagerstroemia fauriei*)	bark	SN, IV, LD, NC, SC
Oregon grape (*Mahonia aquifolium*)	purple-bronze foliage	SN, HD, NC, SC
Nandina (*Nandina domestica*)	red foliage	All
Osmanthus (*Osmanthus*)	foliage, flowers	All
Pieris (*Pieris*)	flowers	SN, IV, NC
Lily-of-the-valley shrub (*Pieris japonica*)	flowers	SN, IV, NC
English laurel (*Prunus laurocerasus*)	foliage	SN, IV, NC, SC
Apache pyracantha (*Pyracantha* 'Apache')	berries	All
Mohave pyracantha (*Pyracantha* 'Mohave')	berries	All
Purple sage (*Salvia leucophylla*)	flowers	IV, NC, SC
Sweet box (*Sarcococca*)	foliage, flowers	SN, IV, NC, SC
Foreman skimmia (*Skimmia foremanii*)	foliage, berries	SN, IV, NC, SC
Snowberry (*Symphoricarpos albus*)	berries	SN, IV, HD, NC, SC
Coralberry (*Symphoricarpos orbiculatus*)	berries	SN, IV, HD, NC, SC
Yew (*Taxus*)	berries	SN, IV, NC, SC

❧ Of the shrubby salvias native to California that are handsome year round, Betsy Clebsch, who wrote *A Book of Salvias* (Timber Press), says "One of my absolute favorites is *Salvia leucophylla,* with its apple-green foliage during winter, when it is in active growth. In late spring, lively pinkish flowers in whorls adorn its mass of soft green leaves." In dormancy, the foliage turns light gray. Betsy notes, "The whorls of flowers desiccate and make an interesting nut-brown decoration extended above the fragrant dove-gray leaves." This salvia is commonly called purple sage.

SHRUBS PRIZED FOR FLORAL ARRANGEMENTS

These shrubs will do double duty as they grace your landscape and provide beautiful flowers, foliage, or berries for interior arrangements. If you keep a few of these plants in your garden, you will have a continuing supply of material for your own indoor decorations and to use in floral gifts. Many of the shrubs listed here will last over a week in floral arrangements.

One thing to keep in mind: When you cut shrub branches for decorative use, you are actually pruning the plants, so be sensible about how you go about it.

Manzanita (*Arctostaphylos*)	SN, IV, NC, SC
Monterey manzanita (*Arctostaphylos hookeri*)	SN, IV, NC, SC
Japanese aucuba (*Aucuba japonica*)	All
Scotch heather (*Calluna vulgaris*)	SN, IV, NC
Camellia (*Camellia*)	SN, IV, NC, SC
Flowering quince (*Chaenomeles japonica*)	All
Wintersweet (*Chimonanthus praecox*)	SN, IV, NC
Scotch broom (*Cytisus scoparius*)	SN, IV, NC, SC
Silverberry (*Eleagnus pungens*)	All
Eucalyptus (*Eucalyptus*)	All
Evergreen euonymus (*Euonymus japonica*)	All
Forsythia (*Forsythia*)	All
Gardenia (*Gardenia jasminoides*)	IV, LD, NC, SC
Canary Island broom (*Genista canariensis*)	SN, NC, SC
Witch hazel (*Hamamelis*)	SN, IV, NC, SC
Hydrangea (*Hydrangea*)	All
Holly (*Ilex*)	All
Jacaranda (*Jacaranda mimosifolia*)	IV, LD, NC, SC
Kerria (*Kerria japonica*)	All
Hybrid osmanthus (*Osmanthus fortunei*)	SN, IV, NC, SC
Sweet olive (*Osmanthus fragrans*)	IV, LD, NC, SC
Tree peony (*Paeonia suffruticosa* hybrids)	SN, IV, HD, NC, SC
Redtip (*Photinia fraseri*)	All
Azalea (*Rhododendron*)	SN, IV, NC, SC
Pink pussy willow (*Salix caprea*)	All
Pussy willow (*Salix discolor*)	All
Rose-gold pussy willow (*Salix gracilistyla*)	All
Senecio, Grey's groundsel (*Senecio greyi*)	SN, IV, NC, SC
Lilac (*Syringa*)	SN, IV, HD, NC, SC
Viburnum (*Viburnum*)	All

❧ Parney cotoneaster is noted for its attractive, long-lasting red berry clusters, used in winter holiday decorations. This arching evergreen makes a good informal hedge in sun or light shade and needs little water once established.

A FEW AZALEAS AND RHODODENDRONS

Among the most popular flowering shrubs that also offer attractive foliage are the evergreen rhododendrons and azaleas, both fitting under the scientific name *Rhododendron*. But not all of these plants do well in all parts of California. They fare badly in areas with alkaline soil, prefering acid soil that is moist but fast draining. They like humidity, too, and generally speaking, they are best if located in the filtered shade of tall trees.

Lucy Tolmach, horticulture director at the Filoli estate gardens in Woodside, says that her favorite azaleas are the Kurume varieties, with their tiered, evergreen habit and brilliant spring flowers. At Filoli these include 'Ward's Ruby,' 'Hinodegiri,' 'Hino-crimson,' and 'Snow.' Among the rhododendrons are 'Mrs. G. W. Leak,' 'Loder's White,' 'Bow Bells,' 'Snow Lady,' 'Else Frye,' and the native western *Rhododendron occidentale*. Lucy notes that in Woodside's Mediterranean climate, their rhododendrons and azaleas are bothered by greenhouse thrips, which attack the epidermis of the leaves, bleaching them out. "We have serious problems with this pest," Lucy notes, "requiring numerous sprays in years with high winter temperatures." Leaves can also be disfigured by the black vine weevil, "a real problem on *Rhododendron yakushimanum*. The weevil chews the edges of the leaves." A problem for some deciduous rhododendrons, such as the Exbury hybrids, is that they mildew badly close to the coast.

Although rhododendrons seem to have more needs than do azaleas, most gardeners would say they are worth the effort. There seems to be a rhododendron or azalea suited to every garden, but assigning the many species and varieties to a particular growing zone is fairly tricky, so this list doesn't try. What it does is present a few azaleas and rhododendrons that are known to do well in California. The final word on which particular plants are best for your area will come through your consultations with the nursery experts where you buy your plants.

Rhododendrons	Bloom Color
Anna Rose Whitney	Deep pink
Blue Ensign	Lilac-blue
Bow Bells	Pink
Cilpinense	Pink
Else Frye	White with pink
Loder's White	White
Mrs. G. W. Leak	Deep pink
Sappho	White with purple
Scarlet Wonder	Red
Snow Lady	White
Taurus	Red
Top Banana	Yellow

Azaleas	
Betty Ann Voss	Pink
Buccaneer	Orange
Fedora	Salmon
George Lindley Taber	Pink
Herbert	Purple
Hino-crimson	Red
Hinodegiri	Cerise
Gumpo	White
Mme. Pericat	Pink
Shinnyo-No-Tsuki	Magenta with white
Snow	White
Ward's Ruby	Red

> "Azaleas do well in California," says Wendy Proud of Monrovia Nursery in Azusa. "The Belgian Indica azaleas usually take shade, but the 'Alaska' variety, which has a white flower, is hardier than the others. It takes full sun, but can take shade too. It's versatile, and it has a spring and fall flowering. 'Red Ruffles' is a Southern Indica azalea, good in full sun. Put it in a high-profile place in your garden. It flowers in spring, fall, and intermittently through the year."

LOW SHRUBS THAT WON'T HIDE WINDOWS

A backdrop of foundation shrubs between the house and its surrounding flower beds always looks nice—but if you find those shrubs blocking light or the view, you may want to replace them with something from this list. These plants will stay low enough to keep out of the way. Also, ask your local nursery professionals about dwarf cultivars of these and other species. In particular, look for more varieties among the Japanese and Chinese hollies, junipers, and low-growing forms of azalea. If your house was built with picture windows that are very low to the ground, you might want to check the list of low-growing shrubs for ground cover, on page 84.

Golden barberry (*Berberis thunbergii* 'Aurea')	All
Scotch heather (*Calluna vulgaris*)	SN, IV, NC
Burkwood daphne (*Daphne burkwoodii*)	SN, IV, NC
Cornish heath (*Erica vagans*)	SN, IV, NC, SC
Forever Pink hydrangea (*Hydrangea macrophylla* 'Forever Pink')	SN, IV, NC, SC
Blue Billow hydrangea (*Hydrangea serrata* 'Blue Billow')	SN, IV, NC, SC
Dwarf Chinese holly (*Ilex cornuta* 'Rotunda')	SN, IV, NC, SC
Soft Touch Japanese holly (*Ilex crenata* 'Soft Touch')	SN, IV, NC, SC
Shamrock inkberry (*Ilex glabra* 'Shamrock')	All
Dwarf yaupon (*Ilex vomitoria* 'Nana')	All
Showy jasmine (*Jasminum floridum*)	SN, IV, LD, NC, SC
Fruitland juniper (*Juniperus chinensis* 'Fruitland')	All
Blue Carpet juniper (*Juniperus squamata* 'Blue Carpet')	All
African boxwood (*Myrsine africana*)	IV, NC, SC
Harbour Dwarf nandina (*Nandina domestica* 'Harbour Dwarf')	All
Montgomery spruce (*Picea pungens* 'Montgomery')	SN, IV, NC
Wheeler's Dwarf pittosporum (*Pittosporum tobira* 'Wheelers Dwarf')	IV, HD, LD, NC, SC
Raffles arborvitae (*Platycladus orientalis* 'Raffles')	All
Dwarf India hawthorn (*Rhaphiolepis indica* 'Ballerina')	IV, LD, NC, SC
Hybrid azalea, low forms (*Rhododendron*)	SN, IV, NC, SC
Skimmia (*Skimmia japonica*)	SN, IV, NC, SC
Spreading English yew (*Taxus baccata* 'Rependens')	SN, IV, NC, SC

> We don't often think about it, but some shrubs provide us with delicious things to eat. Ranging from the dwarf varieties of citrus and avocado, to highbush blueberries, to the shrubby herbs like rosemary, these plants are not only landscape accents, but culinary boons as well. When planning which shrubs to include in your landscape, consider selecting some that are edible. Then consult with your local nursery or cooperative extension agent for more possibilities and to learn what species and varieties are right for your area.

EVERGREEN HEDGES, SCREENS, AND BARRIERS

This list includes shrubs that are for the most part covered in foliage from the ground up. The shrubs in this list overlap those in the windbreak list on page 104, but they are all evergreen and are especially selected for use in screening out unwanted views all year round. Some of them make good barriers as well, because they are either thorny or extremely dense in growth. Some of these plants are technically trees, but they may have dwarf or shrub forms that are sold in nurseries as shrubs. Some, such as boxwood, grow slowly, but every plant in this list should get shoulder height or higher.

Although these shrubs are all evergreen, they vary a great deal in appearance, from the broad shiny leaves of hybrid camellias (some of which will easily top 20 feet or more if unchecked) to the tidy greenery of boxwood. Some come with the added bonus of colorful flowers or attractive berries, while others do stalwart service as virtually unchanging living backdrops to showy deciduous shrubs such as roses or permanently placed statuary or fountains.

For a list of tall, upright evergreen shrubs, suitable for narrow spaces, see page 79. For a list of shrubs best adapted to clipping into formal hedges, see page 102.

Kangaroo thorn (*Acacia armata*)	IV, LD, NC, SC
Barberry (*Berberis*)	All
Weeping bottlebrush (*Callistemon viminalis*)	IV, LD, NC, SC
Lawson cedar (*Chamaecyparis lawsoniana*)	SN, IV, NC
Mexican orange (*Choisya ternata*)	SN, IV, NC, SC
Himalayan cocculus (*Cocculus laurifolius*)	IV, LD, NC, SC
Cotoneaster (*Cotoneaster*)	All
Hop bush (*Dodonaea viscosa*)	SN, IV, LD, NC, SC
Escallonia (*Escallonia*)	SN, IV, NC, SC
Silktassel (*Garrya elliptica, G. fremontii*)	SN, IV, NC, SC
Lavender starflower (*Grewia occidentalis*)	IV, LD, NC, SC
Sweet hakea (*Hakea suaveolens*)	IV, LD, NC, SC
Boxleaf hebe (*Hebe buxifolia*)	IV, NC, SC
Holly (*Ilex*)	All
Juniper (*Juniperus*)	All
Creosote bush (*Larrea tridentata*)	IV, HD, LD
Tea tree (*Leptospermum*)	IV, NC, SC
Texas sage (*Leucophyllum frutescens*)	All
Privet (*Ligustrum*)	All
Melaleuca, Honey myrtle (*Melaleuca*)	IV, LD, NC, SC
Orange jessamine (*Murraya paniculata*)	SC
Myrtle (*Myrtus communis*)	IV, HD, LD, NC, SC
Osmarea (*Osmarea burkwoodii*)	SN, IV, NC
Photinia (*Photinia*)	All
Pittosporum (*Pittosporum*)	IV, LD, NC, SC
Oriental arborvitae (*Platycladus orientalis*)	All
Laurel (*Prunus*)	SN, IV, NC, SC
Firethorn, Pyracantha (*Pyracantha*)	All
Buckthorn (*Rhamnus*)	All
Fuchsia-flowering gooseberry (*Ribes speciosum*)	IV, NC, SC
Brush cherry (*Syzygium paniculatum*)	NC, SC

Yew (*Taxus*)	SN, IV, NC, SC
Yellow bells (*Tecoma stans*)	LD, SC
Cape honeysuckle (*Tecomaria capensis*)	IV, LD, NC, SC
Yellow oleander (*Thevetia peruviana*)	LD, SC
Arborvitae (*Thuja*)	SN, IV, NC, SC

SHRUBS THAT YOU CAN TRAIN INTO SMALL TREES

Some shrubs will grow 10 to 20 feet or more in height, and many of those that do are readily amenable to "limbing up" or removal of lower branches. This treatment turns them into splendid little trees, just perfect for use in small gardens or under power lines where larger trees would be out of scale or simply would not fit. By clearing out around the feet of old hollies, azaleas, and oleanders, you can give these bulky monsters a new, sleek look that will be a real asset in the landscape. Overgrown oleanders—in particular the large, white-flowered variety—take well to this treatment and produce striking trees when trained to an upright form.

Hollyleaf cherry

Fountain butterfly bush (*Buddleia alternifolia*)	All
Japanese sweet shrub (*Clethra barbinervis*)	SN, IV, NC, SC
Texas olive (*Cordia boissieri*)	IV, HD, LD, NC, SC
Fragrant winter hazel (*Corylopsis glabrescens*)	SN, IV, NC
Bronze loquat (*Eriobotrya deflexa*)	IV, HD, LD, NC, SC
Burford holly (*Ilex cornuta* 'Burfordii')	SN, IV, NC, SC
Crape myrtle (*Lagerstroemia indica*)	SN, IV, LD, NC, SC
Japanese privet (*Ligustrum japonicum*)	All
Banana shrub (*Michelia figo*)	IV, NC, SC
Oleander (*Nerium oleander*)	IV, HD, LD, NC, SC
Sweet olive (*Osmanthus fragrans*)	IV, LD, NC, SC
Redtip (*Photinia fraseri*)	All
Tobira (*Pittosporum tobira*)	IV, HD, LD, NC, SC
Hollyleaf cherry (*Prunus ilicifolia*)	IV, LD, NC, SC
English laurel (*Prunus laurocerasus*)	SN, IV, NC, SC
Catalina cherry (*Prunus lyonii*)	IV, LD, NC, SC
Strawberry guava (*Psidium cattleianum*)	IV, NC, SC
Italian buckthorn (*Rhamnus alaternus*)	All
Majestic Beauty rhaphiolepis (*Rhaphiolepis* 'Majestic Beauty')	IV, LD, NC, SC
Sumacs (*Rhus*)	All
Tristania (*Tristania laurina*)	NC, SC
Huron viburnum (*Viburnum japonicum* 'Huron')	SN, IV, HD, NC, SC
Black haw (*Viburnum prunifolium*)	SN, IV, NC, SC
Chaste tree (*Vitex agnes-castus*)	All

SHRUBS FOR A CLIPPED HEDGE

Half the battle of maintaining a clipped hedge is selecting an appropriate shrub to begin with. Some plants take to being cut back, and some don't. The best shrubs for clipping usually have small leaves and don't produce lots of new growth when cut. Cutting into the proper shape helps, too. Instead of trying to get nice, straight sides, or sides that taper towards the ground, what you want is a plant that is narrower at the top. That lets light get to the lower branches, which keeps them from getting woody and sparse of leaf.

Barberry (*Berberis*)	All
Boxwood (*Buxus*)	All
Mirror plant (*Coprosma repens*)	IV, NC, SC
Japanese holly (*Ilex crenata*)	All
Inkberry holly (*Ilex glabra*)	All
Italian jasmine (*Jasminum humile*)	SN, IV, LD, NC, SC
Chihuahua sage (*Leucophyllum laevigatum*)	All
Texas privet (*Ligustrum japonicum* 'Texanum')	All
Pacific wax myrtle (*Myrica californica*)	SN, IV, NC, SC
Devilwood (*Osmanthus americana*)	All
Pittosporum (*Pittosporum*)	IV, LD, NC, SC
Yew pine (*Podocarpus macrophyllus*)	SN, IV, LD, NC, SC
Carolina laurel cherry (*Prunus caroliniana*)	All
English laurel (*Prunus laurocerasus*)	SN, IV, NC, SC
Lemonade berry (*Rhus integrifolia*)	NC, SC
Xylosma (*Xylosma congestum*)	IV, HD, LD, NC, SC
Yew (*Taxus*)	SN, IV, NC, SC

Michael A. Parten of Orchard Nursery & Florist in Lafayette suggests several plants that make good hedges: 'Edward Goucher' abelia, pink princess escallonia, 'Ruby Glow' New Zealand tea tree, 'John Edwards' Italian buckthorn, 'Fern Clouds' African fern pine, and 'Spring Bouquet' laurustinus. The cone-bearing 'Fern Clouds' is also fine for espalier or container growing.

SHRUBS FOR ESPALIER

Espalier is an ancient garden art in which plants are pruned and trained flat against a wall, trellis, or fence. The result can be a formal design such as a candelabra shape, or informal, where the plant assumes a quasi-natural form, but only in two dimensions. Although most people think of trees—especially fruit trees—when they consider espalier, other woody plants adapt well to training and pruning, and they make very interesting espalier subjects in the formal garden or where space is at a premium. In California, evergreen espaliers, such as those made from camellias and pyracanthas, are especially popular due to the extra interest of seasonal flowers or berries. This list is only an introduction to the subject, however, because the possibilities for espalier work are quite large. Also see the list of trees for espalier on page 49.

Red bauhinia (*Bauhinia galpinii, B. punctata*)	IV, LD, NC, SC
Showa-No-Sakae camellia	SN, IV, NC, SC
(*Camellia hiemalis* 'Showa-No-Sakae')	
Chandler camellia (*Camellia japonica* 'Chandler')	SN, IV, NC, SC

Elegans camellia (*Camellia japonica* 'Elegans')	SN, IV, NC, SC
Hana Jiman camellia (*Camellia sasanqua* 'Hana Jiman')	SN, IV, NC, SC
Mine-No-Yuki camellia (*Camellia sasanqua* 'Mine-No-Yuki')	SN, IV, NC, SC
Flowering quince (*Chaenomeles*)	All
Cotoneaster (*Cotoneaster*)	All
Bronze loquat (*Eriobotrya deflexa*)	IV, HD, LD, NC, SC
Bluebush eucalyptus (*Eucalyptus macrocarpa*)	SN, IV, LD, NC, SC
Pineapple guava (*Feijoa sellowiana*)	SN, IV, LD, NC, SC
Gardenia (*Gardenia jasminoides*)	SN, IV, LD, NC, SC
Kerria (*Kerria japonica*)	All
Sweet olive (*Osmanthus fragrans*)	IV, LD, NC, SC
Redtip (*Photinia fraseri*)	All
Pomegranate (*Punica granatum*)	All
Firethorn, Pyracantha (*Pyracantha*)	All
Evergreen pear (*Pyrus kawakamii*)	IV, LD, NC, SC
Burkwood viburnum (*Viburnum burkwoodii*)	SN, IV, HD, NC, SC
Chinese snowball (*Viburnum macrocephalum*)	SN, IV, NC, SC
Shiny xylosma (*Xylosma congestum*)	IV, HD, LD, NC, SC

WELL-BEHAVED BAMBOOS TO USE AS SHRUBS

Bamboos are actually giant grasses, but many of them are put to the same uses that shrubs are in the landscape. Tall bamboos are an effective privacy screen, tall and medium-height bamboos make fine hedges, and some of the shorter bamboos, under 3 feet, can be used as ground covers. "Bamboos have obtained a bad reputation for invasiveness because people plant the wrong bamboos," says George Shor, secretary of the American Bamboo Society. He advises gardeners to be aware of the difference between running bamboos and clumping bamboos. "Running bamboos are suitable for cold climates, and for large estates or farms. When planted on a small suburban lot in a warm climate, they can spread rapidly and, if not controlled, become a nuisance."

George, who lives in La Jolla, provided this list of noninvasive, clumping bamboos, "which do not invade areas where they are not wanted." He notes that the Alphonse Karr and Golden Goddess varieties are frequently used for hedges. If you like bamboo shoots as a vegetable, the shoots of Oldham's and Beechey bamboos are edible. Beechey and the painted bamboos are the tallest in this list, reaching 50 feet. For more information about available bamboos (over 250 species and varieties) and where to get them, write to the American Bamboo Society (750 Krumkill Rd., Albany, NY 12203-5976), include postage to cover 3 ounces, and they'll send you a copy of their annual Bamboo Species Source List. A good place to preview bamboos is the special collection at Quail Botanical Gardens in Encinitas, where you can get an idea of how a particular bamboo might look in your garden.

Beechey bamboo (*Bambusa beecheyana*)	IV, HD, LD, NC, SC
Alphonse Karr bamboo (*Bambusa multiplex* 'Alphonse Karr')	IV, HD, LD, NC, SC
Golden Goddess bamboo (*Bambusa multiplex* 'Golden Goddess')	IV, HD, LD, NC, SC
Oldham's bamboo (*Bambusa oldhamii*)	IV, HD, LD, NC, SC
Painted bamboo (*Bambusa vulgaris* 'Vittata')	NC, SC
Crown bamboo (*Chusquea coronalis*)	IV, LD, NC, SC
Fountain bamboo (*Fargesia nitida*)	SN, HD, NC, SC
Mexican weeping bamboo (*Otatea acuminata aztecorum*)	IV, HD, LD, NC, SC

SHRUBS AS WINDBREAKS

In much of California the wind blows from one direction with predictable regularity at certain times of the day or for certain seasons. To create an effective windbreak, plant up to five rows of shrubs and trees, the lowest on the windward side. This will force the wind to lift over the tallest trees on the leeward side, creating a "wind shadow" around your home. If space is limited, use one row of shrubs and one row of trees.

Evergreen

Coastal wattle (*Acacia cyclopis*)	IV, LD, NC, SC
Prickly acacia (*Acacia verticillata*)	IV, NC, SC
Oldham bamboo (*Bambusa oldhamii*)	IV, NC, SC
Hop bush (*Dodonaea viscosa*)	SN, IV, LD, NC, SC
Silverberry (*Elaeagnus pungens*)	All
Escallonia (*Escallonia*)	SN, IV, NC, SC
Coarse-leaved mallee (*Eucalyptus grossa*)	IV, NC, SC
Square-fruited mallee (*Eucalyptus tetraptera*)	IV, NC, SC
Griselinia (*Griselinia littoralis*)	IV, NC, SC
Sweet hakea (*Hakea suaveolens*)	IV, LD, NC, SC
Junipers, columnar types (*Juniperus*)	All
Malva rosa (*Lavatera assurgentiflora*)	SN, IV, NC, SC
Japanese privet (*Ligustrum japonicum*)	All
Myoporum (*Myoporum laetum*)	IV, NC, SC
Oleander (*Nerium oleander*)	IV, HD, LD, NC, SC
Pittosporum (*Pittosporum*)	IV, HD, LD, NC, SC
Carolina laurel cherry (*Prunus caroliniana*)	All
English laurel (*Prunus laurocerasus*)	SN, IV, NC, SC
Hollyleaf cherry, Catalina cherry (*Prunus ilicifolia, P. lyonii*)	SN, IV, LD, NC, SC
Firethorn, tall forms (*Pyracantha*)	All
Italian buckthorn (*Rhamnus alaternus*)	All
Japanese yew (*Taxus cuspidata*)	SN, IV, NC, SC
Hybrid yew (*Taxus media*)	SN, IV, NC, SC

Deciduous

Quailbush (*Atriplex lentiformis*)	SN, IV, HD, LD
Japanese barberry (*Berberis thunbergii*)	All
Red bird of paradise, Dwarf poinciana (*Caesalpinia pulcherrima*)	HD, LD, NC, SC
Bodinier beautyberry (*Callicarpa bodinieri*)	SN, IV, NC, SC
Siberian peashrub (*Caragana arborescens*)	SN, IV, HD
Flowering quince (*Chaenomeles*)	All
Russian olive (*Elaeagnus angustifolia*)	All
Ocotillo (*Fouquieria splendens*)	HD, LD, SC
Privet (*Ligustrum*)	All
Tatarian honeysuckle (*Lonicera tatarica*)	SN, IV, NC, SC
Tallhedge buckthorn (*Rhamnus frangula* 'Columnaris')	SN, IV, HD
Eglantine, Sweetbriar rose (*Rosa eglanteria*)	All
Father Hugo rose (*Rosa hugonis*)	All
Ramanas rose, Rugosa rose (*Rosa rugosa*)	All
Tamarisk (*Tamarix*)	All

❦ The Mediterranean fan palm, *Chamaerops humilis,* makes a good, wind-resistant hedge. "This is a sucker-ing palm with growth to the sides, so you can get multiple trunks," notes Michael Letzring, lead gardener of the San Diego Zoo. "Although one of the hardiest for cold weather, the Mediterranean fan palm can take the extreme heat in the desert, so full sun is no problem."

SHRUBS WITH FRAGRANT BLOSSOMS

The following list contains shrubs that most people find pleasantly aromatic—but before you select any of these plants, take the time to sniff them at your local nursery. Generally speaking, flower fragrance is strongest before noon on warm and humid days, and least noticeable in the mid-afternoon on hot, dry days. Of course, no fragrant landscape would be complete without a few shrub roses, so be sure to check the rose chapter for the sweetest smelling members of that exceptionally fragrant genus.

Bailey acacia (*Acacia baileyana*)	SN, IV, LD, NC, SC
Bouvardia (*Bouvardia longiflora, B. humboldtii*)	IV, LD, NC, SC
Butterfly bush (*Buddleia davidii*)	All
Orange butterfly bush (*Buddleia globosa*)	All
Natal plum (*Carissa grandiflora, C. macrocarpa*)	SC
Night jessamine (*Cestrum nocturnum*)	IV, LD, NC, SC
Willow-leafed jessamine (*Cestrum parqui*)	IV, LD, NC, SC
Wintersweet (*Chimonanthus praecox*)	SN, IV, NC
Mexican orange (*Choisya ternata*)	SN, IV, NC, SC
Cashmere bouquet (*Clerodendrum bungei*)	SN, IV, LD, NC, SC
Glorybower (*Clerodendrum fragrans pleniflorum*)	IV, LD, NC, SC
Fragrant winter hazel (*Corylopsis glabrescens*)	SN, IV, NC
Daphne (*Daphne*)	SN, IV, NC, SC
Gardenia (*Gardenia jasminoides*)	IV, LD, NC, SC
Sweet hakea (*Hakea suaveolens*)	IV, LD, NC, SC
Honeysuckle (*Lonicera*)	All
Orange jessamine (*Murraya paniculata*)	SC
Sweet olive (*Osmanthus fragrans*)	IV, LD, NC, SC
Mock orange (*Philadelphus*)	All
Tobira (*Pittosporum tobira*)	IV, HD, LD, NC, SC
Frangipani (*Plumeria rubra*)	LD, SC
Wafer ash, Hop tree (*Ptelea trifoliata*)	SN, IV
Western azalea (*Rhododendron occidentale*)	All
Sweet box (*Sarcococca*)	SN, IV, NC, SC
Lilac (*Syringa*)	SN, IV, HD, NC, SC
Ternstroemia (*Ternstroemia gymnanthera*)	SN, IV, LD, NC, SC
Yellow oleander (*Thevetia peruviana*)	LD, SC
Fragrant snowball (*Viburnum carlcephalum*)	SN, IV, HD, NC, SC

❦ "I am especially fond of our fragrant rhododendrons," says Lucy Tolmach, director of horticulture at the Filoli estate gardens in Woodside. "We have a south-facing brick wall in the Walled Garden where *Rhododendron* 'Fragrantissimum' has been trained as a vine. We keep it pruned fairly tight to the wall because it tends to be somewhat rangy otherwise. In April this plant blooms with the most spectacular, fragrant, pale-pink flowers."

SHRUBS THAT WILL ATTRACT BIRDS TO YOUR GARDEN

If you want to attract birds to your garden, select an assortment of shrubs from the list below, which groups the plants by what will attract the birds the most: fruit and seeds, or flowers. The species of birds that come will vary with the plants. Hummingbirds are drawn to flowers in the spring, while a wide variety of birds will arrive on the scene as fruit and seeds ripen in the fall. Remember too that many roses make a fine crop of hips, and birds consider them a delicacy. Check page 126 for a list of roses with great hips.

Fruit, Seeds

Manzanita (*Arctostaphylos*)	SN, IV, NC, SC
Chokeberry (*Aronia*)	SN, IV
Saltbush, Quailbush, Desert holly (*Atriplex*)	All
Beautyberry (*Callicarpa*)	SN, IV, NC, SC
Natal plum (*Carissa grandiflora, C. macrocarpa*)	SC
Night jessamine (*Cestrum nocturnum*)	IV, LD, NC, SC
Willow-leafed jessamine (*Cestrum parqui*)	IV, LD, NC, SC
Dogwood (*Cornus*)	SN, IV, NC, SC
Cotoneaster (*Cotoneaster*)	All
Silverberry, Russian olive (*Elaeagnus*)	All
Euonymus (*Euonymus*)	All
Silktassel (*Garrya*)	SN, IV, NC, SC
Salal, Checkerberry, Wintergreen (*Gaultheria*)	SN, IV, NC, SC
Toyon, California holly (*Heteromeles arbutifolia*)	All
Holly (*Ilex*)	All
Privet (*Ligustrum*)	All
Honeysuckle (*Lonicera*)	All
Mahonia, Oregon grape (*Mahonia*)	All
Pacific wax myrtle (*Myrica californica*)	SN, IV, NC, SC
Photinia (*Photinia*)	All
Carolina laurel cherry (*Prunus caroliniana*)	All
Hollyleaf cherry, Catalina cherry (*Prunus ilicifolia, P. lyonii*)	SN, IV, LD, NC, SC
Firethorn, Pyracantha (*Pyracantha*)	All
Buckthorn, Coffeeberry (*Rhamnus*)	All
Sumac (*Rhus*)	All
Currant, Gooseberry (*Ribes*)	SN, IV, HD, NC, SC
Rosemary (*Rosmarinus officinalis*)	All
Bramble, Blackberry (*Rubus*)	SN, IV, NC
Chilean guava (*Ugni molinae, Myrtus ugni*)	IV, NC, SC
Huckleberry, Cranberry, Blueberry (*Vaccinium*)	SN, IV, NC
Viburnum (*Viburnum*)	All

Flowers

Flowering maple (*Abutilon*)	IV, LD, NC, SC
Acacias (*Acacia*)	IV, HD, LD, NC, SC
Butterfly bush (*Buddleia*)	All
Bird of paradise bush (*Caesalpinia gilliesii*)	IV, HD, LD, NC
Lemon bottlebrush (*Callistemon citrinus*)	IV, LD, NC, SC

Ceanothus, Wild lilac (*Ceanothus*)	SN, IV, NC, SC
Flowering quince (*Chaenomeles*)	All
Desert willow (*Chilopsis linearis*)	HD, LD, SC
Pineapple guava (*Feijoa sellowiana*)	SN, IV, LD, NC, SC
Fuchsia (*Fuchsia*)	SN, IV, NC, SC
Woolly grevillea, Spider flower (*Grevillea lanigera*)	IV, NC, SC
Creambush (*Holodiscus discolor*)	SN, IV, HD, NC, SC
Shrimp plant (*Justicia brandegeana*)	IV, LD, NC, SC
Honeysuckle (*Lonicera*)	All
Melaleuca (*Melaleuca*)	IV, LD, NC, SC
European currant (*Ribes viburnifolium*)	IV, NC, SC

Besides looking to your shrubs for fruit, seeds, and nectar to feast on, birds also depend on them for places to live and hide. Many birds favor the thick greenery of yews, for example, or mahonia or holly. Humans use foundation plantings for insulation and esthetic touches around our homes, but birds also appreciate foundation plantings—a screen of buddleia, bottlebrush, or viburnum near a birdhouse or feeder can offer some protection from sun, winds, and predators.

SHRUBS THAT DRAW BEES

As many gardeners know, the bee population is dropping throughout the United States due to the overuse of insecticides. To create a bee sanctuary in your garden, refrain from spraying and plant shrubs from the following list.

Ceanothus

Chinese abelia (*Abelia chinensis*)	All
Glossy abelia (*Abelia grandiflora*)	All
Acacia (*Acacia*)	IV, HD, LD, NC, SC
Butterfly bush (*Buddleia*)	All
Lemon bottlebrush (*Callistemon citrinus*)	IV, LD, NC, SC
Scotch heather (*Calluna*)	SN, IV, NC
Ceanothus, Wild lilac (*Ceanothus*)	SN, IV, NC, SC
Mexican orange (*Choisya ternata*)	SN, IV, NC, SC
Cotoneaster (*Cotoneaster*)	All
Heath (*Erica*)	SN, IV, NC, SC
Escallonia (*Escallonia*)	SN, IV, NC, SC
Pineapple guava (*Feijoa sellowiana*)	SN, IV, LD, NC, SC
Toyon, California holly (*Heteromeles arbutifolia*)	All
Privet (*Ligustrum*)	All
Orange jessamine (*Murraya paniculata*)	SC
Firethorn, Pyracantha (*Pyracantha*)	All
Rosemary (*Rosmarinus officinalis*)	All
Bush germander (*Teucrium fruticans*)	All

SHRUBS THAT DEER RARELY EAT

If you live in a rural or semirural area, this list of shrubs will be very useful. For one reason or another—usually toxicity or unpleasant flavor—deer will rarely browse them, which means you can relax and enjoy the view.

Butterfly bush (*Buddleia*)	All
Boxwood (*Buxus*)	All
Spice bush (*Calycanthus occidentalis*)	SN, IV, NC, SC
Mexican orange (*Choisya ternata*)	SN, IV, NC, SC
Rockrose (*Cistus*)	SN, IV, NC, SC
Mirror plant (*Coprosma repens*)	NC, SC
Australian fuchsia (*Correa*)	IV, NC, SC
Smoke tree (*Cotinus coggygria*)	All
Scotch broom (*Cytisus scoparius*)	SN, IV, NC, SC
Winter daphne (*Daphne odora*)	SN, IV, NC, SC
Shrubby St. Johnswort (*Hypericum patulum*)	All
Kerria (*Kerria japonica*)	All
Lantana (*Lantana montevidensis, L. sellowiana*)	IV, LD, NC, SC
Mahonia, Oregon grape (*Mahonia*)	All
Honey bush (*Melianthus major*)	IV, LD, NC, SC
Pacific wax myrtle (*Myrica californica*)	SN, IV, NC, SC
Oleander (*Nerium oleander*)	IV, HD, LD, NC, SC
Carolina laurel cherry (*Prunus caroliniana*)	All
Rhododendron, but not azalea (*Rhododendron*)	SN, IV, NC
Sugar bush (*Rhus ovata*)	All
Rosemary (*Rosmarinus officinalis*)	All
Spanish broom (*Spartium junceum*)	All
Brush cherry (*Syzygium paniculatum*)	NC, SC
Bush germander (*Teucrium fruticans*)	All

Scotch broom

Shrubs with small leaves are low on a deer's priority list. Smaller leaves mean less moisture, so deer don't find these plants as attractive as ones with larger, juicy leaves.

A SAMPLER OF SHRUBS FOR INTEREST IN EACH SEASON

Here is a list of shrubs you can use to direct attention to different parts of your garden at different times of the year or to keep attention balanced through a large landscape. Many of these plants appear on other lists in this chapter—for instance, under the type of soil or light conditions they prefer, or by the type of foliage they have—but here you can find them grouped by season, which is a great help in planning a garden. This sampler doesn't include every shrub mentioned in the lists above, so you will find other plants to consider throughout the chapter.

Spring	Interest	Region
Flowering maple (*Abutilon*)	flowers	IV, LD, NC, SC
Acacia (*Acacia*)	flowers	IV, HD, LD, NC, SC
Lemon bottlebrush (*Callistemon citrinus*)	flowers	IV, LD, NC, SC
Camellia (*Camellia*)	flowers	SN, IV, NC, SC

Ceanothus, Wild lilac (*Ceanothus*)	flowers	SN, IV, NC, SC
Palo verde (*Cercidium*)	flowers	HD, LD, NC, SC
Mexican orange (*Choisya ternata*)	flowers	SN, IV, NC, SC
Rockrose (*Cistus*)	flowers	SN, IV, NC, SC
Daphne (*Daphne*)	fragrance	SN, IV, NC, SC
Coral tree (*Erythrina*)	flowers	IV, LD, NC, SC
Apache plume (*Fallugia paradoxa*)	flowers	All
Forsythia (*Forsythia*)	flowers	All
Flannel bush (*Fremontodendron*)	flowers	All
Showy jasmine (*Jasminum floridum*)	flowers	IV, HD, LD, NC, SC
Pacific wax myrtle (*Myrica californica*)	foliage	SN, IV, NC, SC
Nandina, Heavenly bamboo (*Nandina domestica*)	flowers	All
Sweet mock orange (*Philadelphus coronarius*)	fragrance	All
Photinia (*Photinia fraseri*)	foliage	All
Willow pittosporum (*Pittosporum phillyraeoides*)	flowers	IV, LD, NC, SC
Tamarisk (*Tamarix*)	flowers	All
Viburnum (*Viburnum*)	flowers	SN, IV, HD, NC, SC
Weigela (*Weigela*)	flowers	SN, IV, HD, NC

Summer

Chinese abelia (*Abelia chinensis*)	flowers	All
Flowering maple (*Abutilon*)	flowers	IV, LD, NC, SC
Lemon bottlebrush (*Callistemon citrinus*)	flowers	IV, LD, NC, SC
Night jessamine (*Cestrum nocturnum*)	fragrance	IV, LD, NC, SC
Cashmere bouquet (*Clerodendrum bungei*)	fragrance	SN, IV, LD, NC, SC
Russian olive (*Elaeagnus angustifolia*)	flowers, fruit	All
Coral tree (*Erythrina*)	flowers	IV, LD, NC, SC
Fuchsia (*Fuchsia*)	flowers	SN, IV, NC, SC
Gardenia (*Gardenia jasminoides*)	fragrance	IV, LD, NC, SC
Dyer's greenweed (*Genista tinctoria*)	flowers	All
Hibiscus (*Hibiscus*)	flowers	All
Italian jasmine (*Jasminum humile*)	flowers	SN, IV, LD, NC, SC
Brazilian plume flower (*Justicia carnea*)	flowers	IV, LD, NC, SC
Crape myrtle (*Lagerstroemia indica*)	flowers	SN, IV, LD, NC, SC
Oleander (*Nerium oleander*)	flowers	IV, HD, LD, NC, SC
Mock orange (*Philadelphus*)	flowers	SN, IV, HD, LD, NC
Pomegranate (*Punica granatum*)	flowers	All
Princess flower (*Tibouchina urvilleana*)	flowers	NC, SC
Chilean guava (*Ugni molinae, Myrtus ugni*)	flowers	IV, NC, SC

Autumn

Chokecherry (*Aronia*)	berries	SN, IV
Barberry (*Berberis*)	berries	All
Beautyberry (*Callicarpa*)	berries	SN, IV, NC, SC
Lemon bottlebrush (*Callistemon citrinus*)	flowers	IV, LD, NC, SC
Camellia (*Camellia sasanqua*)	flowers	SN, IV, NC, SC
Cleyera (*Cleyera japonica, Eurya ochnacea*)	flowers	SN, IV, NC, SC
Cotoneaster (*Cotoneaster*)	berries	All
Silverberry (*Elaeagnus pungens*)	flowers	All
Natal coral tree (*Erythrina humeana*)	flowers	IV, LD, NC, SC

Winged euonymus (*Euonymus alata*)	foliage	SN, IV, NC
Fuchsia (*Fuchsia*)	flowers	SN, IV, NC, SC
Oakleaf hydrangea (*Hydrangea quercifolia*)	foliage	All
Holly (*Ilex*)	berries	All
Jasmine (*Jasminum*)	flowers	All
Nandina, Heavenly bamboo (*Nandina domestica*)	berries	All
Firethorn, Pyracantha (*Pyracantha*)	berries	IV, HD, LD, NC, SC
Sumac (*Rhus*)	berries, foliage	All
Tea viburnum (*Viburnum setigerum*)	berries	All
Laurustinus (*Viburnum tinus*)	berries	SN, IV, LD, NC, SC

Winter

Chokeberry (*Aronia*)	berries	SN, IV
Camellia (*Camellia*)	flowers	SN, IV, NC, SC
Flowering quince (*Chaenomeles*)	flowers	All
Wintersweet (*Chimonanthus praecox*)	flowers	SN, IV, NC
Redtwig dogwood (*Cornus stolonifera*)	red twigs	SN, IV, NC, SC
Fragrant winter hazel (*Corylopsis glabrescens*)	flowers	SN, IV, NC
Winter daphne (*Daphne odora*)	flowers	SN, IV, NC, SC
Purple hop bush (*Dodonaea viscosa* 'Purpurea')	foliage	SN, IV, LD, NC, SC
Poinsettia (*Euphorbia pulcherrima*)	bracts	IV, LD, NC, SC
Witch hazel (*Hamamelis*)	flowers	All
Winter jasmine (*Jasminum nudiflorum*)	flowers	All
Kerria (*Kerria japonica*)	stems	All
Winter honeysuckle (*Lonicera fragrantissima*)	flowers	SN, IV, NC, SC
Oregon grape (*Mahonia aquifolium*)	foliage	SN, IV, HD, NC, SC
Melaleuca (*Melaleuca*)	bark	IV, LD, NC, SC
Sweet olive (*Osmanthus fragrans*)	flowers	IV, LD, NC, SC
Lily-of-the-valley shrub (*Pieris japonica*)	buds	SN, IV, NC
Willow pittosporum (*Pittosporum phillyraeoides*)	flowers	IV, LD, NC, SC
Rhaphiolepis (*Rhaphiolepis*)	flowers	IV, LD, NC, SC
White flowering currant (*Ribes indecorum*)	flowers	IV, HD, NC, SC
Flame willow (*Salix* 'Flame')	bark	All
Stachyurus (*Stachyurus praecox*)	flowers	SN, IV, NC
Yew (*Taxus*)	berries	SN, IV, NC, SC
Laurustinus (*Viburnum tinus*)	berries	SN, IV, NC, SC

ROSES

Californians have long been rose-lovers, probably because our climate is almost ideally adapted to the requirements of the rose. Mild winters are well suited to the rose's needs, and even a lack of summer rain does not hold back older plants that have developed large root structures. In the lists to come, you will find roses old and new, roses for shade, roses for hedges, roses that naturalize, roses that tolerate drought, roses that grow on massive plants, roses that are some of the best miniatures around, and many more. Whether you are an admitted rosarian or not, you will find a rose in these lists that, once added to your garden, will make you a rosarian at heart.

When selecting roses for your garden, consult with your local nursery about cold-hardiness, cultivation recommendations, and what sort of sprays you might need to help your roses withstand pests and diseases. Also ask them about deadheading blossoms, and cutting back canes.

Generally speaking, roses do best in full sun and where there is good air circulation. They adapt to various soil conditions but prefer good drainage and a soil that is mildly acidic. Roots of roses grow deep into the soil—or should—so prepare the area well when introducing a new rose plant. If your soil is heavy clay that drains poorly, make sure you dig a large hole and improve the soil with organic matter, or try a raised bed. Sandy soil that drains too quickly should be improved as well. In colder areas of California, you may want to plant roses in a sheltered area and provide some additional protection during winter.

Throughout this chapter, fragrant roses are marked with the letter F in parentheses after their names.

ROSES MOST OFTEN FOUND GROWING IN OLD CALIFORNIA GARDENS

Have you ever driven down a two-lane country blacktop road in spring and seen a huge, sprawling, ungainly rose covered with hundreds of tiny bright pink pompons, a rose so eager to reroot itself that it has knocked over a fence and spread into the next property? If you have, it is very likely you have just met Dorothy Perkins, an outstanding, drought-tolerant rambler that was once the most widely planted variety of rose in our state.

The roses in this list are the ones you will find in cemeteries, abandoned farmsteads, and older neighborhoods of long-settled towns. Some were once grown as rootstocks and are found in old gardens because they have outlived the hybrid teas once grafted to them. Many of them are recorded in the book *Our Old-Fashioned Flowers* (published by the Pasadena Humane Society in 1947), in which poet and gardener Olive Percival listed California's favorite oldest plants, including a short list of old roses. If you live in a vintage house, you can enhance your ties to history by planting some of these romantic remnants of the past. For the easiest roses to care for, you can do no better than to choose from the old roses that seem to want to naturalize in California. If you value your fences, however, you might think twice about the Dorothy Perkins and the two Lady Banks varieties, which seem determined to level any impediment to their continued growth.

Roses marked F are fragrant; those marked R were once grown as rootstocks.

Eglantine

Rose	Class	Introduced
American Pillar	Climber	1902
Belle of Portugal	Climber	1903
California Hippolyte	Gallica	19th century
Cherokee Rose, *R. laevigata*	Species	1759
Climbing Cécile Brunner (F)	Polyantha climber	1894
Dorothy Perkins	Rambler	1901
Dr. Huey (F, R)	Rambler	1914
Dr. W. Van Fleet (F)	Rambler	1910
Eglantine, Sweetbriar, *R. eglanteria*	Species	ca. 1551
Excelsa, Red Dorothy Perkins	Rambler	1909
Fortuniana (F)	Banksia climber	1850
Fun Jwan Lo, *R. odorata* (R)	Shrub	1924 in California
Gloire des Rosomanes, Ragged Robin (F, R)	China	1825
Hermosa, Armosa (F)	China	1840
Lady Banks (F)	Banksia	1807
Lady Banks Yellow (F)	Banksia	1824
New Dawn (F)	Rambler	1930
Old Blush (F)	China	1752
Paul's Scarlet Climber	Polyantha climber	1916
Perle d'Or (F)	China	1884
Prosperity	Hybrid musk	1919
Radiance	Hybrid tea	1908
Ramona	Laevigata climber	1913
Russelliana (F)	Polyantha climber	1840

Silver Moon (F)	Laevigata climber	1910
Tausendschoen	Polyantha climber	1906
Veilchenblau (F)	Polyantha climber	1909
White Dorothy	Rambler	1908

Bob Edberg of Limberlost Roses in Van Nuys says that his interest is antique roses. "I don't pay that much attention to the modern roses. Modern roses are inferior in a number of ways. The fragrance is hybridized out of them, for example, and when you look at pictures of them in a catalogue, they all look alike—only the color is different. Old roses have more history, and they have better names, like Comtesse Cecilie de Chabrillant, which is a highly fragrant, light-pink hybrid perpetual introduced in 1858. All hybrid perpetuals are very fragrant repeat bloomers. But everyone interested in roses has a very slanted viewpoint and we can be evangelical about our own area of interest."

ROSES THAT BLOOM ONCE A YEAR ON MASSIVE PLANTS

The roses in this list bloom only once in a season, and although reblooming roses are valued because of their longer period of bloom, these extremely large plants with their once-a-year blooms will give you more flowers at one time than any recurrent roses will. When planted near a road or street, they are traffic stoppers during the three weeks or so that they put on their annual show.

Grow these monsters on heavy-duty pergolas, against rough walls, into trees, or over the top of any small building you want to lose. Give them summer water so that they can reach their greatest potential. Most of them are easy to grow and will require little or no spraying because they are simply too busy putting on size to pause for diseases.

Rose	Class	Color
Albertine (F)	Rambler	Pink
Alchemist	Climber	Yellow
American Pillar	Climber	Pink
Belle of Portugal	Gigantea climber	Pink
Bleu Magenta	Polyantha rambler	Purple
Dorothy Perkins	Rambler	Pink
Excelsa, Red Dorothy Perkins	Rambler	Red
Félicité et Perpétué	Climber	White
Fortuniana (F)	Banksia climber	White
Hiawatha	Polyantha climber	Red
Lady Banks (F)	Banksia	White
Lady Banks Yellow (F)	Banksia	Yellow

Most roses are pruned at the end of their dormant season, before the new growing season begins. Ramblers, however, are usually pruned just after their bloom period. Climbers can be pruned lightly after their blooming period, and then again in spring.

ROSES FOR CUT FLOWERS

Generally speaking, the thicker the petal substance, the longer a rose will last when cut. The roses in this list are just some of those that have good stem length and hold up well as cut flowers. You will doubtless discover many more on your own.

Proper handling of the blossoms will add to their life in arrangements. Cut the flowers in the early morning, choosing those which have not yet fully opened. Recut the stems under water as you make up the final arrangement. Use a commercial flower preservative, or a mixture of distilled water and flat lemon-lime soda. Another old-time trick is dissolving an aspirin tablet in the water. Changing the water daily helps lengthen the beauty of the arrangement.

Rose	Class	Color
Archduke Charles (F)	China	Deep pink
Belle Story (F)	Shrub	Pink
Chrysler Imperial (F)	Hybrid tea	Red
Climbing Sombreuil (F)	Tea climber	White
Cornelia (F)	Shrub	Pink and apricot
Double Delight (F)	Hybrid tea	Cerise on white
Eutin	Floribunda	Red
Fortune's Double Yellow (F)	China	Yellow
Graham Thomas (F)	Shrub	Yellow
Green Rose	China	Green and red
Iceberg (F)	Floribunda	White
Lavender Lassie (F)	Shrub	Lavender-pink
Mme. Hardy (F)	Damask	White
Monsieur Tillier	Tea	Red and white
Mrs. B. R. Cant (F)	Tea	Deep pink
Mrs. Dudley Cross (F)	Tea	Creamy yellow
Mrs. Herbert Stevens (F)	Climber	White
New Dawn (F)	Rambler	Pink
Paul Neyron (F)	Hybrid perpetual	Cerise
Radiance (F)	Hybrid tea	Pink
Souvenir de la Malmaison (F)	Bourbon	Pink
Talisman (F)	Hybrid tea	Copper and yellow
Timeless (F)	Hybrid tea	Deep pink
Touch of Class	Hybrid tea	Orange-pink

"In our area everything grows," notes Donna Bauman of Branscomb Nursery in Healdsburg. "We've got great farming soil!" Donna is particularly fond of long-stemmed tea roses, which if treated right will bloom from the end of March until the end of December in the North Coast region. Deadheading spent blossoms encourages tea roses to set a second or third crop of flowers, says Donna. "Pruning is the key to constant blooms. Cut off the old flowers before they form hips, and deadhead at the fifth leaf that points outward. This keeps the rose open at the center, and it's the fifth leaf that has the bud on it for the next flower."

DROUGHT-TOLERANT ROSES

Alice Flores, of White Rabbit Roses in Elk, has been researching drought-tolerant roses for quite a few years and is currently working on a book about them. Asked for a short list, she says, "Hard choices! They *are* all good roses." Nevertheless, she shortened her extensive catalogue of old garden roses for these pages. "The roses in my list are those which I have found in my rambles through the hills and valleys of Northern California," she notes, adding "They are growing without benefit of fertilizers, pruning, or water." Growing in their natural settings—cemeteries, homesteads, roadsides, and out-of-the-way places—these roses may not be exhibition quality, Alice says, "but they are often spectacularly beautiful—all the more so when they are discovered cascading from a tree or springing from a hillside in the middle of nowhere. With carefully measured amounts of water in a garden situation, these roses will perform with great vigor and produce great beauty."

Alice advises, "No rose prefers growing without water. Any rose will look greener and bloom more reliably and heavily if given a modicum of moisture." The roses in this list can do nicely on the water nature provides, and will do even better if you help out a little.

Rose	Class	Color
Aglaia (F)	Multiflora rambler	Yellow
Alberic Barbier (F)	Luciae rambler	Creamy yellow
Alexander Girault (F)	Wichuraiana rambler	Coral red
Baltimore Belle (F)	Setigera rambler	Pink
Belle of Portugal (F)	Climbing tea	Pink
Climbing Peace (F)	Hybrid tea	Yellow with pink
Cornelia (F)	Hybrid musk	Peach-pink
Dorothy Perkins	Wichuraiana rambler	Pink
Duchesse de Brabant (F)	Tea	Pink
Elsie Poulsen (F)	Floribunda	Red-pink
Francois Juranville (F)	Wichuraiana rambler	Coral
Gardenia (F)	Wichuraiana rambler	Yellow-cream
John Hopper (F)	Hybrid perpetual	Deep pink
Lady Hillingdon (F)	Tea	Apricot
Mermaid (F)	Bracteata hybrid	Yellow
Mme. Gabriel Luizet (F)	Hybrid perpetual	Lilac-pink
Mme. Gregoire Staechelin (F)	Hybrid tea climber	Deep pink
New Dawn (F)	Wichuraiana rambler	Blush pink
Old Blush (F)	China	Pink
Penelope (F)	Hybrid musk	Pink-apricot
R. nutkana (F)	Species	Pink
R. rugosa 'Alba' (F)	Rugosa	White
R. rugosa 'Rubra' (F)	Rugosa	Deep pink
Rambling Rector (F)	Multiflora rambler	White
Veilchenblau (F)	Multiflora rambler	Purple

A DOZEN GREAT MINIATURE ROSES

Bob Coates of Regan Nursery in Fremont, which he says is "the largest retail nursery for roses west of the Rockies," has worked with roses "for a good long time." In fact, "You can say I've worked heavily in roses for the last ten years." Bob gives us this list of a dozen miniature roses.

Pinstripe and Sweet Chariot are very fragrant roses, but Bob notes that most miniatures are not. Gourmet Popcorn, Figurine, and Little Artist are moderately fragrant. Asked about any favorites, Bob says that would be Sweet Chariot, a purple-red, very fragrant, very beautiful, weeping miniature that reaches a diameter of 2 feet. Sweet Chariot also comes in a tree form; it's grafted onto a 36-inch standard.

"Miniatures' main problems," Bob says, "occur in hot weather, when they're susceptible to mites. In July and August, spray them with a miticide."

Rose	Color
Alfi	Lavender-pink
Baby Grand	Pink
Figurine (F)	Pink and white
Gingerbread	Apricot
Golden Sunblaze	Yellow
Gourmet Popcorn (F)	White
Jitterbug	Orange
Little Artist (F)	Red with white center
Pinstripe (F)	Red and white
Sweet Chariot (F)	Purple-red
Texas	Yellow
Winsome	Magenta

Miniature
roses

GREAT PILLAR ROSES

These well-mannered climbing roses won't outgrow their supports. They can be held to 7 to 12 feet and will generally take well to training as moderate climbers on pillars, fences, and trellises. When training roses onto pillars, do not let them reach straight up. Even though they will cover the pillar faster that way, most of the blooms will be at the top. Instead, gently wrap or braid the young canes around the pillar. Not only will they look less leggy, but rose canes trained to the side will bloom more prolifically.

When selecting pillar roses for a gateway, near a door, or where children will be playing, be sure to consider the beautiful and thornless Zephirine Drouhin. Although not a prolific bloomer, it is one of the best mannered, and its bright pink blossoms are sweetly fragrant. For other candidates, see the list of roses with no or few thorns.

Rose	Class	Color
Alister Stella Grey (F)	Noisette	Yellow
Belinda (F)	Shrub	Deep pink
Buff Beauty (F)	Shrub	Yellow
Celine Forestier (F)	Noisette	Yellow
Champney's Pink Cluster (F)	Noisette	Pink
Climbing American Beauty	Climber	Cerise
Climbing Frau Karl Druschki	Perpetual climber	White

Dortmund (F)	Climber	Red with white center
Joseph's Coat	Climber	Orange and yellow
Mme. Ernst Calvat (F)	Bourbon	Pink
Nur Mahal (F)	Shrub	Cerise
Prosperity (F)	Shrub	White
Sombreuil (F)	Tea climber	White
Zephirine Drouhin (F)	Bourbon	Pink

ROSES THAT DO WELL IN POTS

A group or row of roses growing in containers can make a dramatic statement in an intimate garden space. They work especially well on a patio or deck, where the flowers can be examined up close. The varieties listed here average 2 to 3 feet in height and will endure clipping to keep them compact. For the names of even smaller roses, also suitable for container planting, see the list of roses for edging garden beds, immediately below.

Be sure to give roses grown in containers good drainage. Also, water and fertilize them more often than roses planted in the ground. One way to provide water for them is with an inconspicuous automated drip system that runs from pot to pot. Such a set-up will enable you to take extended vacations and return to healthy, thriving plants.

The smaller roses in this list will live happily in a 7-gallon terra-cotta pot; the others may prefer a 15-gallon terra-cotta pot or wooden tub. Large tubs can be wheeled around on a hand truck, which means that you can rearrange the containers at will to bring flowering plants in close and rotate those not in bloom to a rear position.

Rose	Class	Color
All That Jazz	Shrub	Orange-pink
Clotilde Soupert	Polyantha	Pink
Comtesse du Cayla (F)	China	Orange and pink
Dame de Coeur	Hybrid tea	Red
Double Delight (F)	Hybrid tea	Cerise on white
Duchesse de Brabant (F)	Tea	Pink
Gloire des Rosomanes (F)	China	Crimson
Green Rose	China	Green and red
Grüss an Aachen (F)	Floribunda	Pink on cream
Hermosa (F)	China	Pink
Irene of Denmark (F)	Floribunda	Cream
Le Vésuve (F)	China	Pink
Margo Koster	Polyantha	Orange
Marie van Houtte	Tea	Blush and orange
Mme. Lambard (F)	Tea	Pink and salmon
Mrs. Oakley Fisher (F)	Hybrid tea	Orange on yellow
Rosette Delizy (F)	Tea	Yellow and deep pink
Rouletii	China	Pink
The Fairy (F)	Polyantha	Pink
Valentine Heart (F)	Floribunda	Pink

TRAILING ROSES THAT CAN COVER THE GROUND

Roses are not what most people think of when they speak of ground covers, but those with trailing canes perform admirably when planted along steep banks and for erosion control. They also work well on roadside cuts, where they provide seasonal color and don't block the view. Smaller trailing roses—such as Nozomi and Sea Foam—are often used in conjunction with garden water features, massing around fountains or waterfalls, for instance, or overhanging a natural-looking creek.

The most vigorous rose in this list, Dorothy Perkins, is remarkably proficient at erosion control. It was planted along many railroad embankments in the early twentieth century to stabilize the newly cut soil. Its bright pink flowers intrigued the train passengers, and its thorny, mounded mass provided an effective barrier against trespassers.

Rose	Class	Color
Alba Meidiland	Shrub	White
Dorothy Perkins	Rambler	Pink
Excelsa, Red Dorothy Perkins	Rambler	Red
Gardenia (F)	Rambler	Cream
Jeanne Lajoie	Miniature rambler	Pink
Max Graf (F)	Rugosa	Pink
Meillandina	Miniature	Red
Nozomi	Miniature climber	Pink and white
Memorial Rose, R. wichuraiana (F)	Species	White
Raubritter (F)	Shrub	Pink
Scarlet Meidiland	Shrub	Red
Sea Foam (F)	Shrub	White
Surrey	Shrub	Deep pink
The Fairy (F)	Polyantha	Pink

REBLOOMING ROSES ON MASSIVE PLANTS

These plants may not reach the same monstrous size as the ones in the list of once-a-year bloomers on page 113. Still, at 12 to 20 feet in length, they require more space than the average climbing rose. Give them regular summer watering and a sturdy garden structure to lean on. They are not so weighty that they will tear down a fence, but they will most likely be too much for a flimsy, prefabricated lattice-work trellis. These large roses perform admirably when trained up onto stout pergolas.

Rose	Class	Color
Climbing Cécile Brunner (F)	Polyantha climber	Pink
Climbing Crimson Glory	Hybrid tea climber	Red
Climbing Iceberg	Floribunda climber	White
Climbing Lady Hillingdon (F)	Tea climber	Apricot
Climbing Queen Elizabeth	Floribunda climber	Pink
Climbing Souvenir de la Malmaison (F)	Bourbon climber	Blush white
Dortmund (F)	Climber	Red with white center
Jaune Desprez (F)	Noisette	Peach

Kathleen Harrop (F)	Bourbon	Pink
Lamarque (F)	Noisette climber	White
Mermaid (F)	Climber	Yellow
Mme. Alfred Carrière (F)	Noisette	White
New Dawn (F)	Rambler	Pink
Phyllis Bide (F)	Polyantha climber	Variegated
Sally Holmes	Shrub	White
Skyrocket	Shrub	Red

ROSES FOR EDGING GARDEN BEDS

Roses that naturally grow to 1 to 2 feet in height or can be kept to that level by clipping make good container plants, but their diminutive size and repeated blooms also encourage us to use them as accents in the small garden. These roses of small stature make attractive miniature hedges, or borders around beds of taller plants. One pretty use for them is in the front yard, where their thorniness will discourage intruders but their short stature will allow passersby to see past them to beds of annuals or perennials.

Rose	Class	Color
Apricot Sunblaze (F)	Dwarf patio	Orange-red
Baby Faurax	Polyantha	Pink and white
China Doll	Polyantha	Deep pink
Drummer Boy	Dwarf patio	Red
Gingerbread	Miniature	Apricot
Gourmet Popcorn (F)	Miniature	White
Katharina Zeimet	Polyantha	White
Margo Koster	Polyantha	Orange
Marie Pavié (F)	Polyantha	Blush white
Miss Edith Cavell	Polyantha	Red
Pierrine	Miniature	Pink
Rouletii	China	Pink
Starina	Miniature	Orange-red
Sweet Chariot (F)	Miniature	Purple-red
Texas	Miniature	Yellow
White Pet	Polyantha	White
Yvonne Rabier (F)	Polyantha	White

"What's in a name?" Juliet asked, and promptly added, "A rose by any other name would smell as sweet." Just the word "rose" will conjure up sweet fragrances. But when we consider the names of individual roses, we have further associations. Many people experience name recognition when they hear of the roses Dolly Parton, Herbert Hoover, Maria Callas, Ingrid Bergman, and John F. Kennedy. In Great Britain you will find roses named for Queen Elizabeth and the Duke of Edinburgh. A number of roses are named for British actors, such as Susan Hampshire, Nigel Hawthorne, James Mason, Felicity Kendall. Harold Macmillan shows they haven't neglected their politicians either.

ROSES THAT TOLERATE SEA SPRAY AND FOG

Roses grown near the ocean must tolerate some salt spray, and salt-tolerant varieties can be found in many rose classes, but they are universal in the class of rugosas, which derive their breeding from the wild "Ramana Rose" of Japan's beachfront areas. Along California's North Coast, besides the problem of salt spray, misty weather leads to balled blossoms on varieties with soft-textured petals. In spring, when the fog stays away, you may get quite a show from such varieties, but come summer, when the morning and evening fogs settle in, the balled blossoms don't merely fail to open, they become moldy and often rot right on the plant.

The following list of salt-spray and fog-tolerant roses comes from Liselotte Erlanger Glozer, who has grown them in Mendocino for decades, within a few hundred yards of the Pacific Ocean. A cheerful Darwinian, Liselotte loves the old roses best of all, but with the practical wisdom of her 80 years, she declares, "I don't care how beautiful they are. If they don't like it here, I ship them off to my friends in Sacramento!" She says that roses with 25 or fewer petals are less likely to ball, and that most large-flowered white roses have thin and tender petals. "I haven't yet found a large-flowered white rose that succeeds in foggy, wet weather. John F. Kennedy balls badly, and Frau Karl Druschki is a total disaster." Instead, she turns to the stout-blossomed hybrid teas. Their pert, shell-like petals open especially well under trying weather conditions.

Rose	Class	Color
Belle of Portugal	Gigantea climber	Pink
Duchesse de Brabant (F)	Tea	Pink
Golden Showers (F)	Climber	Yellow
Grüss an Aachen (F)	Floribunda	Pink on white
Hansa (F)	Rugosa	Purple-red
Joseph's Coat (F)	Climber	Orange and yellow
Lady Banks (F)	Banksia	White
Lady Banks Yellow (F)	Banksia	Yellow
Margo Koster	Polyantha	Orange
Scabrosa (F)	Rugosa	Cerise
Sutter's Gold (F)	Hybrid tea	Yellow

SUPERIOR OLD ROSES

According to Miriam Wilkins, one of the founders of the Heritage Roses Group and an organizer of the Celebration of Old Roses in El Cerrito, "California rosarians are able to grow any class of the genus *Rosa*. In the south, gardeners revel in teas and noisettes, which bloom all year long and do not mind warm temperatures. Northerners mainly grow the Old European roses and rugosas, which tolerate the cold. Experts can advise you on what to grow in your area."

Miriam notes that the species roses have been around for 50 million years, and fossils found in Colorado date back 35 million years. "This elegant class boasts some glorious roses. If you have a large property, you can grow *R. mulliganii*, which scents the entire yard with its white blossoms." You also need lots of room for the pink-blossomed hybrid gigantea Belle of Portugal, "which goes to 60 feet or more and needs a tree for support. Its seedling, Susan Louise, looks like its parent, is a manageable size, and a repeat bloomer." Miriam says Mermaid, a hybrid bracteata, produces yellow blooms year round and can cover a garage; its seedling, Happenstance, is low growing but has the same large blossoms, although with smaller leaves. She suggests planting the parent behind and above, the seedling below.

When the china roses were crossed with the once-bloomers to produce recurrent blooms, Miriam says the shape and scent suffered, but the all-year bloom was a plus. "The top china for me is Mutabilis, a large bush always full of single-flower roses, which change color from yellow to red, their petals in disarray." She notes, however, that most chinas are not tall and not very fragrant. The old roses Miriam considers especially superior and well suited to California gardens are listed below.

Rose	Class	Color
American Pillar	Rambler	Cerise with white
Belle of Portugal	Gigantea climber	Pink
Charles de Mills (F)	Gallica	Red
Chromatella (F)	Noisette	Yellow
Comte de Chambord (F)	Portland	Pink
Delicata (F)	Rugosa	Cerise
Fantin-Latour (F)	Centifolia	Pale pink
Golden Wings (F)	Shrub	Yellow
Happenstance	Miniature	Yellow
Henri Martin (F)	Moss	Red
Jacques Cartier (F)	Portland	Pink
Kazanlik (F)	Damask	Pink
Konigen von Danemark (F)	Alba	Pink
Lady Hillingdon (F)	Tea climber	Apricot
Lamarque (F)	Noisette climber	White
Louise Odier (F)	Bourbon	Pink
Mermaid (F)	Bracteata hybrid	Yellow
Mme. Hardy (F)	Damask	White
Mme. Louis Lévèque (F)	Moss	Pink
Monsieur Tillier	Tea	Red
Mutabilis	China	Red, pale yellow, copper
Nuits de Young (F)	Moss	Red
Reine des Violettes (F)	Hybrid perpetual	Cerise-violet
Reine Victoria (F)	Bourbon	Pink
Roger Lambelin (F)	Hybrid perpetual	Red with white
R. alba semiplena (F)	Alba	White
R. mulliganii (F)	Species	White
Roseraie de l'Hay (F)	Rugosa	Purple-red
Sombreuil (F)	Tea	White
Susan Louise (F)	Shrub	Pink

"Species roses" are the wild, ancient roses native to many areas of the world. The flowers of species roses are usually flat, with five petals. You will see these five-petal flowers on the Eglantine Rose (R. eglanteria), Dog Rose (R. canina), and Cherokee Rose (R. laevigata). There are double-flowered species roses as well, such as Lady Banks, R. banksiae alba-plena, a double white rose, and R. banksiae lutea, or Lady Banks Yellow.

ROSES FOR NATURALIZING

Almost every growing zone in the Northern Hemisphere can claim at least one species of native rose. Their ubiquitousness and adaptability makes roses a good choice for naturalization, even in tough sites. Take care of them until they are established, then let them take care of themselves. The most obvious choices for naturalization are the species roses, but many vigorous hybrids deliver the toughness of a wild rose with the added flower size or petal count of a domestic variety.

Rose	Class	Color
Cherokee Rose, *R. laevigata* (F)	Species	White
Climbing Cécile Brunner (F)	Polyantha climber	Pink
Cramoisi Superieur (F)	China	Red
Dorothy Perkins	Rambler	Pink
Eglantine, Sweetbriar, *R. eglanteria* (F)	Species	Pink
Escapade (F)	Floribunda	Cerise on white
Fellemberg (F)	China	Red
Gardenia (F)	Rambler	Cream
Lady Banks (F)	Banksia	White
Lady Banks Yellow (F)	Banksia	Yellow
Mermaid (F)	Climber	Yellow
New Dawn (F)	Rambler	Pink
Prairie Rose, *R. setigera* (F)	Species	Cerise
R. multiflora grandiflora (F)	Species	White
R. odorata	Species	Pale pink
Silver Moon (F)	Climber	White
Stanwell Perpetual (F)	Pimpinellifolia	Pink
Trier (F)	Shrub	Cream
Veilchenblau (F)	Polyantha climber	Purple

ROSES THAT MAKE GOOD HEDGES

Rose hedges are not evergreen, but they make up for that with fabulous displays of color. Most landscapers design rose hedges of a single variety, but consider hedges of mixed varieties in harmonious colors (for instance, pink, cerise, and lavender shades, or gold, apricot, and orange). When designing a mixed variety hedge, you will do best if you determine the relative bloom time for each variety. Arrange for early, mid-season, and late bloomers to alternate down the row. This will give a long-lasting display of flowers as the plants successively reach their peak bloom times.

Most varieties of tea roses and china roses make good medium-sized hedges. The twiggy polyanthas can be used for lower, denser hedging. The shrub roses will bloom in both sun and partial shade, so if you are planning a long hedge that wends its way through tree or building shade, they may be the best choice.

Rose	Class	Color
2 to 3 Feet		
Grüss an Aachen (F)	Floribunda	Pink on cream
Marie-Jeanne	Polyantha	Cream
Marie van Houtte	Tea	Pink
Mutabilis	China	Red, pale yellow, copper
Old Blush	China	Pink
Surrey	Shrub	Deep pink
4 to 5 Feet		
Ballerina	Polyantha	Pink on white
Belinda (F)	Shrub	Deep pink
Buff Beauty (F)	Shrub	Yellow
Erfurt	Shrub	Cerise and white
Eutin	Floribunda	Red
Félicité Parmentier (F)	Alba	Pink
Gloire des Rosomanes (F)	China	Crimson
Golden Wings (F)	Shrub	Yellow
Hansa (F)	Rugosa	Purple-red
Le Vésuve (F)	China	Pink
Marjorie Fair (F)	Polyantha	Cerise and white
Nur Mahal (F)	Shrub	Cerise
Penelope (F)	Shrub	Pink-apricot
Sparrieshoop (F)	Shrub	Pink
6 to 7 Feet		
R. rugosa rubra (F)	Rugosa	Purple-red
Great Maiden's Blush (F)	Alba	Pink
Mrs. B. R. Cant (F)	Tea	Deep pink
Pax (F)	Shrub	White
8 Feet or More		
Fortune's Double Yellow (F)	China	Yellow
Nevada (F)	Shrub	White
Sarah Van Fleet	Rugosa	Pink
Zephirine Drouhin (F)	Bourbon	Pink

"Miniature roses are excellent for hedges," notes Ralph Moore, owner of Sequoia Nursery in Visalia. He has been breeding roses for decades and has a special interest in miniatures. "For a hedge, select miniature roses with similar growing habit and size of flower," he advises. "Plant the roses 2 feet apart. Prune to shape as the plants mature, and groom the plants after each flush of bloom to increase flowering." For a miniature rose hedge, Ralph suggests Galaxy, Little Eskimo, Magic Carousel, Judy Fischer, and Lavender Jewel.

ROSES FOR OLD-FASHIONED PEGGING

Pegging is an old way to train roses for optimal bloom. The technique takes advantage of the natural inclination of horizontal rose canes to break into flower along their length. The best roses for pegging are those with flexible canes that reach 5 to 7 feet in length. Let the canes grow out until they have begun to harden up, then gently arch them back to the ground, securing them with a long hook or "peg." Space the canes out evenly, in a sun-wheel effect, interlocking the canes from neighboring roses so that no part of the ground is left entirely bare. Pegged roses look best when viewed on a slight hillside slope or from a second-story window. Although they are a bit unkempt when their new growth is still too tender to train over, a group of well-pegged roses in bloom is an amazing sight, the underlying structure completely hidden by a profusion of flowers.

Rose	Class	Color
Autumn Damask (F)	Damask	Pink
Conrad Ferdinand Meyer	Rugosa	Pink
Constance Spry (F)	Climber	Pink
Dortmund	Climber	Red and white
Frau Karl Druschki	Hybrid perpetual	Pink on white
Honorine de Brabant	Bourbon	Cerise and pink
Mme. Ernst Calvat	Bourbon	Pink
Mme. Isaac Pereire (F)	Bourbon	Cerise
Variegata di Bologna (F)	Bourbon	Red and white

ROSES WITH FEW OR NO THORNS

If a rose has ever drawn blood, you may appreciate the roses in this list. They are good for gardens where children play, or any trafficked areas where people may brush against them. They are also some of the best roses around.

Rose	Class	Color
Alister Stella Gray (F)	Noisette	Yellow
Amadis	Boursault	Red
Blush Noisette (F)	Noisette	Pink
Cécile Brunner (F)	Polyantha	Pink
Charles de Mills (F)	Gallica	Red
Crépuscule (F)	Noisette climber	Peach
Félicité et Perpétué	Climber	White
Golden Wings (F)	Shrub	Yellow
Kathleen Harrop (F)	Bourbon	Pink
La Belle Sultane (F)	Gallica	Purple
Lamarque (F)	Noisette climber	White
Louise Odier (F)	Bourbon	Pink
Mme. Alfred Carrière (F)	Noisette	White
Mrs. Dudley Cross (F)	Tea	Cream and pink
Old Blush (F)	China	Pink
Perle d'Or (F)	Polyantha	Peach and pink
Reine des Violettes (F)	Hybrid perpetual	Cerise-violet
Tausendschoen (F)	Polyantha climber	Pink
Zephirine Drouhin (F)	Bourbon	Deep pink

THE MOST FRAGRANT ROSES

Rose fragrance is a very personal matter. Again and again experience has shown that a variety that is very fragrant to one person will be almost odorless or even unpleasant to another. For many people the "true" rose scent is the one they first smelled when they were young, and many gardeners in their fifties or older believe that the true rose scent belongs only to members of the damask group or to hybrid teas descended from damasks. This is the fragrance one finds most often in rose-scented toiletries and potpourri. To some rose-fanciers, only the hybrid teas with an orange-spice tea aroma (many of them relatives of Talisman) bear the true rose scent reminiscent of a visit to grandmother. It is probable that with the current popularity of the musky and spicy David Austin English roses, a new generation of gardeners will arise for whom the true rose fragrance will only be found in that class, as exemplified in varieties like Tamara and Belle Story.

This list comprises the most fragrant roses according to Gregg Lowery and Philip Robinson of Vintage Gardens in Sebastopol. They rank roses for perfume on a scale of 1 to 4, adjusting the rankings for seasonal variations and by comparing notes with other growers. The following varieties each scored a 4, but that does not mean they smell the same; some have a hint of raspberry, some of apricot, and some smell like . . . a visit to grandmother.

Rose	Class	Color
Blanc Double de Coubert	Rugosa	White
Blanchefleur	Centifolia	White
Blush Noisette	Noisette	Pink
Catalonia	Hybrid tea	Orange
Charles de Gaulle	Hybrid tea	Purple
Condessa de Sástago	Hybrid tea	Coral and yellow
Crimson Glory	Hybrid tea	Red
Deuil de Dr. Reynaud	Bourbon	Deep pink
Double Delight	Hybrid tea	Cerise on white
Duquesa de Peñaranda	Hybrid tea	Orange
Elegant Gallica	Gallica	Purple-pink
Félicité Parmentier	Alba	Pink
Fragrant Cloud	Hybrid tea	Red
Great Maiden's Blush	Alba	Pink
Grüss an Aachen	Floribunda	Pink on cream
Halloween	Hybrid tea	Orange
Lemon Spice	Floribunda	Yellow
Marie Pavié	Polyantha	Blush white
Mme. Lambard	Tea	Pink and salmon
Moonsprite	Floribunda	White
Mrs. B. R. Cant	Tea	Deep pink
Nastarana	Noisette	White
Papa Meilland	Hybrid tea	Red
Rose à Parfum de l'Hay	Rugosa	Red
Sutter's Gold	Hybrid tea	Yellow
Talisman	Hybrid tea	Copper and yellow

 Eglantine is unique among fragrant roses in that its leaves are highly scented. When crushed, they smell like green apples, and the fragrance is especially noticeable during cool or foggy weather, when the scent lingers in the air. For this reason, it was once common to plant eglantines as hedgerows, where passersby could appreciate their aroma from horseback merely by reaching out and crushing a few leaves. Old stands of eglantines are still often found along old California farm driveways, where they have naturalized.

ROSES WITH GREAT HIPS

The rose hip is the seed-containing calyx of the flower, which ripens after the petals drop. Rose hips come in different sizes, shapes, and colors. They can vary from orange to red and even maroon or black. Some are spherical, others vase-shaped or elongated. Many hybrid roses—often those with the most petals—make few or almost no hips. The roses listed below will produce great crops of colorful hips if you don't cut the last batch of flowers.

Rose hips add wonderful winter interest to mixed variety rose hedges, will attract birds to your garden, and are a lovely addition to decorative winter flower arrangements. Their other use is culinary. You frequently see rose hips listed as an ingredient on packages of herbal teas.

Rose	Class
Apothecary's Rose, *R. gallica officinalis*	Gallica
Ballerina	Polyantha
Bonn	Shrub
Carefree Beauty	Shrub
Cherokee Rose, *R. laevigata*	Species
Dog Rose, *R. canina*	Species
Dortmund	Climber
Eglantine, Sweetbriar, *R. eglanteria*	Species
Frau Dagmar Hartopp	Rugosa
Jeanne d'Arc	Alba
Hansa	Rugosa
Herbstfeuer, Autumn Fire	Shrub
Kathleen	Shrub
Kew Rambler	Rambler
La Belle Sultane	Gallica
Lichterloh	Floribunda
Memorial Rose, *R. wichuraiana*	Species
Musk Rose, *R. moschata*	Species
Nur Mahal	Shrub
Old Blush	China
Orangeade	Floribunda
Penelope	Shrub
R. rugosa rubra	Rugosa
Safrano	Tea
Scabrosa	Rugosa
Scharlachglut, Scarlet Fire	Shrub
St. Nicholas	Damask
The Gift	Polyantha
Thérèse Bugnet	Rugosa
Trier	Shrub

Gregg Lowery of Vintage Gardens in Sebastopol highly recommends Orangeade for its prolific and oddly shaped hips. "They are ribbed and for all the world look like tiny pumpkins, which is useful in the fall when you are making Thanksgiving flower arrangements," he says.

The Dog Rose (*R. canina*) is perhaps the best known when it comes to rose hips. This ancient rose is said to be the most common wild rose in the Northern Hemisphere. It tolerates poor soil and shade, and it also does fine in sunny locations with reflected heat. Its fragrant pale-pink or white flowers are succeeded by scarlet hips. This is the hip usually made into jellies or syrups. In fact during World War II, when Great Britain couldn't get hold of much citrus fruit, rose hip syrup was what many relied on as a source of Vitamin C. For rose hip tea, the fruit is usually cut into pieces, dried, and stored until needed.

THE BEST REBLOOMING ROSES

Gregg Lowery and Philip Robinson of Vintage Gardens in Sebastopol propagate thousands of varieties of roses. Since the most-often-asked question they get from their customers is, "What rose will give me the most flowers?" they have kept track of the reblooming patterns of every variety under their care for years, creating a list of sure-fire rebloomers for people who want to have fresh roses at all times of the year. According to Gregg, "These are selected from among our very best performers for superior rebloom. They are ideal choices for the beginner who wants an excellent show of color and the maximum from the rose garden. Most will continue blooming well without any deadheading."

The bloomingest rose in this list may be La Marne. With its small, few-petalled, dark pink and white flowers borne in loose clusters, it is not the prettiest rose in the world, and it is not very fragrant, either, but it tends to outperform the others when it comes to remontancy. Amazingly, it will even do so when planted in partial shade.

Rose	Class	Color
Most China and Noisette roses, and all Tea roses		
Baronne Prévost (F)	Hybrid perpetual	Deep pink
Birdie Blye (F)	Polyantha	Pink
Bouquet d' Or (F)	Climber	Yellow
Buttercup	Hybrid tea	Yellow
Crépuscule (F)	Noisette climber	Peach
Else Poulsen	Floribunda	Cerise
Escapade (F)	Floribunda	Cerise on white
Excellenz von Schubert (F)	Shrub	Purple
Gartendirektor Otto Linne	Shrub	Pink
Grüss an Coburg (F)	Hybrid tea	Apricot-yellow
Grüss an Teplitz	China	Red
Iceberg (F)	Floribunda	White
Irene of Denmark (F)	Floribunda	Cream
Kent	Shrub	White
Kirsten Poulsen	Floribunda	Red
Kitty Kininmonth	Climber	Deep pink
La Marne	Polyantha	Pink
La Tosca (F)	Hybrid tea	Pink
Lady Waterlow (F)	Climber	Pink on pink
Lafayette (F)	Floribunda	Deep pink
Madame Jules Bouché (F)	Hybrid tea	White
Marjorie Fair (F)	Polyantha	Cerise and white
Mistress Bosanquet (F)	Bourbon	Pale pink

Mrs. Herbert Stevens (F)	Climber	White
Mrs. R. M. Finch	Polyantha	Pink
Perle d'Or (F)	Polyantha	Peach and pink
Phyllis Bide (F)	Climber	Variegated
Royal Sunset	Shrub	Orange
Sea Foam (F)	Shrub	White
Surrey	Shrub	Deep pink
White Cap	Climber	White

Timeless, a fragrant and deep-pink hybrid tea, is a favorite of Cindy Milroy of the Red Bluff Garden Center. "It has a beautiful bud, slow to open. In cut arrangements, it outlasts all the other flowers in the mix. It does well in full sun, is good in any climate, and is disease resistant. When all the other roses are taking their rest, this one keeps blooming. Even when the temperature is in the 100s here, the Timeless still keeps opening." Double Delight, another fragrant hybrid tea, is also a favorite. Cindy describes the color as "cream with lots of blushes of pink and red. Each flower on the plant is different from the others. Double Delight is a prolific bloomer, and each bloom is unique."

ROSES FOR PARTIAL SHADE

Although all roses do best with four to six hours of sunlight per day, a few varieties tolerate shade in the form of all-day dappled sunlight under trees or three to four hours of full sun followed by the hard shade of a building or other structure. Chief among shade-tolerating roses are the hybrid musks, or shrub roses, most of which form large bushes that rebloom well, bear small to medium-sized white or pink flowers in clusters, and possess good fragrance.

Three roses in this list deserve special mention. First, the rose most adapted to deep-shade blooming—La Marne—is a hot-pink polyantha, a member of a class not generally known for tolerance for dim light. Another oddity in this list is Eutin, the only truly bright red rose for semi-shade—which also happens to be one of the reddest roses in any class. Finally, Buff Beauty is notable because its fruit-scented, biscuit-colored blooms bleach out to a near-scentless white in less than a day under normal sunlight. If you want to see and smell Buff Beauty at its best, the plants must be situated in partial shade.

To encourage roses to bloom under less than ideal light conditions, feed them extra bonemeal—and be prepared for them to put on a little more size in the shade than they would if grown in full sun.

Rose	Class	Color
Ballerina	Polyantha	Pink on white
Belinda (F)	Shrub	Deep pink
Blush Noisette (F)	Noisette	Pink
Buff Beauty (F)	Shrub	Yellow
Climbing Cécile Brunner	Polyantha climber	Pink
Clotilde Soupert (F)	Polyantha	Pink
Cornelia (F)	Shrub	Pink and apricot
Eutin	Floribunda	Red
Gardenia (F)	Rambler	Cream
Gloire de Dijon	Noisette	Yellow
Hansa (F)	Rugosa	Purple-red

Kathleen (F)	Shrub	Pink
Lady Waterlow (F)	Climber	Pink on pink
La Marne	Polyantha	Pink
Lavender Lassie (F)	Shrub	Lavender-pink
Mme. Alfred Carrière (F)	Noisette	White
Mutabilis	China	Red, pale yellow, copper
Nastarana (F)	Noisette	White
New Dawn (F)	Rambler	Pink
Nur Mahal (F)	Shrub	Cerise
Paul's Scarlet Climber (F)	Polyantha climber	Red
Pax (F)	Shrub	White
Penelope (F)	Shrub	Pink-apricot
Phyllis Bide (F)	Climber	Variegated
Sally Holmes	Shrub	White
Starina	Miniature	Orange-red
Weisse aus Sparrieshoop (F)	Climber	White

For roses that tolerate shade, Miriam Wilkins, one of the founders of the Heritage Roses Group, recommends hybrid musks (a class frequently hidden in the shrub roses category). "They are fragrant, take more shade than most, and bloom continually. Most form large bushes that are fine for background plantings. For yellow, try Buff Beauty. Ballerina is not a tall grower but makes a good showing with vigorous growth and pink blooms. Penelope is one of the best, with pinky-orange roses fading to cream when fully open."

VINES

Vines are among the most dramatic of garden subjects—and the most useful. They soften the harsh lines of fences, posts, and buildings, and they hide unsightly views. They bring fragrance and color to eye level and higher. They create privacy screens and help provide natural air conditioning for homes. Some even work as ground covers when not given anything to climb up onto. To climb, vines need support. Annual vines such as morning glory and scarlet runner beans can grow on any sort of trellis or wire, but permanent, woody landscape vines such as wisteria need something more durable. A long-lasting pergola or arbor built with 4x4s or even thicker lumber is more suitable for their weight.

As the proud designer and owner of a 150-foot-long pergola covered with wisteria, akebia, Virginia creeper, and climbing roses, it may be that my enthusiasm for vines is greater than average—but in my opinion, there is nothing that says "California Gardening" better than a bougainvillea-covered stucco wall or a redwood arbor on which fragrant yellow Lady Banks roses bloom side-by-side with perfumed lavender wisteria.

VINES FOR DRY SITES

Some vines do fine in dry conditions. In fact, hardenbergia would not appreciate any caretaker who has a habit of overwatering. A few, such as queen's wreath, thrive in hot, dry, sunny places. Many of the vines in this list are fairly cold hardy.

Queen's wreath, Rosa de montana (*Antigonon leptopus*)	LD, SC
California clematis (*Clematis lasiantha*)	All
Scarlet clematis (*Clematis texensis*)	All
Lilac vine (*Hardenbergia comptoniana*)	NC, SC
Happy Wanderer hardenbergia (*Hardenbergia violacea* 'Happy Wanderer')	IV, HD, LD, NC, SC
Blue dawn flower (*Ipomoea acuminata*)	IV, LD, NC, SC
Cat's claw (*Macfadyena unguis-cati*)	IV, HD, LD, NC, SC

Cape plumbago (*Plumbago auriculata*)	IV, LD, NC, SC
Pink trumpet vine (*Podranea ricasoliana*)	IV, LD, NC, SC
Cape honeysuckle (*Tecomaria capensis*)	LD, NC, SC

> "Bougainvillea does well in dry sites," advises Wendy Proud of Monrovia Nursery in Azusa. "The new 'Singapore Pink' and 'Singapore White' are compact bush forms with blooms that almost cover the plant from April to October, with some periods of rest." A trumpet creeper variety, *Campsis tagliabuana* 'Madame Galen,' will take dry conditions. "Trumpet creeper is extremely hardy and survives all over the world. A few years ago in Greece, I saw it growing wild. The plant is deciduous, but the show it puts on in one season is amazing. The flowers are 2 to 3 inches long, and vibrant." Wendy notes that a similar plant, *Distictis,* or trumpet vine, is also good for dry sites.

VINES THAT HOLD GROUND ON A SLOPE

Hillside soil may be shallow, and if the hill has been formed by grader work, there may be little or no topsoil left. Because water run-off is dangerous in parts of California where heavy winter rains can lead to mudslides, soil stabilization is both a structural and an esthetic requirement. These fast-growing vines will hold a hillside together, and most will also endure rapid run-off that may leave other plants starving for moisture.

Bougainvillea (*Bougainvillea spectabilis*)	IV, LD, NC, SC
Kangaroo treebine (*Cissus antarctica*)	NC, SC
Winter creeper (*Euonymus fortunei*)	SN, IV, HD, LD, NC
Creeping fig (*Ficus pumila*)	All
Algerian ivy (*Hedera canariensis*)	IV, LD, NC, SC
English ivy (*Hedera helix*)	All
Blue dawn flower (*Ipomoea acuminata*)	IV, LD, NC, SC
Perennial sweet pea (*Lathyrus latifolius*)	All
Japanese honeysuckle (*Lonicera japonica*)	All
Virginia creeper (*Parthenocissus quinquefolia*)	All
Passionflower (*Passiflora*)	All
Knotweed (*Polygonum*)	All
Silver lace vine (*Polygonum aubertii*)	All
Evergreen grape (*Rhoicissus capensis*)	NC, SC
Mexican flame vine (*Senecio confusus*)	LD, NC, SC
Cup-of-gold vine (*Solandra maxima*)	NC, SC
Cape honeysuckle (*Tecomaria capensis*)	IV, HD, LD, NC, SC
Asian jasmine (*Trachelospermum asiaticum*)	All
Star jasmine (*Trachelospermum jasminoides*)	IV, HD, LD, NC, SC

> "Any sort of *Lonicera,* or honeysuckle, does a good job of holding soil on a slope or bank," notes Wendy Proud, a grower at the Monrovia Nursery in Azusa. "Honeysuckle flowers sit up on top of the plant, so you can see them. The 'Halliana' and 'Purpurea' varieties are especially nice because they flower early, about January or February."

VINES FOR ALKALINE SOIL

Alkaline soil can be modified by the regular addition of peat moss and compost, but if the ground water is alkaline as well, you will never be able to permanently correct the condition, and you may just as well plant vines that are adapted to soil alkalinity.

Porcelain berry, Blueberry climber (*Ampelopsis brevipedunculata*)	All
Madeira vine (*Anredera cordifolia*)	All
California dutchman's pipe (*Aristolochia californica*)	SN, IV, NC, SC
Trumpet creeper (*Campsis radicans*)	All
Clematis (*Clematis*)	All
Evergreen clematis (*Clematis armandii*)	All
Scarlet leather flower (*Clematis texensis*)	All
Italian clematis (*Clematis viticella*)	All
Hyacinth bean (*Dolichos lablab*)	All
Creeping fig (*Ficus pumila*)	IV, HD, LD, NC, SC
Perennial sweet pea (*Lathyrus latifolius*)	All
Virginia creeper (*Parthenocissus quinquefolia*)	All
Boston ivy (*Parthenocissus tricuspidata*)	All
Passionflower (*Passiflora*)	All
Knotweed (*Polygonum*)	All
Mexican flame vine (*Senecio confusus*)	LD, NC, SC
Potato vine (*Solanum jasminoides*)	IV, LD, NC, SC
Champanel grape (*Vitis labrusca* 'Champanel')	SN, IV, HD, LD, NC

VINES FOR PARTIAL SHADE

Some vines perform well in partial shade, either in the form of dappled sunlight from tall trees or a building shadow that moves away during the course of the day. Akebia deserves special mention here. A well-mannered vine, it will do quite nicely with its trunk in full shade as long as its canopy has partial sun. Every spring it makes a profusion of bizarre, purple, sticky, fragrant flowers that hang down and catch the eye. For such an easy-growing plant, it is not very common, and if placed around an entrance or gate arbor where visitors are brought face-to-face with the strange flowers, it will be quite a conversation piece.

Five-leaf akebia (*Akebia quinata*)	All
Porcelain berry, Blueberry climber (*Ampelopsis brevipedunculata*)	All
California dutchman's pipe (*Aristolochia californica*)	SN, IV, NC, SC
Climbing snapdragon (*Asarina antirrhinifolia*)	NC, SC
Evergreen clematis (*Clematis armandii*)	All
Violet trumpet vine (*Clytostoma callistegioides*)	IV, LD, NC, SC
Winter creeper (*Euonymus fortunei*)	SN, IV, HD, LD, NC
Fatshedera (*Fatshedera lizei*)	SN, IV, LD, NC, SC
Creeping fig (*Ficus pumila*)	IV, HD, LD, NC, SC
Ivy (*Hedera*)	All
Climbing hydrangea (*Hydrangea anomala*)	All

Climbing snapdragon

Trumpet honeysuckle (*Lonicera sempervirens*)	All
Virginia creeper (*Parthenocissus quinquefolia*)	All
Boston ivy (*Parthenocissus tricuspidata*)	All
Potato vine (*Solanum jasminoides*)	IV, LD, NC, SC
Cape honeysuckle (*Tecomaria capensis*)	LD, NC, SC
Star jasmine (*Trachelospermum jasminoides*)	IV, HD, LD, NC, SC
Chinese wisteria (*Wisteria sinensis*)	All

According to Jacqueline Williams-Courtright of Alden Lane Nursery in Livermore, "Clematis performs very well in the bright shade of a northern or eastern exposure. In the Livermore area, clematis blooms best in morning sun." She recommends anemone clematis (*Clematis montana*), especially the 'Rubens' variety. "Its dogwood-like flower, about 2 inches in diameter, comes in a range of white to pink. It has a huge bloom in spring, then is recurrent, depending on the area." Another favorite that does well in shade is evergreen clematis (*Clematis armandii*). "It has clusters of fragrant white flowers in March, and creates a great backdrop of green against which to set other plants."

VINES FOR HOT SOUTH AND WEST EXPOSURES

Vines that are planted on south or west facing walls or fences must be very tough in order to withstand the cumulative heat built up during the day. Often, this is precisely where a deciduous vine will be most useful, because the leafy shade it provides protects the home from summer sun, and the natural leaf-drop in winter allows sun to shine in when it is most appreciated.

My office is a case in point. It is located in a building with a low ceiling and a long south-facing wall and entry. For the first two years I worked there, my room was intolerably hot during the summer. My friends urged me to buy an air conditioner, but instead I planted wisterias on a stout redwood pergola that followed the line of the wall. Now the entrance to my office is a fantasy-land of fragrant spring flowers, interesting summer fruit pods, and gnarled winter trunks. It is never too hot in summer, and it is cheerfully sunny in winter. The wisteria-laden pergola is a California tradition that makes good sense, saves energy, and above all adds beauty to your property. Just be sure that the structure you use to support it is sturdy; a heavy wisteria vine will destroy lightweight trellis-work supports.

Queen's wreath, Rosa de montana (*Antigonon leptopus*)	LD, SC
Easter lily vine (*Beaumontia grandiflora*)	LD, NC, SC
Bougainvillea (*Bougainvillea*)	LD, NC, SC
Guinea gold vine (*Hibbertia scandens*)	NC, SC
Giant Burmese honeysuckle (*Lonicera hildebrandiana*)	IV, NC, SC
Cat's claw (*Macfadyena unguis-cati*)	IV, HD, LD, NC, SC
Flame vine (*Pyrostegia venusta*)	LD, NC, SC
Cup-of-gold vine (*Solandra maxima*)	NC, SC
Cape honeysuckle (*Tecomaria capensis*)	LD, NC, SC
Sky flower (*Thunbergia grandiflora*)	NC, SC
Japanese wisteria (*Wisteria floribunda*)	All
Silky wisteria (*Wisteria venusta*)	All

VINES THAT MAKE GOOD GROUND COVERS

Where foot traffic is rare and the cover of green is more important than fine texture, the following vines may work well. A few of the plants in this list—notably the ivies and honeysuckles—will abandon the ground and climb trees that are planted among them. You will need to go over the area at least once (or better, twice) a year and remove the adventitious runners. Ivy can be a particular nuisance in this regard, but careful attention to its growth will keep it in bounds.

Bougainvilleas are grown successfully well outside the South Coast area, but their persistence as perennials depends on their finding optimal microclimate conditions. For instance, in the East Bay area (Berkeley, Oakland, and so forth), they are fairly common, but if you check your compass directions, you will notice that most of the large bougainvillea stands are of the purple-bracted species *B. spectabilis*, and they are growing on the south-facing white stucco walls of houses built on the slopes of south-facing hills. Perfect frost-drainage and radiant heat from the walls help them to thrive as if they were an entire region south of where they really are. In addition, the older a bougainvillea is, the more likely it will withstand a freak hard frost. A 10-year-old vine may suffer considerable damage during a hard freeze but come back good as new the next year, while a year-old plant may die completely under the same conditions.

Passionflower

Five-leaf akebia (*Akebia quinata*)	SN, IV, NC, SC
Bougainvillea (*Bougainvillea*)	IV, LD, NC, SC
Winter creeper (*Euonymus fortunei*)	SN, IV, HD, LD, NC
Fatshedera (*Fatshedera lizei*)	All
Carolina jessamine (*Gelsemium sempervirens*)	IV, HD, LD, NC, SC
Algerian ivy (*Hedera canariensis*)	IV, HD, LD, NC, SC
English ivy (*Hedera helix*)	All
Guinea gold vine (*Hibbertia scandens*)	NC, SC
Angelwing jasmine (*Jasminum nitidum*)	IV, HD, LD, NC, SC
Japanese honeysuckle (*Lonicera japonica*)	All
Creeping wire vine (*Muehlenbeckia axillaris*)	IV, HD, NC, SC
Virginia creeper (*Parthenocissus quinquefolia*)	All
Boston ivy (*Parthenocissus tricuspidata*)	All
Passionflower (*Passiflora*)	All
Cape plumbago (*Plumbago auriculata*)	IV, LD, NC, SC
Knotweed (*Polygonum*)	All
Evergreen grape (*Rhoicissus capensis*)	NC, SC
Australian bluebell creeper (*Sollya heterophylla*)	IV, NC, SC
Orange clock vine (*Thunbergia gregorii*)	SC
Asian jasmine (*Trachelospermum asiaticum*)	All
Star jasmine (*Trachelospermum jasminoides*)	IV, HD, LD, NC, SC

VINES FOR THE OCEANFRONT

Salt spray, foggy summer days, persistent winds, and humid air characterize California's oceanfront. Vines in this list will tolerate these conditions. If you can, provide the plants with some protection, such as that on the leeward side of a house or behind a fence or shrubbery windbreak.

Five-leaf akebia (*Akebia quinata*)	All
Porcelain berry, Blueberry climber (*Ampelopsis brevipedunculata*)	All
Bougainvillea (*Bougainvillea*)	IV, LD, NC, SC
Trumpet creeper (*Campsis radicans*)	All
Winter creeper (*Euonymus fortunei*)	SN, IV, HD, LD, NC
Carolina jessamine (*Gelsemium sempervirens*)	IV, HD, LD, NC, SC
Algerian ivy (*Hedera canariensis*)	IV, LD, NC, SC
Hop (*Humulus*)	All
Japanese honeysuckle (*Lonicera japonica*)	All
Virginia creeper (*Parthenocissus quinquefolia*)	All
Silver lace vine (*Polygonum aubertii*)	All
Cup-of-gold vine (*Solandra maxima*)	NC, SC
Cape honeysuckle (*Tecomaria capensis*)	LD, NC, SC
Star jasmine (*Trachelospermum jasminoides*)	IV, HD, LD, NC, SC

ANNUAL VINES

Annual vines have two great virtues. They can provide instant cover on a new pergola or arbor that has been planted with slow-growing perennial vines such as wisteria, and they are fun, friendly, and foolproof for kids. Also consider perennial vines that are not cold-hardy enough for your region. Many will grow fast enough and bloom well enough before cold weather kills them to justify their being treated as annuals, if the price you pay for them is not too high. The vines in this list are mostly annuals suited to all areas of California; some, like cup-and-saucer vine and glory vine, are tender perennials usually treated as annuals.

Climbing snapdragon (*Asarina antirrhinifolia*)
Cup-and-saucer vine (*Cobaea scandens*)
Hyacinth bean (*Dolichos lablab*)
Glory vine (*Eccremocarpus scaber*)
Moonflower (*Ipomoea alba*)
Cardinal climber (*Ipomoea quamoclit*)
Morning glory (*Ipomoea nil, I. tricolor*)
Sweet pea (*Lathyrus odoratus*)
Luffa, Sponge gourd (*Luffa aegyptiaca*)
Canary bird vine (*Nasturtium peregrinum*)
Scarlet runner bean (*Phaseolus coccineus*)
Black-eyed Susan vine (*Thunbergia alata*)
Orange clock vine (*Thunbergia gregorii*)
Twining nasturtium (*Tropaeolum majus*)

Morning glory

VINES THAT CLIMB WITH TENDRILS

To work successfully with vines, you have to give them proper support—and the kind of support they need varies, based on how they climb. The vines in this list send out tendrils and need thin supports like wires, fishing line, or chain-link fencing to climb on.

Porcelain berry, Blueberry climber (*Ampelopsis brevipedunculata*)	All
Queen's wreath, Rosa de montana (*Antigonon leptopus*)	IV, HD, LD, NC, SC
Kangaroo treebine (*Cissus antarctica*)	NC, SC
Grape ivy (*Cissus rhombifolia*)	HD, NC, SC
Violet trumpet vine (*Clytostoma callistegioides*)	IV, LD, NC, SC
Cup-and-saucer vine (*Cobaea scandens*)	All
Perennial sweet pea (*Lathyrus latifolius*)	All
Luffa, Sponge gourd (*Luffa aegyptiaca*)	All
Cat's claw (*Macfadyena unguis-cati*)	IV, HD, LD, NC, SC
Passionflower (*Passiflora*)	All
Chayote (*Sechium edule*)	IV, NC, SC
Grape (*Vitis*)	All

VINES THAT CLIMB BY TWINING

The largest group of vines are those that twine their immature stems around an object and hold fast. The coiled stem then hardens up and becomes a permanent part of the plant. Twining vines can climb wires, like tendril-making vines, but they are just as well adapted to lattice work made of thin wood. The larger ones, like wisteria, need sturdy wooden posts and cross-members, which they will loop around in a snake-like manner.

Twining vines require some guidance to achieve their best form. If an individual stem finds no support during its immature questing phase, it may bunch up into a ball or grab backwards onto another stem of the same plant, making a big, knotted mess that doesn't go anywhere. When working with young twining vines, pay attention during the season of stem growth. Once the stems have extended themselves, "it's twine time" in the words of the old song—and you should physically wrap them into the lattice-work or other supports and check them daily to see that they've taken hold. Older vines need little maintenance of this sort, although it pays to be vigilant with wisterias. The character of their trunks is much improved if you can envision the gnarled and twisted look you want to see in years to come and selectively prune out excess immature shoots that clutter up that ideal form.

Kiwi (*Actinidia*)	SN, IV, NC, SC
Five-leaf akebia (*Akebia quinata*)	All
Madeira vine (*Anredera cordifolia*)	All
California dutchman's pipe (*Aristolochia californica*)	SN, IV, NC, SC
Bittersweet (*Celastrus*)	SN, IV
Clematis (*Clematis*)	All
Hyacinth bean (*Dolichos lablab*)	All
Australian pea vine (*Dolichos lignosus*)	NC, SC
Carolina jessamine (*Gelsemium sempervirens*)	IV, HD, LD, NC, SC
Hardenbergia (*Hardenbergia*)	IV, HD, LD, NC, SC
Lilac vine (*Hardenbergia comptoniana*)	NC, SC

Chilean bellflower (*Lapageria rosea*)	IV, NC, SC
Honeysuckle (*Lonicera*)	All
Mandevilla (*Mandevilla*)	IV, NC, SC
Pink trumpet vine (*Podranea ricasoliana*)	IV, LD, NC, SC
Silver lace vine (*Polygonum aubertii*)	All
Potato vine (*Solanum jasminoides*)	IV, LD, NC, SC
Cape honeysuckle (*Tecomaria capensis*)	LD, NC, SC
Star jasmine (*Trachelospermum jasminoides*)	IV, HD, LD, NC, SC
Wisteria (*Wisteria*)	All

VINES THAT CLIMB BY CLINGING

The vines in this list have adhesive disks or pads that sprout from their stems and grab hold of walls, fences, and tree trunks. Once they get a grip, ripping them down will take house paint with them, so be careful where you plant them. Probably the best use of these plants is on stone or concrete walls, but even then, you should be aware that once they reach roof level, they can cling to gutters and roof shingles and will cause damage if they need to be pulled loose. Although many people grow ivy right up to trunks of trees, this is not encouraged in low-maintenance parts of the garden. Those clinging disks will take hold as soon as your back is turned, and before you know it, the trees will be swathed in green. Ripping 20-foot lengths of stuck-tight ivy down from a dozen trees every year is a tedious chore. I speak as one who knows.

Trumpet creeper (*Campsis radicans*)	All
Winter creeper (*Euonymus fortunei*)	SN, IV, HD, LD, NC
Creeping fig (*Ficus pumila*)	IV, HD, LD, NC, SC
Ivy (*Hedera*)	All
Climbing hydrangea (*Hydrangea anomala*)	All
Virginia creeper (*Parthenocissus quinquefolia*)	All
Boston ivy (*Parthenocissus tricuspidata*)	All
Japanese hydrangea vine (*Schizophragma hydrangeoides*)	SN, IV, NC

"Creeping fig attaches with little grabbers and makes a mat-like wall," says Jacqueline Williams-Courtright of Alden Lane Nursery in Livermore. **"If given support against a wall or shed, it will cling and create a vertical green wall. The more towards the coast they are, the more sun these plants tolerate. Inland they need more protection from heat, so they do well in shade."**

EASY VINES FOR A MAILBOX OR TRELLIS

Try these vines for mailbox posts, lamp posts, or fence posts. They either won't spread very far, or they take well to regular pruning. Also consider one of the annual vines on page 135.

Clematis (*Clematis*)	All
Carolina jessamine (*Gelsemium sempervirens*)	IV, HD, LD, NC, SC
Gold flame honeysuckle (*Lonicera heckrottii*)	All
Chilean jasmine (*Mandevilla laxa*)	SN, IV, NC, SC

EVERGREEN VINES

Many people prefer to plant evergreen vines around entryways, over garden gates, and on patio walls, where visitors see them frequently and where their permanence allows them to be treated as adjuncts to architectural features. Some of the vines in this list will lose their leaves in cold weather; if several growing regions are given for them, you would do well to consider them reliably evergreen only in the warmer areas listed. You can learn much more about how they will behave in your garden by asking a local nursery proprietor to show you a sample in the dead of winter.

Yellow trumpet vine (*Anemopaegma chamberlaynii*)	IV, NC, SC
Queen's wreath, Rosa de montana (*Antigonon leptopus*)	LD, SC
Easter lily vine (*Beaumontia grandiflora*)	HD, LD, NC, SC
Bougainvillea (*Bougainvillea*)	IV, LD, NC, SC
Grape ivy (*Cissus rhombifolia*)	HD, NC, SC
Evergreen clematis (*Clematis armandii*)	All
Bleeding-heart glorybower (*Clerodendrum thomsoniae*)	SC
Violet trumpet vine (*Clytostoma callistegioides*)	IV, LD, NC, SC
Blood-red trumpet vine (*Distictis buccinatoria*)	IV, NC, SC
Vanilla trumpet vine (*Distictis laxiflora*)	NC, SC
Winter creeper (*Euonymus fortunei*)	SN, IV, HD, LD, NC
Fatshedera (*Fatshedera lizei*)	All
Creeping fig (*Ficus pumila*)	IV, HD, LD, NC, SC
Carolina jessamine (*Gelsemium sempervirens*)	IV, HD, LD, NC, SC
Lilac vine (*Hardenbergia comptoniana*)	IV, NC, SC
Happy Wanderer hardenbergia (*Hardenbergia violacea* 'Happy Wanderer')	All
Algerian ivy (*Hedera canariensis*)	IV, LD, NC, SC
Persian ivy (*Hedera colchica*)	All
English ivy (*Hedera helix*)	All
Guinea gold vine (*Hibbertia scandens*)	NC, SC
Wax flower (*Hoya carnosa*)	SC
South African jasmine (*Jasminum angulare*)	NC, SC
Angelwing jasmine (*Jasminum nitidum*)	IV, HD, LD, NC, SC
Chinese jasmine (*Jasminum polyanthum*)	All
Chilean bellflower (*Lapageria rosea*)	NC, SC
Giant Burmese honeysuckle (*Lonicera hildebrandiana*)	IV, NC, SC
Japanese honeysuckle (*Lonicera japonica*)	All
Cat's claw (*Macfadyena unguis-cati*)	IV, HD, LD, NC, SC
Alice du Pont Mandevilla (*Mandevilla* 'Alice du Pont')	SC
Bower vine (*Pandorea jasminoides*)	IV, NC, SC
Passionflower (*Passiflora*)	All
Cape plumbago (*Plumbago auriculata*)	IV, LD, NC, SC
Silver lace vine (*Polygonum aubertii*)	All
Flame vine (*Pyrostegia venusta*)	LD, NC, SC
Evergreen grape (*Rhoicissus capensis*)	NC, SC
Mexican flame vine (*Senecio confusus*)	LD, NC, SC
Cup-of-gold vine (*Solandra maxima*)	NC, SC
Potato vine (*Solanum jasminoides*)	IV, LD, NC, SC
Cape honeysuckle (*Tecomaria capensis*)	LD, NC, SC
Star jasmine (*Trachelospermum jasminoides*)	IV, HD, LD, NC, SC

🌱 Jim Balestreri, owner of the Green Point Nursery, Novato, recommends *Pandorea jasminoides*, or bower vine, as an attractive evergreen vine that is easy to grow. "Bower vine is relatively new for gardens, and long blooming. It will bloom for 6 months with white flowers. There is also a variety that bears pink flowers with a deep-maroon throat. These plants are not for the hottest place in your garden, not for reflected heat or light. Give them medium light, average water, and the support of a trellis or something similar. These vines are pest free and easy to grow. Inland they would need morning or filtered sun."

DECIDUOUS VINES

Deciduous vines—those that drop their leaves in the winter—find their best use where you want some shade from the summer sun but desire solar heat and light during the cold months of the year.

Kiwi (*Actinidia*)	SN, IV, NC, SC
Five-leaf akebia (*Akebia quinata*)	All
Porcelain berry, Blueberry climber (*Ampelopsis brevipedunculata*)	All
Madeira vine (*Anredera cordifolia*)	All
Queen's wreath, Rosa de montana (*Antigonon leptopus*)	LD, SC
California dutchman's pipe (*Aristolochia californica*)	SN, IV, NC, SC
Trumpet creeper (*Campsis radicans*)	All
Clematis (*Clematis*)	All
Common hop (*Humulus lupulus*)	All
Climbing hydrangea (*Hydrangea anomala*)	All
Gold flame honeysuckle (*Lonicera heckrottii*)	All
Chilean jasmine (*Mandevilla laxa*)	SN, IV, NC, SC
Virginia creeper (*Parthenocissus quinquefolia*)	All
Bokhara fleeceflower (*Polygonum baldschuanicum*)	All
Costa Rican nightshade (*Solanum wendlandii*)	NC, SC
Snail vine (*Vigna caracalla, Phaseolus caracalla*)	IV, LD, NC, SC
Wisteria (*Wisteria*)	All

VINES THAT DEER DON'T USUALLY EAT

In rural or suburban areas, foraging deer can cause considerable damage to garden plants. These vines are usually distasteful to deer, so they are rarely browsed. Given the proper conditions for their growth, they can help fill in large planting areas or provide barriers in areas that are unfenced and open onto semi-wild landscapes.

Bougainvillea (*Bougainvillea*)	IV, LD, NC, SC
Carolina jessamine (*Gelsemium sempervirens*)	IV, HD, LD, NC, SC
English ivy (*Hedera helix*)	All
Jasmine (*Jasminum*)	All
Potato vine (*Solanum jasminoides*)	IV, LD, NC, SC
Costa Rican nightshade (*Solanum wendlandii*)	NC, SC
Australian bluebell creeper (*Sollya heterophylla*)	IV, NC, SC
Cape honeysuckle (*Tecomaria capensis*)	LD, NC, SC
Wisteria (*Wisteria*)	All

THE LONGEST VINES YOU'LL EVER SEE

Grouped here by height are some champion growers. The weight of these vines will be in proportion to their length, however, so build a sound structure to support them. Don't be afraid to train them; some of these monsters will take advantage of your good nature and create a jungle if not annually pruned or tied in.

50 Feet or Longer

English ivy (*Hedera helix*)	All
Virginia creeper (*Parthenocissus quinquefolia*)	All
Boston Ivy (*Parthenocissus tricuspidata*)	All
Grape (*Vitis*)	All
Wisteria (*Wisteria*)	All

40 Feet

California dutchman's pipe (*Aristolochia californica*)	SN, IV, NC, SC
Trumpet creeper (*Campsis radicans*)	All
Silver lace vine (*Polygonum aubertii*)	All

20 to 30 Feet

Porcelain berry, Blueberry climber (*Ampelopsis brevipedunculata*)	All
Crimson trumpet creeper (*Campsis tagliabuana*)	All
Cup-and-saucer vine (*Cobaea scandens*)	All
Japanese hop (*Humulus japonicus*)	All
Chinese jasmine (*Jasminum polyanthum*)	SN, IV, LD, NC, SC
Potato vine (*Solanum jasminoides*)	IV, LD, NC, SC

"Potato vine, **Solanum jasminoides**, is in almost perpetual bloom if temperatures are high enough," notes Jacqueline Williams-Courtright of Alden Lane Nursery, Livermore. "In the coldest parts of California in winter, it becomes leafless, but renews quickly." This vine is fast-growing to 30 feet. "It will be more compact in sun. In shade it has a more open character, looking ethereal with its long arms. But it won't bloom as well in shade." This vine in the potato and tomato family has 1-inch, star-shaped white flowers with small yellow beaks.

VINES WITH FRAGRANT FLOWERS

Nothing is more romantic than a veranda or patio overhung by a perfumed vine. A twining vine that casts its aroma into an open bedroom window is even better, for in the early morning, when the fragrance is fresh, there is something magical about awakening to the sensory pleasure of birdsong and blossoms.

Madeira vine (*Anredera cordifolia*)	All
Easter lily vine (*Beaumontia grandiflora*)	LD, NC, SC
Clematis (*Clematis*)	All
Vanilla trumpet vine (*Distictis laxiflora*)	NC, SC
Wax flower (*Hoya carnosa*)	NC, SC
Spanish jasmine (*Jasminum grandiflorum*)	SN, IV, LD, NC, SC

Angelwing jasmine (*Jasminum nitidum*)	IV, HD, LD, NC, SC
Perennial sweet pea (*Lathyrus latifolius*)	All
Honeysuckle (*Lonicera*)	All
Chilean jasmine (*Mandevilla laxa*)	SN, IV, NC, SC
Incense passionflower (*Passiflora* 'Incense')	All
Madagascar jasmine (*Stephanotis floribunda*)	SC
Star jasmine (*Trachelospermum jasminoides*)	IV, HD, LD, NC, SC
Snail vine (*Vigna caracalla, Phaseolus caracalla*)	IV, LD, NC, SC
Wisteria (*Wisteria*)	All

A vine favored by Ernie G. Wasson, of the Berkeley Horticultural Nursery, is Chilean jasmine, *Mandevilla laxa*. "It has white, fragrant, trumpet flowers," Ernie says, "and they *are* fragrant. Some friends of mine have one of these plants on their front porch, and as you walk up, you get a waft of fragrance. The fragrance has a sweetness and a spiciness to it, but more sweet than anything else. Some plants have too sweet a smell, but you can't get enough of this mandevilla." This summer bloomer prefers partial to full sun, and average water. Some mandevillas are evergreen, but *Mandevilla laxa* is deciduous. It can be cut to the ground in winter and will bloom on new growth.

VINES FEARED FOR THEIR VIGOR

There is something beautiful and dangerous about a truly vigorous vine. Left to its own devices, it can tear a trellis apart, lift roof shingles, and pry windows out of their frames. Well managed, it is like a trained circus tiger that will awe you with its magnificent strength and poise. One of the worst offenders is English ivy, which, if not kept within bounds, can undergo a Dr. Jekyll and Mr. Hyde transformation, wrenching apart building mortar and strangling trees. The Druids of ancient England were so impressed by this change that they gave the plant two names: "Ivy" was the mannerly, maple-leafed young ground cover; the mature monster plant was called "The Vine."

The lightweight, graceful Virginia creeper will adhere to a wall or invade nearby flower beds, and a weighty wisteria can crush flimsy supports. Give wisteria a solid support to grow on, however, and it will outlive you and your children, casting the charm of its fragrant, showy flowers on all who pass beneath it.

Porcelain berry, Blueberry climber (*Ampelopsis brevipedunculata*)	All
Trumpet creeper (*Campsis radicans*)	All
American bittersweet (*Celastrus scandens*)	SN, IV, NC, SC
Creeping fig (*Ficus pumila*)	IV, HD, LD, NC, SC
English ivy (*Hedera helix*)	All
German ivy (*Senecio mikanioides*)	NC, SC
Potato vine (*Solanum jasminoides*)	IV, LD, NC, SC
Wisteria (*Wisteria*)	All

"German ivy is the worst pest I have ever seen—worse, even, than pampas grass," says North Coast gardener Liselotte Erlanger Glozer. "I am in my 80s now and I don't have the strength to rip it out of other people's yards, just my own. It is a pretty plant, but it is so sad to see it killing the neighbors' dwarf fruit trees. It has already destroyed their 50-year-old Dorothy Perkins rose, which was enormous. It lay over the top of the rose until the poor thing got no light and died—then it used it as a trellis."

VINES FOR OLD-FASHIONED GARDENS

The plants in grandmother's garden most likely included a fragrant tangle of honeysuckle, and perhaps a somewhat orderly profusion of grapes. Sweet pea and clematis are other vines that would be quite at home in an old-fashioned garden. At the Filoli estate gardens in Woodside, where some of California's floral history is preserved, the horticulturists prize wisteria, which is trained along wrought-iron balconies, balustrades, gates, and garden walls. "Chinese wisteria is the first to bloom, with rich purple blossoms in late March, early April," says Lucy Tolmach, Filoli's director of horticulture. "The white form, 'Alba,' blooms reliably with the late tulips." Silky wisteria, which gets its name from the silken threads on its new leaves, blooms in mid April. "The flower buds are very large and round, with the flowering racemes made up of very large florets. It is a vigorous grower, extremely fragrant, and has beautiful yellow fall color in December." Blooming in mid to late April at Filoli is Japanese wisteria, which has the longest racemes and smallest florets, and is very fragrant. A double form, 'Violacea Plena,' is trained over an arched doorway. "Its flowers look like large clusters of rich purple grapes."

Perennial sweet pea

Lucy advises California gardeners to plant wisteria in full sun in well-drained soil. Once established, the plants can be drought tolerant. "We summer prune the wisterias monthly to keep them tight and encourage more blossoms in the spring. Winter pruning consists of removing dead wood and maintaining the artistic shape of the plant." She also notes that wisterias make excellent pot plants. Filoli's two silky wisteria 'Alba' standards in 20-inch pots are repotted with new fresh soil during their winter dormancy.

This list includes not only Filoli's favorite wisterias, but other vines, many of them fragrant and long blooming, that will help create an old-fashioned effect in your garden.

Madeira vine (*Anredera cordifolia*)	All
Bougainvillea (*Bougainvillea*)	IV, LD, NC, SC
Trumpet creeper (*Campsis radicans*)	All
Downy clematis (*Clematis macropetala*)	All
Golden clematis (*Clematis tangutica*)	All
Blood-red trumpet vine (*Distictis buccinatoria*)	IV, NC, SC
Spanish jasmine (*Jasminum grandiflorum*)	SN, IV, LD, NC, SC
Angelwing jasmine (*Jasminum nitidum*)	IV, HD, LD, NC, SC
Perennial sweet pea (*Lathyrus latifolius*)	All
Japanese honeysuckle (*Lonicera japonica*)	All
Blue crown passionflower (*Passiflora caerulea*)	SN, IV, LD, NC, SC
Champanel grape (*Vitis labrusca* 'Champanel')	SN, IV, HD, LD, NC
Muscat grape (*Vitis vinifera* 'Muscat')	IV, HD, LD, NC, SC
Japanese wisteria (*Wisteria floribunda*)	All
Chinese wisteria (*Wisteria sinensis*)	All
Silky wisteria (*Wisteria venusta*)	All

SOME FRUIT AND VEGETABLE VINES

After reading this list, you may want to head for the kitchen and indulge in one of the items. These vines not only offer attractive foliage or flowers as landscape accents, but they also bear fruit and vegetables you can eat. Annual pumpkin vines, for example, offer large, dramatic leaves, lovely flowers, and an autumn harvest. Some varieties of passionflower—which has one of the most ornate blooms in the vine family—bear delicious fruit that can be eaten fresh or used in beverages or jellies. The vines tend to be vigorous and tolerant of many soil types. Kiwi is a vine with attractive foliage and those odd-looking, hairy brown globes that, when cut open, reveal the delicious lime-green pulp and small black seeds. Unlike passionflower, however, kiwi wants rich soil, and some varieties need cross pollination. Another vine with attractive foliage is grape, which also enriches you with those aromatic clusters of fruit.

Pumpkin

Kiwi (*Actinidia*)	SN, IV, NC, SC
Cucumber (*Cucumis sativus*)	All
Pumpkin (*Cucurbita pepo*)	All
Tomato (*Lycopersicon*)	All
Blue crown passionflower (*Passiflora caerulea*)	IV, LD, NC, SC
Passion fruit (*Passiflora edulis*)	IV, NC, SC
Incense passionflower (*Passiflora* 'Incense')	All
Scarlet runner bean (*Phaseolus coccineus*)	All
Butter bean (*Phaseolus lunatus*)	All
Pole bean (*Phaseolus vulgaris*)	All
Pea (*Pisum sativum*)	All
Chayote (*Sechium edule*)	IV, NC, SC
Grape (*Vitis*)	All

VINES WITH ORNAMENTAL FRUIT, BERRIES, AND SEEDS

These vines, selected for their ornamental fruit or seeds, add interest to the garden when the peak season of bloom is past, and thus do double duty in your landscaping plans.

Fruit, Berries

Kiwi (*Actinidia*)	SN, IV, NC, SC
Porcelain berry, Blueberry climber (*Ampelopsis brevipedunculata*)	All
Chinese bittersweet (*Celastrus rosthornianus*)	SN, IV
American bittersweet (*Celastrus scandens*)	SN, IV
Woodbine (*Lonicera pericylmenum*)	All
Trumpet honeysuckle (*Lonicera sempervirens*)	All

Seeds

Balloon vine, Love-in-a-puff (*Cardiospermum halicacabum*)	NC, SC
Downy clematis (*Clematis macropetala*)	All
Golden clematis (*Clematis tangutica*)	All
Hyacinth bean (*Dolichos lablab*)	All
Japanese wisteria (*Wisteria floribunda*)	All
Chinese wisteria (*Wisteria sinensis*)	All
Silky wisteria (*Wisteria venusta*)	All

VINES WITH SHOWY FLOWERS

If you plant these vines, you will find yourself marking the seasons by your anticipation of their blooming season. To increase the floral display, consult the seasonal sampler on page XXX and interplant several vines on your trellis, arbor, or pergola.

Several Colors Available

Bougainvillea (*Bougainvillea*)	IV, LD, NC, SC
Large-flowered clematis (*Clematis* hybrids)	All
Trumpet vine (*Distictis*)	IV, NC, SC
Honeysuckle (*Lonicera*)	All
Bower vine (*Pandorea jasminoides*)	IV, NC, SC
Passionflower (*Passiflora*)	All
Scarlet runner bean (*Phaseolus coccineus*)	All

Yellow

Yellow trumpet creeper (*Campsis radicans* 'Flava')	All
Golden clematis (*Clematis tangutica*)	All
Carolina jessamine (*Gelsemium sempervirens*)	IV, HD, LD, NC, SC
Cat's claw (*Macfadyena unguis-cati*)	IV, HD, LD, NC, SC
Cup-of-gold vine (*Solandra maxima*)	NC, SC

Orange to Red

Trumpet creeper (*Campsis radicans*)	All
Scarlet clematis (*Clematis texensis*)	All
Glory vine (*Eccremocarpus scaber*)	All
Scarlet runner bean (*Phaseolus coccineus*)	All
Flame vine (*Pyrostegia venusta*)	LD, NC, SC
Mexican flame vine (*Senecio confusus*)	LD, NC, SC
Cape honeysuckle (*Tecomaria capensis*)	LD, NC, SC

Pink to Red

Queen's wreath, Rosa de montana (*Antigonon leptopus*)	IV, HD, LD, NC, SC
Pink Tiara bougainvillea (*Bougainvillea* 'Pink Tiara')	IV, LD, NC, SC
Scarlet clematis (*Clematis texensis*)	SN, IV, NC, SC
Pink trumpet vine (*Podranea ricasoliana*)	IV, LD, NC, SC

Blue

Helsingborg clematis (*Clematis alpina* 'Helsingborg')	All
Lilac vine (*Hardenbergia comptoniana*)	NC, SC
Blue dawn flower (*Ipomoea acuminata*)	IV, LD, NC, SC
Blue crown passionflower (*Passiflora caerulea*)	IV, LD, NC, SC
Australian bluebell creeper (*Sollya heterophylla*)	IV, NC, SC
Chinese wisteria (*Wisteria sinensis*)	All

White or Cream

California dutchman's pipe (*Aristolochia californica*)	SN, IV, NC, SC
Evergreen clematis (*Clematis armandii*)	All
Sweet autumn clematis (*Clematis dioscoreifolia, C. paniculata*)	All
Climbing hydrangea (*Hydrangea anomala*)	All
Chilean jasmine (*Mandevilla laxa*)	SN, IV, NC, SC
Silver lace vine (*Polygonum aubertii*)	All
Japanese hydrangea vine (*Schizophragma hydrangeoides*)	SN, IV, NC
Potato vine (*Solanum jasminoides*)	IV, LD, NC, SC
White Chinese wisteria (*Wisteria sinensis* 'Alba')	All

Purple

Italian clematis (*Clematis viticella*)	All
Violet trumpet vine (*Clytostoma callistegioides*)	IV, LD, NC, SC
Royal trumpet vine (*Distictis* 'Rivers')	NC, SC
Japanese wisteria (*Wisteria floribunda*)	All
Silky wisteria (*Wisteria venusta*)	All

Variegated or Mixed Colors

Angelwing jasmine (*Jasminum nitidum*)	IV, HD, LD, NC, SC
Chinese jasmine (*Jasminum polyanthum*)	SN, IV, LD, NC, SC
Gold flame honeysuckle (*Lonicera heckrotti*)	All
Passion fruit (*Passiflora edulis*)	IV, NC, SC
Snail vine (*Vigna caracalla, Phaseolus caracalla*)	IV, LD, NC, SC

"The bracts are the showy part of the bougainvillea," says Wendy Proud of Monrovia Nursery in Azusa, which may explain why bougainvilleas have no fragrance. "The actual flowers are tiny. The color is in the bract, which is a sort of leaf." Wendy notes that the same is true for poinsettias. To help your bougainvillea put on a good show, Wendy advises cutting back on water and fertilizer just before bloom time. This stresses the plant into bloom. "You can fertilize in spring before the flower season, and again in summer, but not with a fertilizer heavy in nitrogen. Use an even 20-20-20 fertilizer."

Rick Yonkovich of Cameron Park Nursery in Rescue recommends fragrant, fast-growing pink jasmine for showy flowers. "Pink jasmine takes full sun and ample moisture but can't stand in water," he advises. Rick says that Rescue, in the Sierra foothills outside Sacramento, has poor drainage in general, so people there have to be careful about where they place such plants in the garden.

A SAMPLER OF VINE BLOOMS BY SEASON

Spring

Easter lily vine (*Beaumontia grandiflora*)	LD, NC, SC
Evergreen clematis (*Clematis armandii*)	All
Anemone clematis (*Clematis montana*)	All
Violet trumpet vine (*Clytostoma callistegioides*)	IV, LD, NC, SC
Carolina jessamine (*Gelsemium sempervirens*)	IV, HD, LD, NC, SC
Jasmine (*Jasminum*)	All
Sweet pea (*Lathyrus odoratus*)	All
Gold flame honeysuckle (*Lonicera heckrotti*)	All
Cat's claw (*Macfadyena unguis-cati*)	IV, HD, LD, NC, SC
Pink trumpet vine (*Podranea ricasoliana*)	IV, LD, NC, SC
Potato vine (*Solanum jasminoides*)	IV, LD, NC, SC
Wisteria (*Wisteria*)	All

Summer

Queen's wreath, Rosa de montana (*Antigonon leptopus*)	IV, HD, LD, NC, SC
Bougainvillea (*Bougainvillea*)	IV, LD, NC, SC
Trumpet creeper (*Campsis radicans*)	All
Italian clematis (*Clematis viticella*)	All
Violet trumpet vine (*Clytostoma callistegioides*)	IV, LD, NC, SC
Cup-and-saucer vine (*Cobaea scandens*)	All
Hyacinth bean (*Dolichos lablab*)	All
Climbing hydrangea (*Hydrangea anomala*)	All
Morning glory (*Ipomoea*)	All
Spanish jasmine (*Jasminum grandiflorum*)	SN, IV, LD, NC, SC
Perennial sweet pea (*Lathyrus latifolius*)	All
Honeysuckle (*Lonicera*)	All
Chilean jasmine (*Mandevilla laxa*)	SN, IV, NC, SC
Bower vine (*Pandorea jasminoides*)	IV, NC, SC
Scarlet runner bean (*Phaseolus coccineus*)	All
Bokhara fleeceflower (*Polygonum baldschuanicum*)	All
Flame vine (*Pyrostegia venusta*)	LD, NC, SC
Japanese hydrangea vine (*Schizophragma hydrangeoides*)	SN, IV, NC
Australian bluebell creeper (*Sollya heterophylla*)	IV, NC, SC
Star jasmine (*Trachelospermum jasminoides*)	IV, HD, LD, NC, SC

Late Summer

Madeira vine (*Anredera cordifolia*)	All
Golden clematis (*Clematis tangutica*)	All
Scarlet clematis (*Clematis texensis*)	SN, IV, NC, SC
Hop (*Humulus*)	All
Chilean bellflower (*Lapageria rosea*)	IV, NC, SC
Gold flame honeysuckle (*Lonicera heckrotti*)	All
Woodbine (*Lonicera periclymenum*)	All
Silver lace vine (*Polygonum aubertii*)	All

Fall

Madeira vine (*Anredera cordifolia*)	All
Queen's wreath, Rosa de montana (*Antigonon leptopus*)	IV, HD, LD, NC, SC
Sweet autumn clematis (*Clematis dioscoreifolia, C. paniculata*)	All
Climbing hydrangea (*Hydrangea anomala*)	All
Alice du Pont mandevilla (*Mandevilla* 'Alice du Pont')	SC
Japanese hydrangea vine (*Schizophragma hydrangeoides*)	SN, IV, NC

Winter/Early Spring

California dutchman's pipe (*Aristolochia californica*)	SN, IV, NC, SC
Downy clematis (*Clematis macropetala*)	All
Carolina jessamine (*Gelsemium sempervirens*)	IV, HD, LD, NC, SC
Hardenbergia (*Hardenbergia*)	IV, HD, LD, NC, SC
Lilac vine (*Hardenbergia comptoniana*)	NC, SC
Primrose jasmine (*Jasminum mesnyi*)	All
Chinese jasmine (*Jasminum polyantum*)	All
Sweet pea (*Lathyrus odoratus*)	All
Flame vine (*Pyrostegia venusta*)	LD, NC, SC
Cup-of-gold vine (*Solandra maxima*)	NC, SC

FERNS

If the flamboyant colors of flowering plants occasionally strike a nerve, try cutting their impact with the cool and soothing greenery of ferns. The contrast of their graceful fronds can delight the eye and quiet the mind. Easy to grow, these hardy foliage plants add a special texture to any area, from moist ground to dry rocks. Some ferns provide ground cover, while others reach tree stature, and although many prefer shady areas, others do well in the sun.

TALL FERNS

As a dramatic backdrop to colorful annuals and perennials, tall ferns make a statement like no other, turning a simple flower bed into a fantasy wonderland. In a California garden, nothing says "the tropics" like tall ferns. Growing 3 feet or more, they add a glorious "tiki" appeal to even the rawest of new gardens. For even taller ferns, see the tree ferns in the next section.

Mother fern (*Asplenium bulbiferum*)	IV, NC, SC
Lady fern (*Athyrium filix-femina*)	SN, IV, NC, SC
Holly fern (*Cyrtomium falcatum*)	NC, SC
Spreading wood fern (*Dryopteris expansa*)	SN, IV, NC, SC
Male fern (*Dryopteris filix-mas*)	SN, IV, NC
Ostrich fern (*Matteuccia struthiopteris*)	SN, IV, NC, SC
Southern sword fern (*Nephrolepis cordifolia*)	IV, LD, NC, SC
Sword fern (*Nephrolepis exaltata*)	SC
Sensitive fern (*Onoclea sensibilis*)	SN, IV, NC, SC
Royal fern (*Osmunda regalis*)	All
Staghorn fern (*Platycerium bifurcatum*)	NC, SC
Hare's foot fern (*Polypodium aureum*)	NC, SC
Western sword fern (*Polystichum munitum*)	SN, IV, NC, SC
Bracken (*Pteridium aquilinum*)	All
Australian brake fern (*Pteris tremula*)	NC, SC
Giant chain fern (*Woodwardia fimbriata*)	SN, IV, NC, SC

TREE FERNS

Tree ferns are the mop-top aristocrats of the fern world, some reaching 12 to 20 feet in height. All will grow along the South Coast; with protection, the *Dicksonias* can be found quite far into the North Coast region. *Dicksonias* are common around the San Francisco Bay Area, but north of Marin County they require careful placement to survive the occasional freak cold snap. Tree ferns prefer rich soil, moisture, well-drained locations, and shade. My own Tasmanian tree fern is thriving beneath the overhang of a huge redwood tree, a combination of plants that sounds eccentric but gives that part of the garden a decidedly primeval look.

Australian
tree fern

Dwarf tree fern (*Blechnum brasiliense, B. gibbum*)	SC
Hawaiian tree fern (*Cibotium glaucum*)	SC
Mexican tree fern (*Cibotium scheidei*)	SC
Australian tree fern (*Cyathea cooperi*)	NC, SC
Tasmanian tree fern (*Dicksonia antarctica*)	IV, NC, SC
New Zealand tree fern (*Dicksonia squarrosa*)	NC, SC

FERNS FOR SUN

A few ferns, such as sensitive fern and bracken, actually like a full dose of the sun's rays. Along the North Coast, where fog can take the place of shade, some ferns seem to bask in the less intense sun. The ferns in this list don't need full shade to be happy, so check with your local nursery to see which of these you might plant in a sunny spot. Any fern you plant in sun should be given excellent soil, and it will need some water on hot summer days.

Holly fern (*Cyrtomium falcatum*)	NC, SC
Squirrel's foot fern (*Davallia trichomanoides*)	NC, SC
Bear's foot fern (*Humata tyermannii*)	NC, SC
Ostrich fern (*Matteuccia struthiopteris*)	SN, IV, NC, SC
Sensitive fern (*Onoclea sensibilis*)	SN, IV, NC, SC
Coffee fern (*Pellaea andromedifolia*)	SN, IV, NC, SC
Bird's foot fern (*Pellaea mucronata*)	SN, IV, HD, NC, SC
Roundleaf fern (*Pellaea rotundifolia*)	IV, NC, SC
Green cliff-brake (*Pellaea viridis*)	IV, NC, SC
Staghorn fern (*Platycerium bifurcatum*)	NC, SC
Bracken (*Pteridium aquilinum*)	All
Leatherleaf fern (*Rumohra adiantiformis, Aspidium capense*)	IV, NC, SC
Giant chain fern (*Woodwardia fimbriata*)	SN, IV, NC, SC

Coastal conditions in San Diego are difficult for ferns. "They do best in a protected patio," advises Tom Yanagihara Jr. of Ouchi Nursery. Dicksonia tree ferns do well, reaching 6 to 8 feet. "Place them close to the house on the side away from the ocean. People also protect them with a windbreak of melaleuca or other taller trees."

FERNS THAT LIKE MOIST SITES

A walk in Muir Woods, just north of San Francisco, reveals ferns happily at home in the rich decay of leaf mold and other organic matter. Moist and rich, the earth in the quiet darkness beneath the redwoods is ideal sustenance for many ferns. For the ferns in this list, any moist location will do—an area of poor drainage, a septic field. Some fern species are excellent for water overload: sites in flood zones, at the edge of streams, or by small ponds. But beware—a full-on drought may bring drooping death to some species. Talk with your local nursery about which ferns are best for your area.

California maidenhair fern (*Adiantum jordanii*)	SN, IV, NC, SC
Mother fern (*Asplenium bulbiferum*)	IV, NC, SC
Lady fern (*Athyrium filix-femina*)	SN, IV, NC, SC
Japanese painted fern (*Athyrium nipponicum* 'Pictum')	SN, IV, NC, SC
Holly fern (*Cyrtomium falcatum*)	NC, SC
Ostrich fern (*Matteuccia struthiopteris*)	SN, IV, NC, SC
Sensitive fern (*Onoclea sensibilis*)	SN, IV, NC, SC
Royal fern (*Osmunda regalis*)	All
Hare's foot fern (*Polypodium aureum*)	NC, SC
Australian brake fern (*Pteris tremula*)	NC, SC
Chain fern, Woodwardia (*Woodwardia*)	SN, IV, NC, SC

Woodwardia

FERNS THAT DON'T NEED LOTS OF WATER

If you yearn for ferns but think that poor soil conditions or your lack of time for watering will destroy your frond dreams, set your sights on these.

Squirrel's foot fern (*Davallia trichomanoides*)	NC, SC
California wood fern (*Dryopteris arguta*)	SN, IV, NC, SC
Southern sword fern (*Nephrolepis cordifolia*)	IV, LD, NC, SC
Coffee fern (*Pellaea andromedifolia*)	SN, IV, NC, SC
Bird's foot fern (*Pellaea mucronata*)	SN, IV, HD, NC, SC
Roundleaf fern (*Pellaea rotundifolia*)	IV, NC, SC
Green cliff-brake (*Pellaea viridis*)	IV, NC, SC
Staghorn fern (*Platycerium bifurcatum*)	NC, SC
Western sword fern (*Polystichum munitum*)	SN, IV, NC, SC
Bracken (*Pteridium aquilinum*)	All

❧ "One fern not too many people know about," says Ted Mayeda of M & M Nursery in Orange, "is the 'Cancan.' It's like Boston fern or sword fern but divides on the tips, so it's frilly. The full name is *Nephrolepis exaltata* 'Cancan.' Not too many nurseries have it yet, but it is one of the most popular we carry. People come in and notice it." *Nephrolepis* ferns, which include Boston and sword ferns, are all tough plants that are easy to grow. Other ferns popular at M & M are the davallias, staghorns, and *Polypodium* 'Knightiae' (Knight's polypody).

FAVORITE FERNS OF THE SAN DIEGO ZOO

The San Diego Zoo—or as it is more formally known, the Zoological Society of San Diego—is known not only for its animals, but also for its plants. The Zoo is home to more than 6,500 plant species, including many ferns. This list of the ferns most commonly used at the Zoo is from Michael Letzring, the lead gardener. These plants will take coastal sun except for the lace fern, which prefers shade or partial shade. Lace ferns may look delicate, but they are fairly hardy. Michael notes that lace ferns do well in fairly dry soil, and 'Kimberley Queen' sword ferns will tolerate poor soil and erratic watering. These ferns and the leatherleaf fern have a low-growing, spreading form, reaching 2 to 3 feet in height.

The slow-growing, fuzzy-trunked Tasmanian tree fern can reach a height of 15 feet, while the Australian tree fern, a rapid grower, can reach a height of 20 feet from which to display its bright green fronds. Be aware of one caution about the Australian tree fern, however. The brown hairs on the leaf stems and undersides can irritate the skin, so be careful when tending these plants.

Australian tree fern (*Cyathea cooperi*)	NC, SC
Tasmanian tree fern (*Dicksonia antarctica*)	IV, NC, SC
Lace fern (*Microlepia strigosa*)	NC, SC
Kimberley Queen sword fern (*Nephrolepis obliterata*)	IV, LD, NC, SC
Leatherleaf fern (*Rumohra adiantiformis*)	IV, NC, SC

FERNS FOR ROCK WALLS OR ROCK GARDENS

Mudslides are an ever-present danger in the hilly residential areas of California, making retaining walls an imperative for many homeowners. Fortunately, one is not limited to concrete block monstrosities; indeed, with a little extra attention to detail, a rock wall can serve both as protection and an elegant garden feature. Add nicely tipped rocks to your wall design to create a fanciful pocket garden that will delight the eye and, perhaps, save your home in the next deluge. For the finishing touch, try some of these ferns in the rock crannies. Some are also suitable for a rock garden.

Holly fern (*Cyrtomium falcatum*)	NC, SC
Southern sword fern (*Nephrolepis cordifolia*)	IV, LD, NC, SC
Green cliff-brake (*Pellaea viridis*)	IV, NC, SC
Licorice fern (*Polypodium glycyrrhiza*)	SN, IV, NC, SC
Leathery polypody (*Polypodium scouleri*)	SN, IV, NC
Japanese lace fern (*Polystichum setosum*)	SN, IV, NC, SC
Hedge fern (*Polystichum setiferum*)	SN, IV, NC, SC

Tough ferns that do well in the Sierra foothills are woodwardia and Alaskan fern, advises Ron Yonkovich of Cameron Park Nursery in Rescue. Both reach 2 to 2½ feet and require shade. Ron says that ferns do fine in the Rescue area, "but they go deciduous in winter. They turn to a bunch of sticks and go brown."

A FEW FERNS WITH COLORFUL FOLIAGE

Ferns range beyond a monotint of green. The Japanese painted fern, for example, combines purple, lavender, and gray-green. The English painted fern has dark green fronds with purple ribs, while brake ferns have variegated fronds. Japanese shield ferns burst into spring with a beautiful reddish hue, turning to green as the leaves mature. Similarly, the royal fern's 'Purpurascens' variety sports purple new growth and stems. A visit to your local botanical garden is sure to add many other unusual varieties to your fern repertoire.

Japanese painted fern (*Athyrium nipponicum* 'Pictum')	SN, IV, NC, SC
English painted fern (*Athyrium otophorum*)	SN, IV, NC, SC
Japanese shield fern (*Dryopteris erythrosora*)	SN, IV, NC, SC
Purple royal fern (*Osmunda regalis* 'Purpurascens')	All
Coffee fern (*Pellaea andromedifolia*)	SN, IV, NC, SC
Staghorn fern (*Platycerium bifurcatum*)	NC, SC
Brake fern (*Pteris*)	NC, SC

Jim Balestreri, owner of the Green Point Nursery in Novato, says, "The fern we sell most of is the western sword fern, *Polystichum munitum*. It's native to California. But the cleanest, most attractive fern is the leatherleaf fern, *Rumohra adiantiformis*, which is used in floral arrangements. This fern was formerly named *Aspidium capense* but was recently reclassified." Plant names are always undergoing change, but Jim says if you have any confusion about old and new names, use the easiest one.

FERNS THAT MAKE GOOD GROUND COVERS

Some ferns send out sneaky shoots, expanding their territory in a profusion of green. Take advantage of their greedy territoriality to create an unusual ground cover that will provide easy maintenance and rapidly expand to fill a bed.

Squirrel's foot fern (*Davallia trichomanoides*)	NC, SC
Bear's foot fern (*Humata tyermannii*)	NC, SC
Southern sword fern (*Nephrolepis cordifolia*)	IV, LD, NC, SC
Sword fern (*Nephrolepis exaltata*)	SC
Sensitive fern (*Onoclea sensibilis*)	SN, IV, NC, SC
Green cliff-brake (*Pellaea viridis*)	IV, NC, SC
Licorice fern (*Polypodium glycyrrhiza*)	SN, IV, NC, SC
Western sword fern (*Polystichum munitum*)	SN, IV, NC, SC

GROUND COVERS

The plants listed in this chapter include a variety of vines, perennials, shrubs, and grasses with a spreading, dense habit of growth. Many also appear in other chapters, but they are grouped here because they are useful for covering the ground densely. While most of us think of ground cover plants as essentially dwarf or diminutive species, a tightly spaced planting of oleanders along the side of a highway is technically a ground cover as well—after all, they do cover the ground. Still, as used here, the term refers primarily to low-growing, low-maintenance plants that present a uniform surface height when planted in masses.

Before planting ground covers, eliminate weeds from the area. Solarization of the soil with black plastic is a method preferred by those who would rather not use chemical herbicides. If you feel that you must use a weed killer, use one that breaks down fairly quickly without leaving persistent residues in the soil. While your plants are just little green spots on the ground with bare dirt between them, keep weeds out by heavy mulching. Fertilize the plants, and water regularly until they are established.

Ground covers can blanket a hillside and keep the soil in place, or just add a touch of color between the stones of a path. Grass is the ground cover of choice for areas where you welcome steady foot traffic, and this chapter includes a section on warm-season and cool-season turf grasses. For less traveled areas of your landscape, you have a broad selection of plants. Some low-growing ground covers, like the humble but popular carpet bugle (*Ajuga reptans*), will withstand light foot traffic and light mowing. Carpet bugle's round dark-green leaves create a soft mat that in spring and early summer bears tiny purple or blue flowers.

Some ground covers are chosen for their attractive foliage, like silvery artemisia, blue fescue, or deep-green wild ginger (*Asarum*). Epimedium and houttuynia offer variegated leaves. The fragrant foliage and summer flowers of creeping thyme and chamomile make these two plants ideal between stepping stones or along the sides of a path, where the small purple flowers of thyme and the bright yellow heads of chamomile add interest, and the leaves can be brushed against by passersby to release their fragrance.

Native to California are various species of manzanita (*Arctostaphylos*) and wild lilac (*Ceanothus*). These spring bloomers tolerate dry conditions well, and manzanita's tiny fruits will bring birds to your garden.

GROUND COVERS FOR SUN OR SHADE

Sometimes a landscaping plan leaves you with a long bed that for part of its expanse is shaded by a large tree or a building. You want a unified look to the bed, and that calls for a ground cover that will succeed equally well in sun or in shade.

Bishop's weed (*Aegopodium podagraria*)	SN, IV, NC, SC
Carpet bugle (*Ajuga reptans*)	All
Chamomile (*Chamaemelum nobile, Anthemis nobilis*)	All
Winter creeper (*Euonymus fortunei*)	SN, IV, HD, LD, NC
Ivy (*Hedera*)	All
Blue star creeper (*Laurentia fluviatilis*)	SN, IV, NC, SC
Virginia creeper (*Parthenocissus quinquefolia*)	All
Evergreen bramble (*Rubus pentalobus*)	SN, IV, NC, SC
Lamb's ears (*Stachys byzantina*)	All
Asian jasmine (*Trachelospermum asiaticum*)	All
Star jasmine (*Trachelospermum jasminoides*)	IV, HD, LD, NC, SC
Barren strawberry (*Waldsteinia*)	SN, IV, NC
Wedelia (*Wedelia trilobata*)	LD, SC

Amacker Bullwinkle, a Palo Alto gardener who has created an English garden feel to her clay-bogged mid-Peninsula domain, recommends lamb's ears, "the wonderfully tactile silvery gray-green ground cover preferred by people with children. It is durable, irresistible, and beautiful and will take both full sun and light shade. It also is flexible in its soil and water requirements, tolerating sandy dry soil as well as heavy clay."

GROUND COVERS FOR FULL SUN

The most popular ground cover for sunny areas is, of course, the lawn. A ground cover is an alternative if you want to cut down on lawn maintenance, reduce water use, or break up the "sheep pasture" look of a vast lawn. Ground covers provide delineating beds of texture and color and a transition to more heavily designed beds of flowers. This list comprises ground covers that will happily grow where a lawn would also thrive. Included are evergreen perennials, dwarf shrubs, and ornamental grasses. For even more choices, check the chapters on shrubs, perennials, roses, and vines, where additional specialized ground covers are listed.

Prostrate abelia (*Abelia grandiflora* 'Prostrata')	All
Carpet bugle (*Ajuga reptans*)	All
Rockcress (*Arabis*)	SN, IV, NC, SC
Bearberry (*Arctostaphylos uva-ursi*)	SN, IV, NC, SC
Silver spreader artemisia (*Artemisia caucasica*)	All
Chamomile (*Chamaemelum nobile, Anthemis nobilis*)	All
Bearberry cotoneaster (*Cotoneaster dammeri*)	All
Rock cotoneaster (*Cotoneaster horizontalis*)	SN, IV, HD, NC, SC
Winter creeper (*Euonymus fortunei*)	SN, IV, HD, LD, NC
English ivy (*Hedera helix*)	All
Creeping St. Johnswort (*Hypericum calycinum*)	All
Prostrate juniper (*Juniperus chinensis* 'Parsonii')	All
Creeping juniper (*Juniperus horizontalis*)	All
Spreading juniper (*Juniperus sabina*)	All

Trailing lantana (*Lantana montevidensis*)	IV, LD, NC, SC
Blue star creeper (*Laurentia fluviatilis*)	SN, IV, NC, SC
Creeping lily turf (*Liriope spicata*)	SN, IV, LD, NC, SC
Oriental fountain grass (*Pennisetum orientale*)	SN, IV, NC, SC
Ribbon grass (*Phalaris arundinacea* 'Dwarf Garters')	SN, IV, NC, SC
Prairie phlox (*Phlox pilosa*)	SN, IV, HD, LD, NC
Creeping phlox (*Phlox stolonifera*)	SN, IV, HD, LD, NC
Moss pink (*Phlox subulata*)	SN, IV, HD, LD, NC
Knotweed (*Polygonum capitatum*)	All
Creeping cinquefoil (*Potentilla tonguei*)	All
Lowboy firethorn (*Pyracantha* 'Lowboy')	All
Ruby Mound firethorn (*Pyracantha* 'Ruby Mound')	SN, IV, LD, NC, SC
Lamb's ears (*Stachys byzantina*)	All
Caraway-scented thyme (*Thymus herba-barona*)	All
Creeping thyme (*Thymus praecox*)	All

For full-sun areas, "verbena is your answer," Amacker Bullwinkle of Palo Alto states. "It spreads like wildfire and can live well enough without regular water, but still manages to thrive in a damp, clay soil." Amacker also likes artemisia, a shrubby ground cover with soft, ferny, velvety, silver-green foliage and a purple flower. "The foliage smells of sage and spice. Elegant in the full sun."

GROUND COVERS FOR LIGHT SHADE

Under the light shade of trees, these plants will do well. For really dark places, see the next list. Ferns also make good ground covers for shaded areas; they can be found in their own chapter.

Carpet bugle (*Ajuga reptans*)	All
Marlberry (*Ardisia japonica*)	IV, NC
Wild ginger (*Asarum caudatum*)	SN, IV, NC, SC
Chamomile (*Chamaemelum nobile, Anthemis nobilis*)	All
Ivy (*Hedera*)	All
Yellow archangel (*Lamium galeobdolon*)	All
Dead nettle (*Lamium maculatum*)	All
Blue star creeper (*Laurentia fluviatilis*)	SN, IV, NC, SC
Creeping lily turf (*Liriope spicata*)	SN, IV, LD, NC, SC
Moneywort, Creeping Jenny (*Lysimachia nummularia*)	SN, IV, NC, SC
Mondo grass (*Ophiopogon japonicus*)	SN, IV, NC, SC
Pachysandra (*Pachysandra terminalis*)	SN, IV, NC, SC
Prairie phlox (*Phlox pilosa*)	SN, IV, HD, LD, NC
Moss pink (*Phlox subulata*)	SN, IV, HD, LD, NC
Yerba buena (*Satureja douglasii, Micromeria chamissonis*)	SN, IV, NC, SC
Saxifrage (*Saxifraga rosacea*)	SN, IV, NC
Strawberry geranium (*Saxifraga stolonifera*)	IV, NC, SC
Baby's tears (*Soleirolia soleirolii, Helxine soleirolii*)	All
Lamb's ears (*Stachys byzantina*)	All
Piggyback plant (*Tolmiea menziesii*)	SN, IV, NC, SC
Dwarf periwinkle (*Vinca minor*)	All
Wedelia (*Wedelia trilobata*)	LD, SC

GROUND COVERS FOR MOIST, POORLY DRAINED SITES

Although most Californians complain about dry soil rather than wet soil, in some regions low spots that retain moisture and drain slowly pose a real problem. Poor drainage leads to poor soil oxygenation and less than optimal conditions for root growth. In the winter rainy season, these areas can become muddy, and walking through them will damage overwintering lawns. One solution is to create stepping stone paths and landscape the rest with moisture-tolerant ground covers.

Bog rosemary (*Andromeda polifolia*)	SN
Wild ginger (*Asarum caudatum*)	SN, IV, NC, SC
Blue sedge (*Carex flacca, C. glauca*)	SN, IV, NC, SC
Turtlehead (*Chelone obliqua*)	SN, IV, NC
Golden star (*Chrysogonum virginianum*)	SN, IV, NC
Dwarf horsetail (*Equisetum scirpoides*)	All
Creeping Jenny (*Lysimachia nummularia*)	SN, IV, NC, SC
Partridgeberry (*Mitchella repens*)	SN, IV
Cranberry (*Vaccinium macrocarpon*)	SN, IV
Cowberry (*Vaccinium vitis-idaea*)	SN, IV, NC

Turtlehead

"A dwarf horsetail could be used as a ground cover in boggy areas," notes Cindy Braley of Foothill Nursery in Shingle Springs. "It grows to 8 inches tall, and it spreads." But use horsetails with caution, she advises, because they have an invasive nature.

GROUND COVERS FOR DEEP SHADE

Here are some ground covers that can be planted beneath the dense shade of trees, or even under decks, as long as they have sufficient water and fertilizer. Remember that many ferns will tolerate deep shade. As a last resort, if it seems that only moss will grow in a very shady area of your garden, then by all means, let the moss grow! Taking plugs and spreading them out will speed up the coverage.

Creeping Jenny

Marlberry (*Ardisia japonica*)	IV, NC
Wild ginger (*Asarum caudatum*)	SN, IV, NC, SC
Lily-of-the-valley (*Convallaria majalis*)	SN, IV, NC, SC
Holly fern (*Cyrtomium falcatum*)	SN, IV, NC, SC
Sweet woodruff (*Galium odoratum*)	SN, IV, NC
Yellow archangel (*Lamium galeobdolon*)	All
Dead nettle (*Lamium maculatum*)	All
Moneywort, Creeping Jenny (*Lysimachia nummularia*)	SN, IV, NC, SC
Pachysandra (*Pachysandra terminalis*)	SN, IV, NC, SC
Rohdea (*Rohdea japonica*)	IV, HD, LD, NC, SC
Sweet box (*Sarcococca humilis*)	SN, IV, NC, SC
Foamflower (*Tiarella cordifolia*)	SN, IV, NC, SC
Piggyback plant (*Tolmiea menziesii*)	SN, IV, NC, SC
Asian jasmine (*Trachelospermum asiaticum*)	All
Star jasmine (*Trachelospermum jasminoides*)	IV, HD, LD, NC, SC
Sweet violet (*Viola odorata*)	All

GROUND COVERS TO STABILIZE A SLOPE

Except for the Inland Valley and Low Desert regions, most of California is hilly or even downright mountainous. As suburban development spreads into rural areas, more and more homes are being built on sites where the land slope is extreme. These areas are impossible to mow, so a lawn is out of the question, and many such sites present the new owner with the problem of potential erosion or mudslides during prolonged rainy weather. The only practical solution when you own an area like this is to plant the slope with a ground cover that has a strong root system to hold the soil and that will stay low enough—say, under three feet—to allow you to enjoy the view from your windows or deck. Some of the plants below require water during the dry summer months; they are not drought-proof natives adapted to hilly land, but civilized ground covers that require tending and care.

Prostrate abelia (*Abelia grandiflora* 'Prostrata')	All	Jasmine
Bearberry (*Arctostaphylos uva-ursi*)	SN, IV, NC, SC	
Blue sedge (*Carex flacca, C. glauca*)	SN, IV, NC, SC	
Crown vetch (*Coronilla varia*)	All	
Bearberry cotoneaster (*Cotoneaster dammeri*)	All	
Rock cotoneaster (*Cotoneaster horizontalis*)	SN, IV, HD, NC, SC	
Emerald Carpet cotoneaster (*Cotoneaster salicifolius* 'Emerald Carpet')	All	
Autumn Fire cotoneaster (*Cotoneaster salicifolius* 'Autumn Fire')	All	
Rosea ice plant (*Drosanthemum floribundum*)	IV, NC, SC	
Winter creeper (*Euonymus fortunei*)	SN, IV, HD, LD, NC	
Carolina jessamine (*Gelsemium sempervirens*)	All	
Ivy (*Hedera*)	All	
Daylily (*Hemerocallis*)	All	
Horseshoe vetch (*Hippocrepis comosa*)	IV, HD, LD, NC, SC	
Creeping St. Johnswort (*Hypericum calycinum*)	All	
Jasmine (*Jasminum*)	All	
Creeping juniper (*Juniperus horizontalis*)	All	
Spreading juniper (*Juniperus sabina*)	All	
Creeping mahonia (*Mahonia repens*)	All	
Japanese honeysuckle (*Lonicera japonica*)	All	
Mexican evening primrose (*Oenothera speciosa*)	All	
Virginia creeper (*Parthenocissus quinquefolia*)	All	
Santa Cruz firethorn (*Pyracantha koidzumii* 'Santa Cruz')	All	
Memorial rose (*Rosa wichuraiana*)	All	
Periwinkle, Myrtle (*Vinca major*)	All	

Wendy Proud of Monrovia Nursery in Azusa says, "An evergreen plant that shopping centers use on slopes is *Trachelospermum*, or star jasmine. You can cut it back to keep it really low, or you can let it grow wild on a bank but it won't take over your house." Wendy also recommends *Jasminum polyanthum*, or pink jasmine, which takes its name from the color of its buds. "It buds up in January and has a fine foliage texture. Grow it on a stake as a vine, or use it as a ground cover. The white, star-shaped flowers are what we call intensely fragrant."

GROUND COVERS FOR THE OCEANFRONT

As those who own sandy oceanfront property know, ground covers are very important around the home to help keep sand in its place. Even for those who live along the North Coast, where cliffs tend to separate houses from the beach, ground cover is an asset. The ground covers listed below will withstand salt spray; they will also work well when interplanted with the oceanfront perennials and shrubs listed in other chapters. All will grow well in both Northern and Southern California, with the possible exception of the ice plants, which may find extreme northern coastal winters a little rough unless they receive some protection.

Bearberry (*Arctostaphylos uva-ursi*)
Chilean ice plant (*Carpobrotus chilensis*)
Carmel creeper (*Ceanothus griseus horizontalis*)
Sageleaf rockrose (*Cistus salviifolius*)
Ice plant (*Delosperma*)
Winter creeper (*Euonymus fortunei*)
Creeping fig (*Ficus pumila*)
Sand strawberry (*Fragaria chiloensis*)
Carolina jessamine (*Gelsemium sempervirens*)
Ivy (*Hedera*)
Sunrose (*Helianthemum nummularium*)
Horseshoe vetch (*Hippocrepis comosa*)
Creeping St. Johnswort (*Hypericum calycinum*)
Winter jasmine (*Jasminum nudiflorum*)
Chinese jasmine (*Jasminum polyanthum*)
Shore juniper (*Juniperus conferta*)
Creeping juniper (*Juniperus horizontalis*)
Golden ice plant (*Lampranthus auranticus*)
Redondo creeper (*Lampranthus filicaulis*)
Purple ice plant (*Lampranthus productus*)
Trailing ice plant (*Lampranthus spectabilis*)
Privet honeysuckle (*Lonicera pileata*)
India hawthorn (*Rhaphiolepis indica*)
Lavender cotton (*Santolina chamaecyparissus*)
Asian jasmine (*Trachelospermum asiaticum*)

Creeping juniper

"Good, low-growing ground covers for oceanfront areas are ice plants," advises Tom Yanagihara Jr. of Ouchi Nursery in San Diego. "That's the *Delosperma* family. They get up to 6 inches high, have flowers in different colors, and are repeat bloomers. 'Disneyland' is very nice with its dime-size white flowers. Another good choice would be small junipers, about 10 to 12 inches high. You won't have any flowers, just the green, but they do well in salt air."

GROUND COVERS FOR DRY SITES

Few of the plants listed below are absolutely drought-proof, but most will survive on very little water. Make sure, however, that these plants get enough water until they are established in your garden.

Woolly yarrow (*Achillea tomentosa*)   All
Cast-iron plant (*Aspidistra elatior*)   SN, IV, LD, NC, SC

Sageleaf rockrose (*Cistus salviifolius, C. villosus* 'Prostratus')   All
Crown vetch (*Coronilla varia*)   All
Bearberry cotoneaster (*Cotoneaster dammeri*)   All
Rock cotoneaster (*Cotoneaster horizontalis*)   SN, IV, HD, NC, SC
Autumn Fire cotoneaster (*Cotoneaster salicifolius* 'Autumn Fire') All
Emerald Carpet cotoneaster   All
    (*Cotoneaster salicifolius* 'Emerald Carpet')
Evergreen broom (*Genista lydia*)   SN, IV, NC
Algerian ivy (*Hedera canariensis*)   IV, LD, NC, SC
Persian ivy (*Hedera colchica*)   All
Creeping St. Johnswort (*Hypericum calycinum*)   All
Creeping juniper (*Juniperus horizontalis*)   All
Trailing lantana (*Lantana montevidensis*)   IV, LD, NC, SC
Japanese honeysuckle (*Lonicera japonica*)   All
Harbour Dwarf nandina (*Nandina domestica* 'Harbour Dwarf') All
Blue-eyed Mary (*Omphalodes verna*)   SN, IV, NC, SC
Jerusalem sage (*Phlomis russelliana, P. samia*)   All
Silver lace vine (*Polygonum aubertii*)   All
Evergreen bramble (*Rubus pentalobus*)   SN, IV, NC, SC
Yerba buena (*Satureja douglasii, Micromeria chamissonis*)   SN, IV, NC, SC
Sedum (*Sedum*)   All
Creeping thyme (*Thymus praecox*)   All

WARM-SEASON AND COOL-SEASON TURF GRASSES

For walk-on expanses of your landscape, turf grass is no doubt the best ground cover. This list is from Vic Gibeault, a cooperative extension specialist with the University of California at Riverside. "Californians benefit from turf grasses in many ways," Vic says. "Turf grasses reduce soil erosion, prevent dust problems, dissipate heat, abate noise, and reduce glare and air pollution. They also provide the low-cost, durable, smooth surface required for many recreational activities, while at the same time giving a safety cushion that is appealing."

Both warm-season and cool-season turf grasses are used in California. According to Vic, "Cool-season species prefer an environment that is relatively cool and at no time is continuously hot both day and night." Cool-season turf grasses would be used in Northern California, Central and Northern Coastal California, and the high-elevation areas of Eastern California. Hot summers in Southern California would stress them. "Warm-season grasses grow best in warm to hot climates," Vic says, which would be in the Central Valley and much of interior Southern California. Warm-season grasses go dormant or lose color during winter months. Both cool-season and warm-season turf grasses are used in the transitional climate zone, along the Southern California coast and around San Francisco Bay.

What follows is a short list of turf grasses that are most suited to California lawns. Vic advises that when buying turf grasses, you should base your choice not only on the climate in your area, but on soil conditions at your site as well.

Cool-Season Grasses
Fine-leaved fescue
Kentucky bluegrass
Perennial ryegrass
Tall fescue

Warm-Season Grasses
Common bermuda grass
Hybrid bermuda grass
St. Augustine grass
Zoysia grass

GROUND COVERS THAT DRAPE AND TRAIL

Many of California's towns were built on hills before heavy earth-moving equipment was available, which in turn resulted in many homes being built on sloping lots. This combination of factors gave rise to one of the most pleasant sights to be found in the older neighborhoods of our coastal and foothill towns and cities: the retaining wall that overlooks a sidewalk, from which drapes and trails a colorful ground cover. The following ground covers will spill and sprawl downward, carrying color and form down the side of a wall and softening its appearance.

Red Apple ice plant (*Aptenia cordifolia* 'Red Apple')	NC, SC
Bearberry (*Arctostaphylos uva-ursi*)	SN, IV, NC, SC
Bearberry cotoneaster (*Cotoneaster dammeri*)	All
Emerald Carpet cotoneaster (*Cotoneaster salicifolius* 'Emerald Carpet')	All
Rosea ice plant (*Drosanthemum floribundum*)	IV, NC, SC
Winter creeper (*Euonymous fortunei*)	SN, IV, HD, LD, NC
Trailing gazania (*Gazania rigens*)	IV, HD, LD, NC, SC
English ivy (*Hedera helix*)	All
Shore juniper (*Juniperus conferta*)	SN, IV, NC, SC
Creeping juniper (*Juniperus horizontalis*)	All
Dead nettle (*Lamium maculatum*)	All
Trailing ice plant (*Lampranthus spectabilis*)	IV, NC, SC
Trailing lantana (*Lantana montevidensis*)	IV, HD, LD, NC, SC
Silver-vein creeper (*Parthenocissus henryana*)	SN, IV, NC
Trailing phlox (*Phlox nivalis*)	SN, IV
Creeping phlox (*Phlox stolonifera*)	SN, IV, HD, LD, NC
Knotweed (*Polygonum capitatum*)	IV, LD, NC, SC
Creeping thyme (*Thymus praecox*)	All
Periwinkle, Myrtle (*Vinca major*)	All
Dwarf periwinkle (*Vinca minor*)	All

Cindy Braley of Foothill Nursery, Shingle Springs, prizes *Rosmarinus officinalis* 'Prostratus,' a fragrant, trailing ground cover with a spread of 4 to 8 feet. It is "very carefree and drought tolerant," Cindy says, and "absolutely resistant to deer." Though slow to start, Cindy advises, rosemary is beautiful when it attains maturity.

GROUND COVERS FOR STEPPING STONES AND CRANNIES

These fairly low-growing plants lend a softening effect to rock walls and stone or brick paths. Plants such as thyme and chamomile will release their scents when passersby brush against them.

Woolly yarrow (*Achillea tomentosa*)	SN, IV, HD, NC, SC
Aubrieta (*Aubrieta deltoidea*)	SN, IV, NC, SC
Chamomile (*Chamaemelum nobile*, *Anthemis nobilis*)	All
Creeping morning glory (*Dichondra micrantha*)	IV, LD, NC, SC
Sweet woodruff (*Galium odoratum*)	SN, IV, NC
Sunrose (*Helianthemum nummularium*)	SN, IV, NC, SC

Green carpet (*Herniaria glabra*)	All
Little Gem candytuft (*Iberis sempervirens* 'Little Gem')	All
Blue star creeper (*Laurentia fluviatilis*)	SN, IV, NC, SC
White cup flower (*Nierembergia repens*)	SN, IV, NC, SC
Creeping phlox (*Phlox stolonifera*)	SN, IV, HD, LD, NC
Irish moss (*Sagina subulata*)	SN, IV, HD, NC, SC
Goldmoss sedum (*Sedum acre*)	All
Baby's tears (*Soleirolia soleirolii, Helxine soleirolii*)	All
Caraway-scented thyme (*Thymus herba-barona*)	All
Woolly thyme (*Thymus pseudolanuginosus*)	All

GROUND COVERS THAT CAN QUICKLY GET OUT OF CONTROL

No one appreciates vigorous plants more than I do; the easier a plant is to grow and the better it adapts to my garden, the more its praises will be sung. But sometimes you can have too much of a good thing, and in the case of ground covers, that means plants that jump their bed boundaries or overtake the companions with which they have been interplanted. Probably the worst offenders in this category in California are ivy, Virginia creeper, honeysuckle, and periwinkle. All four will climb trees, reach across driveways, strangle perennials and small shrubs, and generally get out of hand. Limit their use to large beds, and avoid interplanting them with other plants. If there are trees in their beds, be prepared to trim their exploratory tendrils off the trunks twice a year.

Bishop's weed (*Aegopodium podagraria*)	SN, IV, NC, SC
Crown vetch (*Coronilla varia*)	All
Horsetail (*Equisetum hyemale*)	All
English ivy (*Hedera helix*)	All
Yellow archangel (*Lamium galeobdolon*)	All
Dead nettle (*Lamium maculatum*)	All
Japanese honeysuckle (*Lonicera japonica*)	All
Virginia creeper (*Parthenocissus quinquefolia*)	All
Baby's tears (*Soleirolia soleirolii, Helxine soleirolii*)	All
Periwinkle, Myrtle (*Vinca major*)	All

ANNUALS

When you plant perennials, you count on them coming back again next year and the year after. Annuals you aren't going to see again unless they self-sow and provide you with their descendants. You might think of annuals as the accessories of the garden. By changing them every year, you provide your garden with different accents. Among the perennials—the constant elements of a garden bed—add some annuals that can vary year to year, depending on your changing tastes or new plants you become aware of. The lists in this chapter may introduce you to something you never heard of before, or remind you of an old favorite.

These annuals should do fine in all growing zones in California, so no zone codes have been included in the lists. Some of the plants in these lists are botanically perennials; in cold-winter areas of California they will die at the first frost, but they will live on for years in areas of no frost or where winters are mild. Some are biennials; they will overwinter and bloom in their second year.

ANNUALS THAT DO WELL IN SHADE

Most people associate annual flowers with bright, splashy, sunlit meadows, but plenty of annuals grow and bloom dependably in areas of shade.

Begonia (*Begonia*)
Browallia, Amethyst flower (*Browallia speciosa*)
Caladium (*Caladium bicolor*)
Coleus (*Coleus hybridus*)
Foxglove (*Digitalis purpurea*)
Gerbera daisy (*Gerbera jamesonii*)
Impatiens (*Impatiens wallerana*)
Jacobinia (*Justicia carnea*)
Lobelia (*Lobelia*)
Monkey flower (*Mimulus hybridus*)
Forget-me-not (*Myosotis*)
Nicotiana, Flowering tobacco (*Nicotiana alata*)

Begonia

Woodland nicotiana (*Nicotiana sylvestris*)
Star clusters (*Pentas lanceolata*)
Salvia (*Salvia coccinea*)
Scarlet sage (*Salvia splendens*)
Lilac sage (*Salvia verticillata*)
Schizanthus, Poor-man's orchid (*Schizanthus pinnatus*)
Cineraria, Annual dusty miller (*Senecio hybridus*)
Black-eyed Susan vine (*Thunbergia alata*)
Wishbone flower (*Torenia fournieri*)
Johnny-jump-up (*Viola tricolor*)

> There aren't many truly blue flowers, but Cyndee Carvalho of Alden Lane Nursery in Livermore says that one of the prettiest is *Browallia*, or amethyst flower. "It's a real periwinkle-blue flower, and it does well in shade in the summer months." Suitable for hanging baskets and pots, *Browallia* is also used in cut arrangements.

ANNUALS YOU CAN PLANT IN THE HEAT OF SUMMER

It's the middle of summer and you are behind on your gardening. How will you fill those empty beds? It's vacation time and you've just moved the family to the cabin. How are you going to bring some quick color to the front yard? Nursery proprietors are ready for people with problems like yours; in early summer they begin heavily advertising their 4-inch pots of color—small annuals ready to plant out, some already in flower. These are quick-growing plants selected for their ability to overcome a late start. When planting them out, prepare the soil well and give them a steady supply of water so their growth will not be checked. If buying pots of color seems a bit like cheating, you can raise them up in flats yourself and set them out when they are ready.

Begonia (*Begonia*)
Caladium (*Caladium bicolor*)
Madagascar periwinkle (*Catharanthus roseus, Vinca rosea*)
Chinese woolflower (*Celosia* 'Childsii')
Crested cockscomb (*Celosia* 'Cristada')
Plume cockscomb (*Celosia* 'Plumosa')
Cleome (*Cleome*)
Coleus (*Coleus hybridus*)
Hyacinth bean (*Dolichos lablab*)
Blue daze (*Evolvulus glomeratus*)
Globe amaranth (*Gomphrena globosa*)
Sunflower (*Helianthus annuus*)
Impatiens (*Impatiens wallerana*)
Moonflower (*Ipomoea alba*)
Morning glory (*Ipomoea tricolor*)
Blackfoot daisy (*Melampodium leucanthum*)
Star clusters (*Pentas lanceolata*)
Marigold (*Tagetes*)
Mexican sunflower (*Tithonia rotundifolia*)
Verbena (*Verbena* hybrids)
Zinnia (*Zinnia elegans*)

ANNUALS TO GROW FROM SEEDS IN SUMMER

If you've missed the main buying season for those 4-inch pots of color at the garden center, that doesn't mean you have to be without flowers in your garden. Or maybe you just enjoy the therapeutic value of working the soil and planting seeds. In this list you will find some annuals that can get a late start but still produce respectable plants and flowers.

Joseph's-coat (*Amaranthus tricolor*)
Cosmos (*Cosmos*)
Hyacinth bean (*Dolichos lablab*)
Impatiens (*Impatiens wallerana*)
Moonflower (*Ipomoea alba*)
Butter daisy (*Melampodium paludosum*)
Marigold (*Tagetes*)
Zinnia (*Zinnia elegans*)

Zinnia

ANNUALS FOR SUNNY, HOT, DRY PLACES

Sandy soil that doesn't hold water, bright locations next to south-facing stucco walls, and small beds surrounded by heat-retaining pavement are difficult places for many annuals—except these. All of the annuals listed here are adapted to heat, light, and minimum water. These are not drought-proof flowers, but they can be left while you're on vacation for a week, and although they may be wilted when you return, they'll spring back.

Desert marigold (*Baileya multiradiata*)
Madagascar periwinkle (*Catharanthus roseus*, *Vinca rosea*)
Cleome (*Cleome hasslerana*)
Annual coreopsis (*Coreopsis tinctoria*)
Yellow cosmos (*Cosmos sulphureus*)
Blanket flower (*Gaillardia pulchella*)
Globe amaranth (*Gomphrena*)
Lantana (*Lantana*)
Portulaca, Rose moss (*Portulaca grandiflora*)
Purslane (*Portulaca oleracea*)
Black-eyed Susan (*Rudbeckia hirta*)
Gloriosa daisy (*Rudbeckia hirta* 'Gloriosa Daisy')
Mexican bush sage (*Salvia leucantha*)
Scaevola (*Scaevola aemula* 'Blue Wonder')
Peruvian verbena (*Verbena peruviana*)

"The Davis area is more regularly Mediterranean than the Mediterranean itself," says Warren Roberts of the UC Davis Arboretum, explaining why Mediterranean plants do so well in California. "The true Mediterranean climate has significant rain only in winter. May to December, sometimes we have a soaking rain, but usually no rain at all. In the Davis area during the long dry season, we may only water plants to wash off dust."

ANNUALS THAT BLOOM UNAIDED FROM SPRING UNTIL FROST

The plants in this list will keep on blooming for a long season, from spring until the first frost, and can do it without your having to do any deadheading (removing the spent blooms).

Ageratum (*Ageratum houstonianum*)
Wax begonia (*Begonia semperflorens*)
Gomphrena (*Globe amaranth*)
Impatiens (*Impatiens wallerana*)
Moonflower (*Ipomoea alba*)
Morning glory (*Ipomoea tricolor*)
Lantana (*Lantana*)
Pentas (*Pentas lanceolata*)
Narrowleaf zinnia (*Zinnia angustifolia*)

ANNUALS THAT BLOOM FROM SPRING TO FROST IF YOU DEADHEAD

Deadheading is what gardeners call removing the dead blooms from plants. As soon as annuals set seed, they begin shutting down operations, which means they won't be producing more flowers. By removing the faded blossoms before the seeds begin to ripen, you trick annuals into producing more flowers in an effort to make seeds. Here is a list of annuals that you can keep flowering by snipping off the old blooms.

Cleome (*Cleome hasslerana*)
Annual coreopsis (*Coreopsis tinctoria*)
Cosmos (*Cosmos bipinnatus*)
Yellow cosmos (*Cosmos sulphureus*)
Sweet William (*Dianthus barbatus*)
Chinese pink (*Dianthus chinensis*)
Blanket flower (*Gaillardia pulchella*)
Geranium, Pelargonium (*Pelargonium*)
Petunia (*Petunia hybrida*)
Mealycup sage (*Salvia farinacea*)
Scarlet sage (*Salvia splendens*)
African marigold (*Tagetes erecta*)
Mexican sunflower (*Tithonia rotundifolia*)
Zinnia (*Zinnia elegans*)

For a long season of bloom and minimal care, Michael A. Parten of Orchard Nursery & Florist in Lafayette recommends tuberous begonias, perennials frequently treated as annuals. "They require zero deadheading," Michael says, and notes that impatiens also need no removal of spent blooms. Other suggestions for plants that get by with minimal or no deadheading are violas, pansies, and Madagascar periwinkle. Annuals that do better if deadheaded but can be left on their own are cosmos, petunias, and zinnias. Michael notes, "Marigolds are excellent if deadheaded, but you can also let them grow."

ANNUALS THAT DO AND DON'T WITHSTAND OVERHEAD WATERING

The summer rains, hails, and thunderstorms that can smash blooming plants to the ground are rarely a problem in California the way they are in the east—but unless you have a water-saving drip system or low-output sprinklers, you will be watering by hose or with high-volume rotating sprinklers, and the latter can do just as much damage to annuals as a driving rain. Tall plants with heavy flower heads, such as zinnias and snapdragons, often get badly beaten by overhead watering, so if you water with a "Rainbird" type sprinkler, you'll find annuals here that can tolerate the downpour.

Annuals That Withstand Overhead Watering
Silk flower (*Abelmoschus sakensis*)
Ageratum (*Ageratum houstonianum*)
China aster (*Callistephus chinensis*)
Madagascar periwinkle (*Catharanthus roseus, Vinca rosea*)
Crested cockscomb (*Celosia* 'Cristata')
Chinese pink (*Dianthus chinensis*)

Annuals That Suffer From Heavy Overhead Watering
Snapdragon (*Antirrhinum majus*)
Plume cockscomb (*Celosia* 'Plumosa')
Bachelor's button, Cornflower (*Centaurea cyanus*)
Cosmos (*Cosmos bipinnatus*)
Roselle, Jamaica sorrel (*Hibiscus sabdariffa*)
Flanders poppy (*Papaver rhoeas*)
Opium poppy (*Papaver somniferum*)
Petunia (*Petunia hybrida*)
Zinnia (*Zinnia elegans*)

ANNUALS FOR ALKALINE SOIL

Alkaline soil has a pH level above 7, which is a measure of the chemical composition of the soil. Alkaline soil, usually found in areas of little rainfall, is high in calcium carbonate (lime) and sodium. Many plants tolerate or even prefer alkaline conditions, and the annuals in this list will do fine in such soil. However, you can reduce your soil's alkalinity by working in organic matter, and you can apply periodic infusions of an acid-type fertilizer.

Snapdragon (*Antirrhinum majus*)
China aster (*Callistephus chinensis*)
Basket flower (*Centaurea americana*)
Bachelor's button, Cornflower (*Centaurea cyanus*)
Clarkia (*Clarkia unguiculata*)
Cleome (*Cleome hasslerana*)
Larkspur (*Consolida ambigua*)
Cosmos (*Cosmos bipinnatus*)
Dahlberg daisy (*Dyssodia tenuiloba*)
California poppy (*Eschscholzia californica*)
Lisianthus (*Eustoma grandiflorum*)

Black-eyed
Susan

Blanket flower (*Gaillardia pulchella*)
Globe amaranth (*Gomphrena globosa*)
Baby's breath (*Gypsophila elegans*)
Sunflower (*Helianthus annuus*)
Candytuft (*Iberis umbellata*)
Scarlet flax (*Linum grandiflorum*)
Lobelia (*Lobelia erinus*)
Sweet alyssum (*Lobularia maritima*)
Money plant, Honesty (*Lunaria annua*)
Texas bluebonnet (*Lupinus texensis*)
Stock (*Matthiola incana*)
Butter daisy (*Melampodium paludosum*)
Forget-me-not (*Myosotis sylvatica*)
Love-in-a-mist (*Nigella damascena*)
Iceland poppy (*Papaver nudicaule*)
Opium poppy (*Papaver somniferum*)
Annual phlox (*Phlox drummondii*)
Gloriosa daisy, Black-eyed Susan (*Rudbeckia hirta*)
Mexican sunflower (*Tithonia rotundifolia*)
Narrowleaf zinnia (*Zinnia angustifolia*)
Zinnia (*Zinnia elegans, Z. haageana*)

EASY ANNUALS FOR POOR, SANDY SOIL

Most gardeners prepare a special bedding soil for annuals, rich in organic matter for fertilization and moisture retention. However, here are some annuals that don't require all that fuss and bother. These will grow in poor, sandy soil, and may also make do with a less-than-generous ration of summer watering.

Annual coreopsis, Calliopsis (*Coreopsis tinctoria*)
Cosmos (*Cosmos bipinnatus*)
Livingstone daisy (*Dorotheanthus bellidiformis*)
Mexican fire plant (*Euphorbia heterophylla*)
Blanket flower (*Gaillardia pulchella*)
Sunflower (*Helianthus annuus*)
Butter daisy (*Melampodium paludosum*)
Petunia (*Petunia*)
California bluebells (*Phacelia campanularia*)
Portulaca, Rose moss (*Portulaca grandiflora*)
Mexican sunflower (*Tithonia rotundifolia*)
Nasturtium (*Tropaeolum majus*)

The California native clarkias and godetias like poor, sandy soil and full sun. Reaching heights of 1 to 2 feet, these annuals sport single or double flowers in a range of colors, including pink, lavender, white, red, and yellow. The flowers can be used in cut arrangements.

ANNUALS THAT SELF-SOW

In the wild, annuals must reseed themselves or they will die out—but getting them to perform that feat in your garden is not always easy. The closer your soil conditions, weather, and temperature patterns are to a flower's natural habitat, the more likely it is that it will reseed. The following annuals can be expected to perform in a wide range of temperature and soil conditions.

Hollyhock (*Alcea rosea*)
Bachelor's button, Cornflower (*Centaurea cyanus*)
English wallflower (*Cheiranthus cheiri*)
Oxeye daisy (*Chrysanthemum leucanthemum*)
Feverfew (*Chrysanthemum parthenium*)
Larkspur (*Consolida ambigua*)
Annual coreopsis, Calliopsis (*Coreopsis tinctoria*)
Cosmos (*Cosmos bipinnatus*)
Chinese forget-me-not (*Cynoglossum amabile*)
Sweet William (*Dianthus barbatus*)
Siberian wallflower (*Erysimum alpinum*)
California poppy (*Eschscholzia californica*)
Globe amaranth (*Gomphrena globosa*)
Baby blue eyes (*Nemophila menziesii*)
Nicotiana (*Nicotiana*)
Love-in-a-mist (*Nigella damascena*)
Flanders poppy (*Papaver rhoeas*)
Petunia (*Petunia purpurea*)
Black-eyed Susan (*Rudbeckia hirta*)
Johnny-jump-up (*Viola tricolor*)
Zinnia (*Zinnia elegans*)

"Baby blue eyes (*Nemophila menziesii*), an annual native, is a nice little plant," says Ernie G. Wasson of the Berkeley Horticultural Nursery. "The flowers—sky blue with white centers—form open cups. This is a plant for a sunny spot. They are easy to grow, and if they like a spot, they'll reseed and come back. I used to see them growing only naturally in California, but when I went to England, I saw them in English gardens. They are used in California gardens more now. Sometimes English gardeners recognize a plant's horticultural value before the original country does. The exotic is tried before the native. People are recently realizing that natives are some of the most beautiful flowers." Baby blue eyes is available as seeds or as 4-inch annuals.

ANNUALS FOR THE OCEANFRONT

As with any plant grown along the coast, oceanfront annuals must be able to withstand steady winds, foggy days, and salt spray. The plants that can take it generally form neat, low mounds and have sturdy stems or rugged leaves that can shrug off salty air. Some of them, such as the calendulas that have naturalized along the Mendocino coast, seem to actually enjoy the cooler temperatures afforded them by this niche climate.

Floss flower (*Ageratum houstonianum*)
Wax begonia (*Begonia semperflorens*)

Ornamental cabbage (*Brassica oleracea*)
Ornamental kale (*Brassica oleracea*)
Calendula (*Calendula officinalis*)
Clarkia (*Clarkia*)
Sweet William (*Dianthus barbatus*)
California poppy (*Eschscholzia californica*)
Blanket flower (*Gaillardia pulchella*)
Gazania (*Gazania rigens*)
Impatiens (*Impatiens wallerana*)
Lantana (*Lantana*)
Sweet alyssum (*Lobularia maritima*)
Lady Washington pelargonium (*Pelargonium domesticum*)
Ivy geranium (*Pelargonium peltatum*)
Portulaca, Rose moss (*Portulaca grandiflora*)
Annual dusty miller (*Senecio hybridus*)
Verbena (*Verbena hybrida*)

ANNUALS GROWN FOR COLORFUL FOLIAGE

The annuals in this list are grown for the color of their foliage, although some have pretty flowers as well. The dense green leaves of the burning bush kochia turn vibrant red in the fall. Snow-on-the-mountain's pale green and white leaves contrast well with the bright colors of zinnias and the darker begonias. What would our winters be without the spectacular purples, whites, grays, and greens of ornamental kale and cabbage?

Joseph's coat (*Amaranthus tricolor*)
Red-leafed begonia (*Begonia*)
Ornamental cabbage (*Brassica oleracea*)
Ornamental kale (*Brassica oleracea*)
Coleus (*Coleus*)
Snow-on-the-mountain (*Euphorbia marginata*)
Polka-dot plant (*Hypoestes phyllostachya*)
Bloodleaf (*Iresine*)
Burning bush, Kochia (*Kochia scoparia*)
Shiso (*Perilla frutescens*)
Castor bean (*Ricinus communis*)
Annual dusty miller (*Senecio hybridus*)

Vegetables are annuals too, notes Tom Yanagihara Sr. of Ouchi Nursery in San Diego. Most gardeners don't think of these as suitable candidates for the front yard, but Tom sells mustard, turnip, and collard seeds by the scoop, and they are extremely popular in his area. "These plants fare well along the South Coast, due to our mild winters and year-round growing season. They don't burn in the summer, although they may go to seed if it's too hot. If you're worried about the heat, offer them 50 percent shading, and you can take these crops from seed to table in about two months."

ANNUAL WILDFLOWERS FOR A MEADOW MIX

Here is a mixture of wildflowers that will do well throughout most of California. Already prepared mixtures are available for the mountains, oceanfront areas, and inland valleys, so check with your local nursery for their regional recommendations.

Bachelor's button (*Centaurea cyanus*)
Annual coreopsis, Calliopsis (*Coreopsis tinctoria*)
California poppy (*Eschscholzia californica*)
Blanket flower (*Gaillardia pulchella*)
Tidytips (*Layia platyglossa*)
Annual lupine (*Lupinus hartwegii*)
Sky lupine (*Lupinus nanus*)
Forget-me-not (*Myosotis sylvatica*)
Baby blue eyes (*Nemophila menziesii*)
California bluebells (*Phacelia campanularia*)
Annual phlox (*Phlox drummundii*)
Gloriosa daisy, Black-eyed Susan (*Rudbeckia hirta*)

Carol Bornstein, horticulture director at the Santa Barbara Botanic Garden, suggests several native annuals for a meadow or natural effect: California poppy, clarkia, phacelia, tidytips, Chinese houses, lupines, and baby blue eyes. Chinese houses have flowers stacked on the stalk for an interesting effect. "They look like the tops of pagodas. The flowers are pretty, open throated, and can be blue, lavender, or pink. These plants do well in shade or sun."

ANNUALS FOR BEGINNERS

If you are just starting with annuals, here are some that are very easy to grow, especially if they are given well-drained soil enriched with compost or other organic matter. Many nurseries sell these old-stand-bys in flats at the beginning of the year, or as 4-inch pots of color as the summer progresses. Beginning gardener's should note one thing, however, about the very easy marigold. In much of California, these flowers can be little more than high-priced snail-food when they are bedded out in summer. It is exquisitely disappointing for a beginning gardener to set out a blooming bed of marigolds and come back the next day to find them stripped of their leaves.

Snapdragon (*Antirrhinum majus*)
Wax begonia (*Begonia semperflorens*)
Madagascar periwinkle (*Catharanthus roseus, Vinca rosea*)
Sweet William (*Dianthus barbatus*)
California poppy (*Eschscholzia californica*)
Globe amaranth (*Gomphrena globosa*)
Impatiens (*Impatiens wallerana*)
Lantana (*Lantana*)

Snapdragon

Butter daisy (*Melampodium paludosum*)
Petunia (*Petunia*)
Salvia, Sage (*Salvia*)
Pincushion flower (*Scabiosa atropurpurea, S. grandiflora*)
Marigold (*Tagetes*)
Verbena (*Verbena*)
Pansy (*Viola wittrockiana*)

Don Rodrigues of Pacific Horticulture Consultants in Ventura says, "This area of California has its best weather in winter. The rains start around January and continue through March. Summer is when the fog rolls in." For popular, easy annuals Don advises, "Impatiens do incredibly well here year round. They don't freeze in winter, so they act like a perennial here." Impatiens are probably the top-selling annual in California, Don says, with petunias close behind, followed by pansies and marigolds. To combat snail attacks on marigolds and other plants, Don says pastes containing metaldehyde are effective. "In the Ventura area, snails are so bad, people put 3-inch copper bands around tree trunks. Snails won't cross copper, and this saves the tree's leaves and fruit. For a biological approach, there's a snail that eats immature garden snails."

ANNUALS THAT MAKE GOOD CUT FLOWERS

When you have a garden of your own, the question of whether a plant makes good cut flowers—ones that will last more than a day in an arrangement—is not terribly important. However, if you want to make arrangements for others from flowers you grow yourself, this list should help.

Snapdragon (*Antirrhinum majus*)
China aster (*Callistephus chinensis*)
Bachelor's button, Cornflower (*Centaurea cyanus*)
Cleome (*Cleome hasslerana*)
Larkspur (*Consolida ambigua*)
Cosmos (*Cosmos bipinnatus*)
Yellow cosmos (*Cosmos sulphureus*)
Sunflower (*Helianthus annuus*)
Strawflower (*Helichrysum bracteatum*)
Sweet pea (*Lathyrus odoratus*)
Toadflax (*Linaria maroccana*)
Butter daisy (*Melampodium paludosum*)
Poppy (*Papaver*)
Gloriosa daisy, Black-eyed Susan (*Rudbeckia hirta*)
Scarlet sage (*Salvia splendens*)
Pincushion flower (*Scabiosa atropurpurea*)
Marigold (*Tagetes*)
Nasturtium (*Tropaeolum majus*)
Pansy (*Viola wittrockiana*)
Zinnia (*Zinnia*)

SUPER EASY FLOWERS FROM A PACKET OF SEEDS

These annuals are easy to start from seed, and they develop quickly. Just follow the directions on the seed packet, which will tell you when to sow the seeds, how much soil cover to give them, and what light conditions they require. Give them water to get them started.

Calendula (*Calendula officinalis*)
Bachelor's button (*Centaurea cyanus*)
Annual coreopsis, Calliopsis (*Coreopsis tinctoria*)
Cosmos (*Cosmos bipinnatus*)
Yellow cosmos (*Cosmos sulphureus*)
Sweet William (*Dianthus barbatus*)
Hyacinth bean (*Dolichos lablab*)
California poppy (*Eschscholzia californica*)
Globe amaranth (*Gomphrena globosa*)
Sunflower (*Helianthus annuus*)
Moonflower (*Ipomoea alba*)
Sweet pea (*Lathyrus odoratus*)
Toadflax (*Linaria maroccana*)
Scarlet runner bean (*Phaseolus coccineus*)
Marigold (*Tagetes*)
Mexican sunflower (*Tithonia rotundifolia*)
Nasturtium (*Tropaeolum majus*)
Zinnia (*Zinnia elegans*)

ANNUALS FOR FRAGRANCE

Many annuals attract pollinators through their bright colors, and although some have a slight fragrance, as a class of plants, annuals are not known for their alluring perfumes. This list contains the exceptions: annuals that emit beautiful aromas. Plant them were you will walk near them and get the benefit of their fragrance—by the front door, in containers on the steps, or in window boxes. Nicotiana's fragrance will be strongest in the evening.

Sweet William (*Dianthus barbatus*)
Heliotrope (*Heliotropium arborescens*)
Moonflower (*Ipomoea alba*)
Sweet pea (*Lathyrus odoratus*)
Sweet alyssum (*Lobularia maritima*)
Stock (*Matthiola*)
Four o'clock (*Mirabilis jalapa*)
Nicotiana, Flowering tobacco (*Nicotiana alata*)
Woodland nicotiana (*Nicotiana sylvestris*)
Petunia (*Petunia*)
Nasturtium (*Tropaeolum majus*)

Sweet
William

ANNUALS THAT TRAIL OVER EDGES

Trailing annuals are usually grown in hanging basket containers or window boxes, but they may also be used to edge larger containers filled with upright annuals or perennials or for raised beds. Use them anywhere you want a cascading effect.

Firetail (*Acalypha pendula*)
Climbing snapdragon (*Asarina*)
Swan River daisy (*Brachycome iberidifolia*)
Dahlberg daisy (*Dyssodia tenuiloba*)
Licorice plant (*Helichrysum petiolare*)
Polka-dot plant (*Hypoestes phyllostachya*)
New Guinea impatiens (*Impatiens* New Guinea hybrids)
Trailing lantana (*Lantana montevidensis*)
Trailing lobelia (*Lobelia erinus*)
Lady Washington pelargonium (*Pelargonium domesticum*)
Ivy geranium (*Pelargonium peltatum*)
Petunia (*Petunia hybrida*)
Swedish ivy (*Plectranthus*)
Creeping zinnia (*Sanvitalia procumbens*)
Scaevola (*Scaevola aemula*)
Purple Heart (*Setcreasea pallida* 'Purple Heart')
Nasturtium (*Tropaeolum majus*)
Verbena (*Verbena hybrida*)

Annual alyssum is a trailing plant that gets about a foot tall, grows in almost any soil, and has a long bloom season. "Alyssum comes in a variety of colors," says Michael A. Parten of Orchard Nursery & Florist in Lafayette. "You'll find white, pink, purple, and mixed colors. There are also apricot and coral in the new mixes."

ANNUALS FOR CLAY SOIL

Of course you are working to improve your soil every year, but if you have just moved into a new house, what do you do with that heavy adobe right now? Well, add some compost, leaf mold, or manure, plus a bit of sterile sand, and in the meantime, plant these annuals that will endure clay soil.

Silk flower (*Abelmoschus moschatus*)
Love-lies-bleeding (*Amaranthus caudatus*)
Yellow cosmos (*Cosmos sulphureus*)
Globe amaranth (*Gomphrena globosa*)
Sunflower (*Helianthus annuus*)
Moonflower (*Ipomoea alba*)
Cypress vine (*Ipomoea quamoclit*)
Morning glory (*Ipomoea tricolor*)

ANNUALS FOR WINTER AND EARLY SPRING

In California, we are lucky enough to have a climate that allows us to plant annuals in the fall and early winter for bloom throughout the cool season. In most parts of the state except the cold-winter Sierra, these plants will need no winter protection at all. In marginal areas, a light covering of straw may benefit them.

Snapdragon (*Anthirrhinum majus*)
English daisy (*Bellis perennis*)
Ornamental cabbage (*Brassica oleracea*)
Ornamental kale (*Brassica oleracea*)
Calendula (*Calendula officinalis*)
Bachelor's button, Cornflower (*Centauria cyanus*)
English wallflower (*Cheiranthus cheiri*)
Godetia (*Clarkia amoena*)
Larkspur (*Consolida ambigua*)
Chinese forget-me-not (*Cynoglossum amabile*)
Dianthus (*Dianthus purpurea*)
Foxglove (*Digitalis*)
California poppy (*Eschscholzia californica*)
Sweet pea (*Lathyrus odorata*)
Stock (*Matthiola*)
Forget-me-not (*Myosotis sylvatica*)
Poppy (*Papaver*)
Cineraria, Annual dusty miller (*Senecio hybridus*)
Viola (*Viola cornuta*)
Johnny-jump-up (*Viola tricolor*)
Pansy (*Viola wittrockiana*)

Tulips are a good choice for containers to provide color in March and April, advises Lucy Tolmach, director of horticulture at the Filoli estate gardens in Woodside. "California gardeners use tulips as annuals in pots. They don't bloom reliably the second year because the winter temperatures aren't cold enough to keep the bulb dormant." For Filoli, the best tulips are late-bloomers "like the peony types, cottage, single late, or French tulips. These bloom better with less chilling, and they bloom late enough to miss the rains, which batter tulip blossoms in California." Some of the late March and early April bloomers at Filoli are 'Renown,' 'Angelique,' and 'Mrs. John Scheepers.'

One shade-tolerant perennial frequently treated as a winter annual is primrose. Cyndee Carvalho of Alden Lane Nursery in Livermore recommends fairy primrose, *Primula malacoides,* for its light-green leaf and fluffy, feathery blooms. She also likes English primrose, *Primula vulgaris,* which has attractive dark-green leaves and bold, bright colors. But her favorite might be *Primula obconica,* or German primrose. "It has cabbage-like leaves at the base, and trumpet-like flowers in pastel pink, blue, or peach."

TALL ANNUALS FOR THE BACK OF
A BORDER

In the "English garden" style, the tallest plants will be at the back of a border that follows a wall or pathway. If the bed is made in the French "parterre" style, so that the viewer will walk all around it, the tallest plants go at the center.

Hollyhock (*Alcea rosea*)
Love-lies-bleeding (*Amaranthus caudatus*)
Joseph's coat (*Amaranthus tricolor*)
Snapdragon (*Antirrhinum majus*)
Plume cockscomb (*Celosia* 'Plumosa')
Cleome (*Cleome hasslerana*)
Cosmos (*Cosmos bipinnatus*)
Foxglove (*Digitalis purpurea*)
Sunflower (*Helianthus annuus*)
Roselle, Jamaica sorrel (*Hibiscus sabdariffa*)
Mallow (*Lavatera trimestris*)
Woodland nicotiana (*Nicotiana sylvestris*)
Opium poppy (*Papaver somniferum*)
Castor bean (*Ricinus communis*)
Mexican sunflower (*Tithonia rotundifolia*)

Annual
sunflower

WAIT TILL IT'S WARM TO PLANT THESE

If you live in a region with cold winters, this list may spell the difference between success and failure. These annuals don't like cool spring weather, and if you set them out too early, even though frost has passed, they won't grow well. Wait until two to three weeks after the last frost to plant them, though, and they will do just fine.

Love-lies-bleeding (*Amaranthus caudatus*)
Joseph's coat (*Amaranthus tricolor*)
Madagascar periwinkle (*Catharanthus roseus, Vinca rosea*)
Chinese woolflower (*Celosia* 'Childsii')
Crested cockscomb (*Celosia* 'Cristata')
Plume cockscomb (*Celosia* 'Plumosa')
Cleome (*Cleome hasslerana*)
Globe amaranth (*Gomphrena globosa*)
Impatiens (*Impatiens*)
Morning glory (*Ipomoea nil, I. tricolor*)
Zinnia (*Zinnia elegans*)

 Ted Mayeda of M & M Nursery, Orange, takes the concept of the vegetable as an ornamental annual one step further. Ted encourages his customers to try vegetables in patio baskets. "Treat them as if they were ground plants," Ted says. "Just water them, and spray once in a while for insects. You can grow tomatoes, herbs, beans, zucchini, eggplant, and even the compact watermelons just as successfully in baskets as you can flowers like lobelia and impatiens."

ANNUALS THAT ATTRACT HUMMINGBIRDS

Hummingbirds prefer brightly colored flowers—especially those that are red and deep pink—with plenty of nectar. Here is a list of annuals that hummingbirds will feed on. Try to supplement such a planting with some of their favorite perennials (see page 32) and be sure to supply them with a source of water, too.

Hollyhock (*Alcea rosea*)
Indian paintbrush (*Castilleja coccinea*)
Clarkia (*Clarkia*)
Cleome (*Cleome hasslerana*)
Godetia (*Godetia*)
Impatiens (*Impatiens*)
Cardinal climber, Cypress vine (*Ipomoea quamoclit*)
Morning glory (*Ipomoea tricolor*)
Monkey flower (*Mimulus hybridus*)
Four o'clock (*Mirabilis jalapa*)
Nicotiana, Flowering tobacco (*Nicotiana alata*)
Geranium (*Pelargonium*)
Star clusters (*Pentas lanceolata*)
Petunia (*Petunia*)
Phlox (*Phlox drummundii*)
Scarlet sage (*Salvia splendens*)
Nasturtium (*Tropaeolum majus*)
Zinnia (*Zinnia*)

Cleome

ANNUALS WITH SEEDS FOR BIRDS TO EAT

Birds will flock to your garden to eat the seeds of these annuals, as long as you don't deadhead the spent flowers. If you decide to grow these plants for birdseed, you will reduce the number of flowers, because annuals like zinnia, cosmos, and tithonia will produce many more blossoms if deadheaded. Consider growing a group in your flower bed, which you will deadhead, and plant a birdseed group in your vegetable garden, where it can go to seed naturally.

Bachelor's button, Cornflower (*Centaurea cyanus*)
Annual coreopsis, Calliopsis (*Coreopsis tinctoria*)
Cosmos (*Cosmos bipinnatus*)
Yellow cosmos (*Cosmos sulphureus*)
California poppy (*Eschscholzia californica*)
Blanket flower (*Gaillardia pulchella*)
Sunflower (*Helianthus annuus*)
Black-eyed Susan (*Rudbeckia hirta*)
Marigold (*Tagetes*)
Mexican sunflower (*Tithonia rotundifolia*)
Zinnia (*Zinnia elegans*)

ANNUALS THAT ATTRACT BUTTERFLIES

To have a steady population of butterflies in your garden, plant nectar-producing flowers for the adult butterflies, and host plants for the baby caterpillars to grow on (and don't spray those caterpillars with pesticides).

Flowers for Butterflies
Snapdragon (*Antirrhinum majus*)
Yellow cosmos (*Cosmos sulphureus*)
Pink (*Dianthus*)
Globe amaranth (*Gomphrena globosa*)
Heliotrope (*Heliotropium arborescens*)
Impatiens (*Impatiens wallerana*)
Lantana (*Lantana*)
Sweet pea (*Lathyrus odoratus*)
Sweet alyssum (*Lobularia maritima*)
Star clusters (*Pentas lanceolata*)
Phlox (*Phlox drummondii*)
Gloriosa daisy, Black-eyed Susan (*Rudbeckia hirta*)
Marigold (*Tagetes*)
Mexican sunflower (*Tithonia rotundifolia*)
Verbena (*Verbena*)
Zinnia (*Zinnia elegans*)

Hosts for Caterpillars
Hollyhock (*Alcea rosea*)
Dill (*Anethum graveolens*)
Snapdragon (*Antirrhinum majus*)
Cleome (*Cleome hasslerana*)
Queen Anne's lace (*Daucus carota*)
Foxglove (*Digitalis purpurea*)
Sunflower (*Helianthus annuus*)
Mallow (*Lavatera trimestris*)
Lupine (*Lupinus hartwegii*)
Parsley (*Petroselinum crispum*)
Rue (*Ruta graveolens*)
Nasturtium (*Tropaeolum majus*)

Michael A. Parten of Orchard Nursery & Florist in Lafayette advises that aster, zinnia, schizanthus, alyssum, and snapdragon are good choices if you want to draw butterflies to your garden. For hummingbird attraction, he suggests Victoria blue sage (*Salvia victoria*) and notes that hummingbirds seem to like snapdragons as much as butterflies do.

RESOURCES

FOR PLANTS & INFORMATION

Adachi Florist & Nursery
5166 Sobrante Ave
El Sobrante, CA 94803
510-223-6711

Alden Lane Nursery
981 Alden Lane
Livermore, CA 94550
510-447-0280

Berkeley Horticultural Nursery
1310 McGee Ave
Berkeley, CA 94703
510-526-4704

Branscomb Nursery
14685 Grove St
Healdsburg, CA 95448
707-433-1856

Cameron Park Nursery
3151 Green Valley Rd
Rescue, CA 95672
530-677-6293
530-677-0961 fax

Filoli
Canada Rd
Woodside, CA 94062
415-364-2880

Foothill Nursery
3931 Durock Rd
Shingle Springs, CA 95682
530-676-6555

Green Point Nursery
133 H Lane
Novato, CA 94945
415-892-2442

Green Thumb Nursery
301 Wilson St
Petaluma, CA 94952
707-762-8187

Hida Bonsai Garden & Tools
1333 San Pablo Ave
Berkeley, CA 94702
510-524-3700
800-443-5512

Huntington Botanical Gardens
1151 Oxford Rd
San Marino, CA 91108
818-405-2141

La Verne Nursery
642 E Baseline
San Dimas, CA 91773
909-599-0815
800-822-1117
909-592-1541 fax

Limberlost Roses
7304 Forbes Ave
Van Nuys, CA 91406
818-901-7798
818-997-6421

M & M Nursery
380 N Tustin Ave
Orange, CA 92867
714-538-8042
800-644-8042
www.mmnursery.com

Millards Florist & Nursery
13050 Mono Way
Sonora, CA 95370
209-532-3454

Monrovia Nursery
18331 E Foothill Blvd
Azusa, CA 91702
818-334-9321

Orchard Nursery & Florist
4010 Mt Diablo Blvd
Lafayette, CA 94549
510-284-4474

Ouchi Nursery
5003 Imperial Ave
San Diego, CA 92113
619-263-6114
619-263-8364 fax

Pacific Horticulture Consultants
3352 Loma Vista Rd
Ventura, CA 93003
805-644-1336

Quail Botanical Gardens
230 Quail Gardens Dr
Encinitas, CA 92024
760-436-3036

Red Bluff Garden Center
766 Antelope Blvd
Red Bluff, CA 96080
530-527-0886
530-528-2492 fax

Regan Nursery
4268 Decoto Rd
Fremont, CA 94555
510-797-3222

Santa Barbara Botanic Garden
1212 Mission Canyon Rd
Santa Barbara, CA 93105
805-682-4726

Seedhunt
PO Box 96
Freedom, CA 95019-0096
408-763-1523
seedhunt@aol.com

Sequoia Nursery
2519 E Noble Ave
Visalia, CA 93292
209-732-0309
209-732-0192 fax

Strybing Arboretum & Botanical Gardens
9th Ave and Lincoln Way
San Francisco, CA 94122
415-661-1316

Vintage Gardens
2833 Old Gravenstein Hwy S
Sebastopol, CA 95472
707-829-2035

White Rabbit Roses
PO Box 191
Elk, CA 95432
707-877-1888
roses@mcn.org
www.mcn.org/b/roses/

Zoological Society of San Diego
San Diego, CA 92112-0551
619-231-1515
www.sandiegozoo.org

INDEX